THEORETICAL DEVELOPMENTS IN HISPANIC LINGUISTICS
Javier Gutiérrez-Rexach, Series Editor

Advances in the Analysis of Spanish Exclamatives

Edited by Ignacio Bosque

THE OHIO STATE UNIVERSITY PRESS • COLUMBUS

Copyright © 2017 by The Ohio State University.
All rights reserved.

Library of Congress Cataloging-in-Publication Data
Names: Bosque, Ignacio, editor.
Title: Advances in the analysis of Spanish exclamatives / edited by Ignacio Bosque.
Other titles: Theoretical developments in Hispanic linguistics.
Description: Columbus : The Ohio State University Press, [2017] | Series: Theoretical developments in Hispanic linguistics | Includes bibliographical references and index.
Identifiers: LCCN 2016041476 | ISBN 9780814213261 (cloth ; alk. paper) | ISBN 081421326X (cloth ; alk. paper)
Subjects: LCSH: Spanish language—Exclamations. | Spanish language—Syntax. | Spanish language—Semantics.
Classification: LCC PC4395.A35 2017 | DDC 465—dc23
LC record available at https://lccn.loc.gov/2016041476

Cover design by AuthorSupport.com
Text design by Juliet Williams
Type set in Minion and Formata

♾ The paper used in this publication meets the minimum requirements of the American National Standard for Information Sciences—Permanence of Paper for Printed Library Materials. ANSI Z39.48-1992.

9 8 7 6 5 4 3 2 1

The series Theoretical Developments in Hispanic Linguistics was conceived and directed by Javier Gutiérrez-Rexach, whose sudden and unexpected passing has meant a tremendous loss for the international linguistics community. The extraordinary significance of Javier's contributions to the field of Hispanic linguistics over the past twenty-five years will inspire the work of many researchers in the future. This book, which contains one of his last contributions, is dedicated to his memory.

Contents

Chapter 1 · Spanish Exclamatives in Perspective: A Survey of
Properties, Classes, and Current Theoretical Issues   1
  Ignacio Bosque

Chapter 2 · *Más*-Support   53
  Luis Sáez

Chapter 3 · Optative Exclamatives in Spanish   82
  Cristina Sánchez López

Chapter 4 · Exclamatives in (Argentinian) Spanish and Their Next of Kin   108
  Pascual José Masullo

Chapter 5 · At-Issue Material in Spanish Degree Exclamatives:
An Experimental Study   139
  Xavier Villalba

Chapter 6 · Exclamative Sentences and Extreme Degree Quantification   159
  Raquel González Rodríguez

Chapter 7 · Embedded Exclamatives and the Ingredients of
Grounded Belief   181
  Javier Gutiérrez-Rexach and Patricia Andueza

References   *211*
List of Contributors   *229*
Index   *232*

Spanish Exclamatives in Perspective
A Survey of Properties, Classes, and Current Theoretical Issues

Ignacio Bosque

1. Introduction

Exclamative constructions are the result of the rather intricate (and not fully understood) crossing of several syntactic, semantic, and pragmatic variables. Even so, substantial progress in all of these factors has been achieved in recent years, both from theoretical linguistics and the specific grammar of Romance languages. A large number of recent theoretical studies, most of them mentioned below, constitute substantial contributions to our understanding of the semantic import of the grammatical ingredients of these peculiar constructions. Results of this abundant research touch on the projections that articulate their syntax, the specific processes of variable binding in structures of degree quantification, the interpretation of mirative and evidential particles, the behavior of exclamatives in negative and subordinate contexts, and the grammatical consequences of the very significant differences between interrogative and exclamative patterns, among others.

I would have liked to express my deep gratitude to Javier Gutiérrez-Rexach for inviting me to participate in this series. I am also very grateful to Cristina Sánchez López and two anonymous reviewers for their comments on a previous version of this chapter. This research has been partially supported by grant UCM-930590 from the Complutense University, Madrid.

The specific ways in which these theoretical issues are relevant for the grammar of Romance languages have been analyzed with much detail in recent years. Main contributions include research on French (Gérard, 1980; Bacha, 2000; Rys, 2006; Beyssade & Marandin, 2006; Marandin, 2008, 2010; Burnett, 2009; Kellert, 2010), Portuguese (Bastos-Gee, 2011), Catalan (Castroviejo, 2006, 2007, 2008a, 2008b; Villalba, 2001, 2003, 2004, 2008b), and Italian (Benincà, 1995, 1996; Zanuttini & Portner, 2000, 2003; Porter & Zanuttini, 2000, 2005; Munaro, 2003, 2005, 2006; Benincà & Munaro, 2010; Zanuttini et al., 2012), among other languages. As regards Spanish, main references are mentioned and discussed in this overview and the rest of the book. General presentations of exclamative structures in current theoretical grammar include Michaelis (2001), Heycock (2006), and Villalba (2008b).

This book on Spanish exclamatives intends to constitute a contribution to Romance linguistics, as well as a general picture of settled, new, and pending issues in this important, as well as traditionally neglected, domain of grammar. The necessary comparison of exclamative structures (either present, absent, or lost) in the Romance languages family is yet to be done. The present overview aims to be a guide into the intricate jungle of exclamative patterns in Spanish. It is also meant to be a threshold to welcome the reader to the main theoretical issues and controversies standing out of the considerable existing current literature on this topic.

2. Exclamatives as Speech Acts

Exclamatives are speech acts, and they are addressed as such in classical typologies of utterances. For example, Searle (1976, 1979) distinguishes assertive, directive, commissive, declarative, and expressive speech acts and subdivides the latter into exclamatives and optatives (for developments and refinements, see also Sadock & Zwicky, 1985; Zaefferer, 2001; Abels, 2005; and Boisvert & Ludwig, 2006). Being speech acts, exclamative utterances have illocutionary force, lack truth values, and are exclusively attributed to the speaker, even if—as happens in questions—they lose these features when embedded (§ 6.5.).

Whereas promises or commands are addressed to a hearer, exclamatives do not require one, unless reinterpreted as rhetorical questions or commands. There is little doubt that the speech act that exclamatives perform constitutes the manifestation of an emotional reaction of the speaker. In fact, in the literature it is often assumed that the key notion behind exclamatives is the speaker's surprise (Elliott, 1971, 1974; Castroviejo, 2006; Rett, 2007, 2009, 2011; Andueza, 2011; and many others). This concept is both accurate in many cases and too restrictive in others. The reason is that surprise is bound to counterexpectation, and this requirement is not always fulfilled in exclamatives. If I get up and open my window, I may utter (1):

(1) ¡Qué bonita mañana!
     'What a beautiful morning!'

This utterance may be fully felicitous in complete absence of any previous (explicit or implicit) bad weather forecast on my part. One may say that the emotional reaction expressed by (1) is complacency and also that other exclamative utterances express disappointment, frustration, excitement, surprise, enthusiasm, or amazement, among other subtle notions. Such a large list of possible emotional reactions, together with a similarly extended paradigm of grammatical structures able to express them, have lead specialists to raise the natural question whether exclamatives are a unified speech type, or rather constitute one or several varieties of a more comprehensive one, sometimes called "expressive." See Abels (2005), Allan (2006), Potts (2007), Merin and Nikolaeva (2008), Schlenker (2007), and Castroviejo (2008a) on this issue.

Whether or not this reduction is possible, it must be stressed that, according to Zanuttini and Portner's (2003) influential analysis, surprise and similar concepts are somehow derived notions in the grammar of exclamatives, in fact a consequence of what they call "widening" processes. These authors argue that by using an exclamative sentence such as, say, *How X she is!* (X being a qualifying adjective), the speaker implies that the extent in which X is predicated exceeds or outranks the range of possibilities under consideration. In their analyses, a fundamental property of wh-exclamatives is the fact that they widen or enlarge the domain of quantification for the wh-operator,[1] and this operation gives rise to the set of alternative propositions denoted by the sentence. Being extreme, values expressed by degree quantifiers in exclamatives are associated with typical entailment monotonicity processes (Castroviejo, 2008b).

The contrast between questions and exclamations is rather sharp, as regards this essential aspect of their meaning: whereas wh-words in questions pick up one alternative in an implicit set, as *cómo* 'how' does in

---

1. Following a standard convention, in this chapter I will use the term wh- (wh-operator, wh-exclamatives, wh-words) for Spanish instead of *qu-*, *cu-* or *q-*.

(2a), their exclamative counterparts, as *cómo* in (2b), behave in a rather different way:

(2) a. ¿Cómo canta María?
 'How does M. sing?'
 b. ¡Cómo canta María!
 'How M. sings!'

In fact, exclamative *cómo*—a different word from its interrogative counterpart in French and other languages—refers to an implicit set of nonstandard ways of singing (see § 6.1 for a more precise characterization). Since the denotation of exclamative wh-phrases involves a widening process, the characteristic form of the illocutionary force associated with them must be crucially related to this particular sort of variable binding and domain denotation. Chernilovskaya and Nouwen (2012) argue that widening—a notion usually applied to the semantics or free-choice indefinites (Kandom & Ladman, 1993)—is not exactly the relevant concept to be grasped in exclamatives, and they suggest noteworthiness, a notion related to saliency, prominence, and similar concepts, as a better candidate (on this issue, see also Brown, 2008). In any case, the fact that only extreme values in implicit scales are implied by wh-exclamatives, so that intermediate extents are disregarded, has been repeatedly pointed out in the literature as a defining feature of these utterances (see Elliott, 1971, 1974; Milner, 1978; Gérard, 1980; and Rett, 2008, 2009; among many others).

The speaker's emotional reaction is, thus, related to the non-standard set of extreme values associated with the domain of wh-words, but these two notions must be kept apart. The main reason to do so is the fact that the choice of the emotion expressed in exclamative wh-utterances is mostly a pragmatic issue, whereas the quantification domain obtained for wh-expressions may be either overt (as in the «*How* + adjective» pattern[2]) or calculated from a restricted set, as in (2b). That is, the ways of singing to which some emotional reaction is addressed in (2b) are placed at the

---

2. Notice that adjectives in so-called "closed scales" (Kennedy & McNally, 2005a) are gradable, as in *lleno* 'full' (cf. *muy lleno, llenísimo* 'quite full'), even if the highest extent of the relevant property seems to be interpreted on the subject's extension: "full in all their parts." These adjectives allow for adversative tags such as ... *pero no del todo* '... but not quite', disallowed by other gradable adjectives (*interesante* 'interesting', *caro* 'expensive', etc.). On the interpretation of wh-APs such as *qué lleno*, see Castroviejo (2006) and Villalba (this volume). González Rodríguez (this volume) argues that adverbs such *extremadamente* 'extremely' close Kennedy and McNally's (2005a) open scales.

opposite extremes of an implicit scale built of pragmatic information: either beautifully, marvelously, etc., or awfully, out of tune, etc. This set of extreme values may be extended to *¡Qué + N!* 'What a N' exclamatives (§ 4.1). Some contextual factors, such as those pointed out by Potts and Schwarz (2008), might help one decide on the correct polarity of the extreme values involved.

Closer looks at different types of exclamatives (particularly those built of a series of non wh-exclamative particles) show that their syntactic structures may be associated with particular meanings and intentions in much more specific ways. For example, quantificational expressions, such as *vaya si* 'sure, definitely' in (3a) are not compatible with low degrees. Similarly, by using *mira* in (3b) the speaker expresses that he or she considers a certain fact to be both surprising and inadequate; the grammatical structure of (3c) is inextricably linked to the expression of some disappointment, etc.

(3) a. ¡Vaya si me gusta!
        'I sure like it.'
     b. ¡Mira que haber dejado tu empleo! (from Sánchez López, 2014b)
        'I can't believe you've left your job.'
     c. ¡Y pensar que te creí!
        'And to think I believed you!'

Many other similar cases exist, and some of them have been addressed in detail in the large descriptive literature on Spanish exclamatives (González Calvo, 1984–88, 1998; Carbonero Cano, 1990; Alonso-Cortés, 1999a, 1990b; Casas, 2005; Vigara Tauste, 2005; etc.). See also the literature referred to in § 5.2.

Two modal notions developed recently have important consequences for the analysis of exclamative utterances: mirativity and evidentiality. The first (DeLancey, 2001; Aikhenvald, 2012; on Spanish, see Sánchez López, 2014a, 2014b; Olbertz, 2009, 2012; and Torres Bustamante, 2013) refers to the novelty of the propositional contents and the emotional reaction that unawareness, surprise, or lack of information causes in the speaker. Sánchez López (2014b) argues that exclamatives headed by Sp. *mira* involve mirative information—see also Ocampo (2009) and Gutiérrez-Rexach and Andueza (this volume) on this issue. Other potential candidates include *cuidado (que)* and *vaya (que)* (both, 'sure, no doubt'). See Casas (2005), Sancho Cremades (2008), and Tirado (2013, 2015a, 2015b) on these exclamative particles.

Evidentiality (Plungian, 2001; Aikhenvald, 2004) is a different notion, although not entirely unrelated to mirativity, as argued by Lazard (1999,

2001) and Rett and Murray (2013). It concerns the source of the information and specifically whether it is direct or indirect (that is, obtained through witness experience, hearsay, etc.), as well as whether or not it is taken to be reliable or established. Rodríguez Ramalle (2008a, 2008b) and Demonte and Soriano (2014) argue that the non-subordinated *que* in expressions such as *¡Que ha dimitido el decano!* 'Hey, the dean has just resigned!' is an evidential particle, then signaling the reported status of the propositional content of the sentence. I will return to this in § 5.3.

The emotional nature of expressive speech acts has some other grammatical consequences. Emotive predicates are factive (Kiparsky & Kiparsky, 1970; Giannakidou, 2006; De Cuba, 2007; and many more). Since exclamative sentences express an emotive reaction, the natural question is whether or not exclamatives are factives as well. Most answers are affirmative: Elliott (1971, 1974), Grimshaw (1979), Michaelis (2001), and Michaelis and Lambrecht (1996). Even so, some indications suggest that the notion "factivity" might be understood in a somehow extended sense in these cases. First of all, there is little doubt that indirect exclamatives (§ 6.5), such as (4a), presuppose the truth of their complement:

(4) a. Es sorprendente lo bien que se porta el niño.
 'It's amazing how well the child behaves himself.'
 b. ¡Qué listo es Juan!
 'How smart Juan is!'

But notice that a similar conclusion would be obtained from a non-exclamative complement clause of the same predicate. Factivity is not so straightforward as regards main clause exclamatives. Sentence (4b) reflects some belief of the speaker (namely, "Juan is very smart"), which can be refuted by the hearer (as argued by Rett, 2008; Abels, 2010), a situation not expected in factive patterns. Villalba (this volume) shows that speakers tend to interpret that refusal as a rejection of the property itself, rather than its high degree.

Beyssade (2009) claims that standard tests on factivity are not applicable to main exclamatives, which—she argues—are not presupposition triggers, but rather expressive speech acts whose content is speaker-only oriented. In a similar vein, notice that interjective expressions manifest a speaker's emotions (then, personal reactions toward true state of affairs), but this does not imply that they are factive constructions. Zanuttini and Portner (2003) suggested that the relationship between wh-exclamatives and their propositional contents is not presupposition, but conventionally implicature. Villalba (this volume) argues that it is neither, but one of projective meaning, in Tonhauser et al.'s (2013) sense.

3. A Classification of Exclamative Expressions in Spanish

The very existence of quite a number of general descriptions of Spanish exclamatives (González Calvo, 1984–88, 1998, 2001; Alonso-Cortés, 1999a, 1999b; Casas, 2005; RAE-ASALE, 2009, § 42.13–16; and Villalba, 2016, among others) does not imply that it is easy, or even possible, to come up with a classification of exclamatives able to be generally accepted. We may classify exclamative expressions on the basis of two factors: (1) their grammatical structure and (2) whether or not this structure is exclusively exclamative. According to the former, an expression may be signaled as exclamative by some lexical and/or syntactic clue ("primary exclamatives"); in the latter group, only intonation and the proper interpretation of the exclamative illocutionary force associated with it are the linguistic markers of exclamative import ("secondary exclamatives"). The following groups are obtained by applying these criteria:

(5) A classification of Spanish exclamative expressions

	Primary	Secondary
Lexical	• Interjections • Phrasal and sentential idioms	• Vocatives?
Phrasal	• Interjective phrases • Wh-phrasal exclamatives • DPs with other exclamative particles	• Imprecatives (insults, compliments, etc.) • Intonation-only exclamative phrases
Sentential	• Wh-exclamative sentences and definite determiner exclamatives • Focal exclamatives • Polarity exclamatives • Matrix complementizer exclamatives • Binomial exclamatives • Suspended exclamatives • Optative exclamatives	• Intonation-only exclamative sentences (= Declarative exclamatives)

Exclamative intonation, which applies to all types in (5), is often characterized by a number of features: hyperarticulation, increasing intensity and quantity in stressed syllables (in polysyllabic expressions), changes in individual tonal range (more specifically, movement of the general range of pitch over or below standard levels), and a perceptible acceleration or retardation of "tempo." For a technical description of Spanish exclamative intonation patterns in ToBi parameters, see Prieto and Roseano (2010). A more traditional, but still quite accurate, account in a number of respects is Navarro Tomás (1918).

Interjections, not addressed in this book, are lexical units associated with a number of (fixed but often fuzzy) emotional reactions: ¡vaya! 'what a . . . , oh,' ¡toma ya! 'wow,' ¡ni modo! 'no way.' General descriptions of Spanish interjections include Sánchez Royo (1976), Almela Pérez (1982), Alonso-Cortés (1999a, 1999b), Montes (1999), Torres Sánchez (2000), López Bobo (2002), Edeso (2009), and RAE-ASALE (2009, ch. 32), among others.

Phrasal and sentential idioms are in the lexical group in (5) because they are expected to be in the lexicon, even if some of them allow for morphological variants. Phrasal idioms are expressions such as ¡La madre que {me/te/lo/la . . . } parió! 'By the mother who bore {me/you/him/her}.' Examples of sentential idioms include ¡Qué le {voy/vas/vamos} a hacer}! 'What can {I/you/we} do!' or ¡(No) {faltaría/faltaba} más! 'By all means, of course.'

Primary phrasal exclamatives are divided into three groups in (5). The first one corresponds to interjective phrases, that is, phrases headed by interjections (RAE-ASALE, 2009, § 32.8; Alonso-Cortés, 1999a; Rodríguez Ramalle, 2007b), as in ¡Vaya con el muchacho! 'What a (disgusting) boy!'; ¡Ay de la que se retrase! 'Woe unto the woman who is late!'; ¡Bien por el equipo! 'Good for our team!' The second group is that of wh-phrasal exclamatives (§ 4.1), as in ¡Qué calor! 'It's so hot!'; ¡Qué bonito! 'How nice!'; ¡Qué deprisa! 'How fast!' The third group includes other exclamative particles (§ 4.2), as in ¡Menudo lío! 'What a mess!'; ¡Vaya día! 'What a day!'; or ¡Valiente tontería! 'What nonsense!'

Grammatical expressions with exclamative intonation and no other identifying syntactic structure are called "intonation-only exclamatives" in (5) and may be phrasal or sentential. The former are expressions such as ¡Las tostadas! 'The toast!'; ¡Muy interesante! 'Quite interesting!'; or ¡Bien dicho! 'Well said!' Some might be reduced to other groups. For example, exclamative APs such as ¡Muy interesante! can be a variant of binomial (that is, predicate-subject) exclamatives, such as ¡Muy interesante, este libro! 'Quite interesting, this book!,' addressed in § 5.4. Other items in this class include emphatic answers or replies, fragments, etc.

Intonational-only exclamative sentences, sometimes called *declarative exclamatives*, may be easily exemplified: *¡Se están quemando las tostadas!* 'The toasts are burning!'; *¡Tienes razón!* 'You are right!'; or *¡La respuesta estaba ahí mismo!* 'The answer was right there!' Notice that the lack of a grammatical marker (distinct from intonation) that signals these expressions as exclamative does not dismiss the need to analyze the specific import of their illocutionary force. In fact, this import lies in the process of assigning the propositions they contain to the extremes of implicit pragmatic scales of standardness, expectation, relevance, or plausibility. From this point of view, it is not extreme degrees that are valued, but extreme states of affairs. On this perspective, see Gutiérrez-Rexach (1996, 1998, 2008), Rett (2008), and Andueza and Gutiérrez-Rexach (2011).

But exclamative intonation and its correlates in exclamative force are not a default option for all assertions. When they are not, the natural question is which specific propositional contents are, and are not, suitable to be freely converted into secondary exclamative utterances. Modal information is one of the possible restricting factors. Notice that the utterance in (6a) is a good candidate to be an impossible secondary exclamative sentence (that is, an intonational-only exclamative); (6b) might be one as well, but (6c) is not:

(6) a. *¡Estás equivocado probablemente!
Most probably, you are wrong!
b. ??¡Tal vez estés equivocado!
Maybe you are wrong!
c. ¡Puedes equivocarte!
You may be wrong!

Possible constraints on secondary exclamatives are worth exploring, but they will not be considered here.

It is not obvious that lexical exclamatives exist (that is, non-phrasal lexical items giving rise to exclamative speech acts through intonation patterns only), but perhaps vocatives and empathic one-word answers might fit here. As regards secondary phrasal exclamatives, they include imprecatives, which, according to Sadock and Zwicky (1985), constitute a specific type of speech act. Imprecatives are exclamative expressions only indirectly, since they require addressees, as imperatives do, but unlike imperatives, they do not expect answers. On their relationship with exclamatives utterances, see Alonso-Cortés (1999a, 1999b).

The main difficulty in classifying primary sentential exclamatives is the fact the structural considerations and semantic import may unavoidably overlap in some groups (as in matrix complementizer exclamatives and optative exclamatives). The tentative classification in (5) is as follows:

a) Wh-sentential exclamatives (§ 5.1) are sentences built with phrasal wh-exclamatives, as in *¡Qué calor hace hoy!* 'How hot it is today!' Extreme degree exclamatives with definite articles, as in *¡Lo fuertes que son!* 'How strong they are!' (§ 5.1.2), may be associated with this group as well.
b) Focal exclamatives involve focus movement of a phrase to a left peripheral position. Focus preposing is not necessarily bound to exclamative intonation, since not all sentences involving this process are necessarily exclamative (e.g., *De algo hay que vivir* 'One has to make a living'). Focal exclamatives with overt complementizers, as in *¡Buenos bocadillos que te comías tú!* 'You used to eat so many wonderful sandwiches!,' are no doubt primary, but those without them, as in *¡En buen lío (??que) me he metido!* 'What a mess I got myself into!,' might be secondary. See § 5.2 below.
c) "Polarity exclamatives" is the term that Batllori and Hernanz (2013) apply to exclamative utterances built out of emphatic particles such as *bien* 'well' or *sí* 'for sure, no doubt,' which display some quantificational properties, as shown in § 5.2.
d) Matrix complementizer exclamatives are headed by *que* 'that' or unstressed *si* 'if.' Both are functional heads, but they give rise to quite different meaning depending on verbal mood. See § 5.3.
e) Binomial exclamatives are predicative sentences with no copula, as in *¡Muy bueno, tu artículo de ayer en el periódico!* 'Quite good, your article in yesterday's newspaper.' They may be divided into several subclasses, as shown in § 5.4.
f) Suspended exclamatives (§ 5.5) exhibit a rising final intonation, quite close to that of consecutive sentences with omitted codas, as in *¡Estoy tan cansado . . . !* 'I am so tired . . . !' or *¡Tienes unas cosas . . . !* 'You come up with such ideas . . . !'
g) Optative or desiderative exclamatives (§ 5.6) express the speaker's desire, as in *¡Quién fuera rico!* 'Whish I were a rich man!'

This list is by no means exhaustive. Other exclamative types include those headed by *con* 'with' or *conque* 'so that,' as in *¡Conque no quieres comer!*

'So, you don't want to eat!,' as well as infinitival exclamatives such as ¡Tener que aguantar yo esto! 'I can't believe I have to put up with this!,' among others. On infinitival exclamatives, see Herrero (1991) and Grohmann and Etxeparre (2003).

Even if we take the basic tenets of the classification in (5) to be on the right track, a number of objective factors make it difficult to trace a sharp boundary between primary and secondary exclamatives in some cases:

1) Predicates lexically denoting extreme values, sometimes called *elatives,* cannot be dissociated from the emotional content expressed by exclamations—hence, some evaluation of the speaker—as in *Mary is marvelous.* This is a natural consequence of the fact that extreme degree values of properties are associated with exclamative illocutionary force (Zanuttini & Portner, 2003; Rett, 2008). In fact, the speaker's involvement in those judgements is much stronger than the one we may attest in other predications, as in *Mary is a chemical engineer.* Morphological elatives may be marked by prefixes in Spanish (*re-, requete-, super-, archi-, hiper-*) or suffixes (*-ísimo, -érrimo*); they are subject to dialectal variation (Masullo, this volume) and belong to various word classes. Spanish elatives are described in detail in González Calvo (1984–88), Arce Castillo (1999), Vigara Tauste (2005, ch. 3), and Casas (2005), among others. They share a number of properties with exclamatives, as Masullo (1999, 2003, 2012, this volume) and González Rodríguez (2006, 2008, 2009, 2010) have very explicitly argued. But even so, elatives are not illocutionary expressions, even less so root constructions. They also bear a close relationship with so-called *qualifying nouns* (Milner, 1978; Gandon, 1988), which are typical of predicative nominal structures, such as *El imbécil de Juan* 'That idiot, Juan.' In fact, this pattern is one option for wh-phrasal exclamatives, as in *¡Qué maravilla de película!* 'What a marvelous film!'

2) Exaggerations are also typically associated with exclamative patterns, as in *Te lo he dicho mil veces* 'I've told you that a thousand times.' Some ironic statements, as in *Me voy a preocupar yo por eso . . .* 'I do not intend to worry about that' and emphatic comparisons, such as *Vives como un rajá* 'You live like a rajah,' also bare a close relationship with exclamations. All these expressions introduce personal statements resulting from subjective assessments that present states of affairs as non-actual or non-standard,

often as resources to convey humor. In any case, they do not quite assimilate to the specific grammatical type of exclamatives.

3) The close relationship between rhetorical questions and exclamations has been pointed out on many occasions. As Spanish grammar is concerned, see Gutiérrez-Rexach (1998), Escandell-Vidal (1984, 1999), Casas (2005), and Andueza (2011) on the difficulties of telling them apart in a number of cases. Nevertheless, grammatical factors still make the distinction possible, as I will discuss in the pages to follow.

4. Phrasal Exclamatives

4.1. WH-PHRASAL EXCLAMATIVES

The main characteristics of wh-exclamative words in Spanish have been analyzed in both the synchronic and the diachronic literature. The most detailed descriptions are found in Casas (2005), Octavio de Toledo and Sánchez López (2009, 2010), and RAE-ASALE (2009, ch. 22). See also Bosque (1984a, 1984b) and Andueza (2011). Since it would be out of the question to cover such a huge amount of information here, I will merely attempt to clarify the general picture as regards some fundamental conceptual issues. First of all, wh-exclamative phrases may be quantitative or qualitative, the former being degree or amount exclamatives:

(7) Quantitative wh-exclamative phrases
    a. ¡Qué caro! [Degree]
       'How expensive!'
    b. ¡Cuán lejos! [Degree]
       'How far!'
    c. ¡Cuántos coches! [Amount]
       'How many cars!'
    d. ¡Cuánto calor! [Amount]
       'So much heat!; It's so hot!'
    e. ¡Cuánto trabajas! [Amount]
       'How hard you work!'

(8) Qualitative wh-exclamative phrases
    a. ¡Qué casa! [Type]
       'What a house!'

b. ¡Qué fruta! [Type]
'What a (piece of) fruit!'

The term *degree exclamatives* is sometimes applied to all types in (7) and (8), which suggests an (perhaps deliberate) extended interpretation of the notion of "degree." Indeed, *qué* and *cuán* (the latter, an apocope variant of *cuánto* restricted to a very formal literary style) form degree phrases with adjectives and adverbs. The phrases in (7a, b) express the extreme extent of some property, but notice that no property is graded in (7c). This phrase denotes the speaker's emotional reaction toward the fact that the number of cars in a certain place exceeds the average. In a broader sense, (7c) implies that the amount is high or excessive, therefore reaching a high level in a scale of possible implicit amounts. But this does not exactly mean that *cuántos* 'how many' denotes degree, nor does it imply that "amount" and "degree" are interchangeable concepts.

As regards qualitative wh-phrases, possible interpretations of the notion of degree depend on their grammatical analysis, as we will see in a minute. The DP in (8a) expresses the fact that a certain house is unique because of some remarkable properties, which somehow make it singular or special.

There is little doubt that quantitative DPs such as (7c) involve at least two components, both of which are overt in English ("how" and "many"): one corresponds to the wh-operator, and another one represents a measure projection. Interestingly, both are overt in Spanish if the utterance is about some small amount, as in *¡Qué pocos coches!* 'How few cars!,' and both might be overt as well in medieval Spanish, as pointed out by Octavio de Toledo and Sánchez López (2009, p. 1014), as in *¡Qué muchas avellanas!* 'How many hazelnuts!' (Juan Ruiz, *Libro de Buen Amor*, CORDE). Even so, many more examples of this pattern are attested to in interrogatives than in exclamative sentences. For example, Eng. *how many/much* corresponds to Italian *ché tanto* in exclamatives (Zanuttini & Portner, 2003), a pattern also occasionally attested to in American Spanish texts (Octavio de Toledo & Sánchez López, 2009, p. 1026).

Quantitative exclamative wh-DPs are headed by *cuánto* (or its morphological variants) or by *qué de* (lit. "what of"), with no interrogative counterpart, both followed by mass or plural nouns. As an adverb, *cuánto* 'how much/many' is decomposed as *qué mucho* in some medieval texts: *¡Qué mucho pesas!* 'How much you weigh!' (Juan Ruiz, *Libro de Buen Amor*, CORDE), a pattern still present in some varieties of Caribbean Spanish (RAE-ASALE, 2009, § 22.14r), together with *qué tanto*:

(9) a. ¡Qué tanto ha cambiado eso! 'How very much all this has changed!' (Oral Corpus, Venezuela, CREA).
b. ¡Qué tanto sabía Nicanor! '¡How very many things Nicanor used to know!' (T. Carrasquilla, *Hace tiempo*, CORDE).

"*Qué tan* + Adj/Adv." is the standard pattern for wh-degree questions in present-day American Spanish. This does not hold for exclamatives, which are formed as in (7a), but it did in medieval Spanish, as attested by Octavio de Toledo and Sánchez López (2009, p. 1019). It must be pointed out that *qué* in (7a) is not a degree modifier, since, as opposed to *muy* 'very,' it allows for interposed adverbs, such as *increíblemente* or *extraordinariamente*, as well as high degree adjectives (*qué carísimo ~ *muy carísimo* 'How expensive'). As in the case of nominals, *mucho* or *muy* do not appear in this position nowadays, but they did in Old Spanish:

(10) Muy repetido es entre todos . . . cuán muy nutritivo es el vino a los que le beben.
'It is much repeated among people how nutritious wine is for those who drink it.'
(J. de Pineda [1585], CORDE)

According to Sáez (this volume; see also Corver, 1997), the *muy-tan* alternation might be a mirage: if a degree projection (as Eng. *so*) takes an orientational measure complement, as in Eng. *very* in *so very happy*, these two grammatical components might not necessarily be in the same paradigm. Even so, notice that some explanation should be given for the absence of the "*qué tan mucho/muy*" pattern in all time periods and dialects.

Acknowledging that more research is needed to account for the strong asymmetry between interrogative and exclamative patterns on both a historical and geographical basis, there is enough evidence to conclude that at least a measure projection separates the wh-degree word for quantitative adverbs, adjectives, and nominals in the lexical structure, whether or not it is visible in overt syntax.

Let us turn to qualitative wh-phrases now, such as those in (8). Interestingly, *qué* does not agree with N, which may be plural (even overtly quantified), in this pattern:

(11) ¡Qué (tres) casas!
'Check out those (three) houses!'

The relationship between qualitative and quantitative exclamative DPs is intriguing for both lexical and semantic reasons. The interpretation of mass nouns in Spanish wh-exclamative DPs is subject to some lexical restrictions. As seen in (8), N in the "*Qué*-N" pattern can be count or mass. In Bosque (1984a, 1984b) it is observed that *qué* exclamative DPs apparently give rise to quantitative readings with some mass nouns, but not with others:

(12) a. ¡Qué dolor! 'What a pain!' = ¡Cuánto dolor! 'How much pain!'
 b. ¡Qué fruta! 'What fruit!' ≠ ¡Cuánta fruta! 'How much fruit!'

In the group with *dolor* we find *suerte* 'luck,' *calor* 'heat,' and *fuerza* 'strength'; in the group with *fruta* one might place *arroz* 'rice,' *locura* 'madness,' or *verdad* 'truth.' It is suggested that the key factor in these two lexical classes is whether or not mass nouns quantifiers allow for paraphrases with size adjectives; that is, *mucho dolor* = *dolor grande* 'much pain = a big pain.' See also Marandin (2008, 2010) on other aspects of this relationship. Notice that an explanation of the pattern in (12a) along these lines does not necessarily imply that *qué dolor* receives a quantitative reading, but rather that qualitative readings in these cases (as in *severe pain*) cannot be sharply distinguished from quantitative interpretations (as in *much pain*). An argument in support of this conclusion[3] comes from the fact that paraphrases with «*Qué de* + N», restrictive to quantitative readings, are rejected in the pattern in (12a), but allowed in that of (12b). This implies that the qualitative reading can then be preserved in (12a) if the extreme values applicable to the noun denotation are expressed through seize adjectives, since these adjectives are used to grade intensity, not just size.[4] The fact that the equivalences in (12a) do not hold for questions may be seen as a simple consequence of the fact that widening processes do not hold for them either.

How are then qualitative exclamative wh-DPs, such as (8a), to be grammatically analyzed? Here are some possibilities:

(13) a. We may suppose that *qué* is an inherently qualitative determiner. Octavio de Toledo and Sánchez López (2009) remark that Lat. *quantus* could be used in this way, as in *Quantus homo* 'What a man!' In this exclamative NP, *quantus* does not quantify

---

3. Thanks to C. Sánchez López for pointing it out to me (personal communication).
4. An independent question, not addressed here, is when exactly are "*qué*-N" exclamatives allowed to receive polarized interpretations. Notice that (8a) is about a wonderful or an awful house, and (8b) is about juicy or rotten fruit, but (12a) is not about some mild pain, nor is *qué injusticia* (in the b group) about some minor injustice.

homo, but qualifies it, then highlighting a number of implicit non-standard properties that therefore make someone outstanding as a singular individual. Exclamative *cuál* 'which' had this very meaning in Old Spanish (RAE-ASALE, § 22.14h).

b. We may interpret a silent qualitative determiner. In present-day Peruvian Spanish, (8a) alternates with *¡Qué tal casa!* (lit. "what such house"), a variant also registered in Old Spanish (RAE-ASALE, 2009, § 22.14v; Octavio de Toledo & Sánchez López, 2009). The qualitative determiner *tal* 'such' is, then, parallel to the quantitative *tan* 'so much'.

c. We may suppose that the qualitative interpretation is obtained through a silent measure coda with *tan* 'so much' or *más* 'more', plus an elative adjective that is contextually determined, since (8a) is equivalent to *¡Qué casa {tan/más} + ADJ!*

Notice that option (13a) places the proper interpretation of the wh-word in the lexicon, whereas the two other analyses locate it in the syntax. Option (13b), suggested in Octavio de Toledo and Sánchez López (2009), is particularly interesting. It somehow reproduces Zanuttini and Portner's (2003) idea that a hidden high degree modifier is present (in fact, optional) in exclamative sentences such as *How (very) long this bridge is!*, an option not available for interrogatives (**How very long this bridge is?*). An additional indirect argument for (13b) is the free omission of *tal* in present-day standard wh-qualitative questions in Spanish, as in *¿Qué (tal) tiempo hace?* 'How's the weather?'

Sáez's (this volume) analysis of (8a) is as follows

(14) [$_{DegP}$ Qué [$_{Deg^{\circ}}$ ϵ] [$_{QRP}$ ∅ [casa]]]

In (14), *qué* occupies the specifier of a Degree projection headed by ϵ. This is Zanuttini and Porter's (2003) exclamative operator, that is, the operator that these authors associate with the specific illocutionary force of exclamatives. ∅ in (14) is a measure quantifier oriented in polar opposite directions, such as those implied by *mucho* 'much' vs. *poco* 'little'.

Notice that the lexical solution in (13a) might be reduced to (13b)—or some variety of it—if we suppose that all that makes them different is whether the information corresponding to the wh- and the qualitative (measure) projections is separated in the syntax or conflated in the lexicon.[5]

---

5. In any case, identification of the relevant non-standard required properties of qualified nouns is not a straightforward matter. One might guess that these properties include exoticism

As for solution (13c), which does not necessarily imply an unrecoverable ellipsis, it provides a good paraphrase of these expressions, as Anscombre (2013) argued for French. In RAE-ASALE (2009, § 42.13l) it is suggested that *¡Qué vestido tan bonito!* and *¡Qué bonito vestido!* (both 'What a nice dress!') are derivationally related, since the latter might contain a Ø variant of *tan* 'such.' There is another interesting contact point between (13b) and (13c). As Sáez (this volume) argues, the measure complement in (15a) is headed by a false comparative. In fact, quantificational degree words such as *tan* 'such' and *más* 'more' may be omitted here, with a certain range of historical and dialectal variation:

(15) a. ¡Qué obra {tan/más} maravillosa! [Standard Spanish]
    'What a marvelous work!'
  b. ¡Qué obra maravillosa! [Classical Spanish; also many varieties of American Spanish and present-day European literary Spanish]
    'What a marvelous work!'
  c. *¡Qué {tan/más} maravillosa obra! [All dialects]
    'What a marvelous work!'
  d. ¡Qué maravillosa obra! [Standard Spanish]
    'What a marvelous work!'

Numerous examples of the pattern in (15b) with elative adjectives, such as *¡Qué sitio deprimente!* 'What a depressing place' or *¡Qué idea absurda!* 'What an absurd idea!,' are attested in RAE-ASALE (2009, § 22.13w), Carbonero Cano (1990), and Casas (2005), among others. Non-elative adjectives (as in *¡Qué cosa rara!* 'What a strange thing') are less common in this pattern, but also possible in certain geographical varieties.

Sáez (this volume) argues that *más* receives no interpretation in (15a) and behaves as a last-resort item inserted in order to support ∈ (the exclamative operator). According to this analysis, the DP with *más/tan* cannot be

---

for countries in (ia), but the verbal predicate is a crucial deciding factor, since exoticism is not the required property in (ib):

(i) a. ¡Qué países visitas en vacaciones!
    'What countries you usually visit on vacation!'
  b. ¡Qué países se endeudan en estos tiempos!
    'What countries get into debt nowadays!'

Arguably, "non-standardness" is all the grammar needs to build qualitative wh-phrases, so that its specific realization will depend on pragmatic variables relative to world knowledge. See Zanuttini and Portner (2003) and Rett (2008, 2009) on these issues.

preposed, since ε is properly identified by its overt specifier *qué*. On the possibility that the wh-word may be null in some qualitative wh-exclamative DPs, as in *¡Cosa más rara!* 'What a strange thing!', see Alonso-Cortés (1999b, p. 54).

4.2. OTHER PHRASAL EXCLAMATIVES

DP phrasal exclamatives may be headed by *vaya* 'what a' with no inflection, as well as a number of grammaticalized but fully inflected qualifying adjectives acting as exclamative determiners: *menudo* (lit. 'small'), *valiente* (lit. 'courageous'), *bonito* (lit. 'nice'), etc. For a longer list, see Casas (2005, pp. 148ff.), who calls them *ironic adjectives*.

(16) a. ¡Vaya casa!
    'What a house!'
 b. ¡Menudo chasco!
    'What a big disappointment!'
 c. ¡Valiente mequetrefe!
    'S/he is such a pipsqueak!'

These exclamative words behave as qualifying determiners (such as Lat. *quantus* or Old Spanish *cuál*), rather than quantifiers. In fact, *vaya* does not quantify over houses in (16a), just as Eng. *what* does not do so in its English counterpart. As we have seen, qualifiers may indirectly be seen as degree words, insofar as they call for the highest or the lowest values of properties in implicit scales. The phrases in (16) are root exclamatives (§ 5.2). The fact that they reject subordination is an argument against the idea that these determiners are wh-items:

(17) a. ¡Vaya lata es eso!
    'What a nuisance that is!'
 b. *Sé muy bien vaya lata es eso.
    'I know quite well what a nuisance that is.'

The syntactic projections of the exclamative words in (16) do not quite coincide. Only *vaya* optionally allows for indefinite NPs, as in *Vaya (una) casa* 'What a house.' Sáez (this volume) argues that *a/una* occupies the place of the exclamative operator ε in these expressions. *Vaya* precedes nouns, but in the Spanish of Asturias and León (northern Spain) it allows for adjectives

(¡*Vaya caro!* 'How expensive!') and adverbs (¡*Vaya despacio!* 'How slowly!'). It does not inflect, but it allows for plural nominals, as the adjectives in (16) do. It differs from them in admitting interposed adjectives, a property shared by wh-words (Tirado, 2013, 2015a, 2015b):

(18) ¡{Vaya/*Menuda} curiosa coincidencia!
'What a curious coincidence!'

On the behavior of these phrases in exclamative sentences, see § 5.2. On the grammaticalization of *vaya* (a subjunctive form of the verb *ir* 'go'), see Octavio de Toledo (2001–2002) and Tirado (2015b). On other properties of the exclamative words in (16), and the paradigm they constitute, see Sancho Cremades (2001–2002, 2008), Casas (2005), Rodríguez Ramalle (2008a, 2008b, 2011), Escandell-Vidal and Leonetti (2014), Tirado (2013, 2015a, 2015b), and Gutiérrez-Rexach and Andueza (this volume).

5. Sentential Exclamatives

5.1. WH-EXCLAMATIVES AND RELATED STRUCTURES

5.1.1. Wh-Exclamatives

Wh- sentential exclamatives are exclamative sentences built with wh-words and phrases moved at the specifier of some position at the left periphery. As opposed to English wh-exclamatives, their Spanish counterparts require V-preposing, a property shared by focus fronting. A well-known characteristic of root Spanish wh-exclamatives, rejected by their interrogative counterparts, is the fact that they apparently display doubly filled COMPs on an optional basis, as in (19):

(19) a. ¡Qué bien (que) canta María!
'How well M. sings!'
b. ¡Qué raro (que) eres!
'How strange you are!'

There is no disagreement on the fact that (19) involves wh-movement, but no consensus exists on the specific projection targeted by the wh-phrase in these structures. The main alternatives are presented in (20):

(20) a. The wh-phrase moves to Spec/CP: Bosque (1984a), Brucart (1994), and Masullo (2012); also Castroviejo (2006, 2007) for the Catalan counterparts of (19).
  b. The wh-phrase moves to Spec/FocusP: Hernanz (2006) and Hernanz and Rigau (2006).
  c. The wh-phrase moves to Spec/CP1, a low CP under CP2: Zanuttini and Portner (2003) for Italian.
  d. Wh-phrases are split, as in Kayne's (1994) analysis of relatives: Gutiérrez-Rexach (2008).

The analysis in (20d) requires some clarification. Gutiérrez-Rexach extends Kayne's (1994) anti-symmetric analysis of relatives to exclamatives. This means that *qué bien* 'how well' or *qué raro* 'how strange' are not syntactic constituents in (19). Just as a D° head selects for a CP in Kayne's well-known analysis of relatives and the internal NP is the operator that moves out of IP and reaches Spec/CP, *bien* and *raro* are moved from their propositional constituent, so that wh-phrases split along the derivation. The four options in (20) are depicted in (21):

(21) a. $[_{CP}\ [_{WH\text{-}DEGP}$ qué bien$]\ [_{C'}\ [_{C°}$ que $[_{IP}$ canta María $[_{WH\text{-}DEGP}$ e ...$]]]]$
  b. $[_{FocusP}\ [_{WH\text{-}DEGP}$ qué bien$]\ [_{Foc'}\ [_{Foc°}$ que $[_{FinP}$ canta María $[_{WH\text{-}DEGP}$ e ...$]]]]]$
  c. $[_{CP2}\ [_{WH\text{-}DEGP}$ qué bien$]\ [_{C'}\ [_{C°}\ [_{CP1}\ [_{C'}\ [_{C°}$ que $[_{IP}$ canta María $[_{WH\text{-}DEGP}$ e ...$]]]]]]]$
  d. $[_{ForceP}\ [_{WH\text{-}DEGP}$ qué$_i]\ [_{Force'}\ [_{FocusP/DegP°}\ [e_i]$ bien$]\ [_{TopicP'}$ que canta María $[_{WH\text{-}AdvP}$ e ...$]]]]$

In none of these structures does a syntactic relation hold between the wh-phrase and the indicative mood of the verb. Bosque (1984a) compares (19a) with its subjunctive counterpart, *¡Qué bien que cante María!* 'How nice (that) M. is singing!,' and argues that the interpretive difference follows from the predicative or binomial structure (§ 5.4) of the latter, since predicates select the mood of their sentential arguments. See Casas (2004, 2005) on other aspects of the optionality of *que* in (20).

In all the exclamatives above some wh-phrase moves as a whole, with the exception of (20d), where *qué bien* still has to be considered a constituent in regard to coordination processes. Apparently, the possibility exists that wh-exclamative phrases are overtly split in syntax. This might happen when the wh-word preposes, leaving the rest of the phrase behind. But some doubts persist on the existence of this splitting process. First of all, two main varieties of these (apparently split) wh-exclamatives may be recognized. Both involve *cómo* 'how much' and adjectives and adverbs. The first pattern is illustrated in (22):

(22) a. ¡Cómo eres bella!
      'How beautiful you are!'
   b. ¡Cómo es grande mi pueblo! (M. Viezzer [Bolivia, 1977], CREA)
      'How big my town is!'
   c. ¡Oh, cómo canta bien y sabe bien italiano! (J. de Pasamonte [1605], CORDE)
      'How well s/he sings and knows Italian!'

The type in (22), widespread in Old Spanish, is still alive in some literary variants of American Spanish. See Octavio de Toledo and Sánchez López (2009) for examples, as well as for other comments on the history of this pattern. This is the unmarked form in present-day French (*Comme tu est belle!*) and Italian (*Come sei bella!*).

The second pattern is standard in European Spanish and less common in present-day American Spanish:

(23) a. ¡Cómo eres de bella!
      'How beautiful you are!'
   b. ¡Cómo canta de bien!
      'How well s/he sings!'

Although it is tempting to see (22) as extraposed wh-exclamatives (more specifically, as instances of a wh-word moved out of an AP), the fact that *cómo* 'how' is not a wh-degree word for APs (*¡Cómo bella eres!* 'How beautiful you are!') is an argument against this option. This analysis could be applied to old variants of (22) with *cuánto*, instead of *cómo*, as in (24):

(24) Quánto fue engañado aquel hombre (J. de Ortega [1512], CORDE)
     'How deceived that man was!'

In Bosque (1984a, 1984b) it is suggested that wh-exclamative words in (22) might be VP adjuncts instead of degree modifiers inside APs. VP adjuncts of this sort in present-day Spanish include *hasta qué punto* 'to what extent'. Interestingly, *mucho* 'much' was freely focalized in Old Spanish in similar contexts, as in (25a), and still is in some varieties of oral speech, mostly with ironic interpretations, as in (25b):

(25) a. Mucho es desseado de aquella que lo ha menester (Anonymous [1522], CORDE)
'He is very much desired by she who needs him'
b. ¡Mucho estás tú en crisis!⁶
'No doubt you are in a deep crisis, for sure!'

To all this one may add that cases are found of focalized *mucho* displaying a lack of nominal agreement in Old Spanish: if (26) were an instance of focal movement out of an NP, the feminine *mucha* would be expected.

(26) Mucho es marauilla (Anonymous [1470], CORDE)
'This is most wonderful.'

5.1.2. Definite Article Degree Exclamatives

It has been traditionally recognized that there is a close link between wh-sentential exclamatives and "definite article degree exclamatives" (DADEs), sometimes also called "degree relatives" and "exclamatives with emphatic articles." These are exclamatives headed by a definite determiner followed by a projection denoting degree or amount. DADEs may vary according to the categorial features of the degree projection they host, which may optionally admit modifiers. Possible hosted categories are nouns (27a), adjectives (27b), adverbs (27c), and prepositions (27d):

(27) a. ¡Los (incontables) sitios que ha visitado este hombre!
'The (innumerable) places that this man has visited!'
b. ¡Lo (muy) inteligente que es María!
'How very clever M. is!'
c. ¡Lo (increíblemente) rápido que va este coche!
'How (incredibly) fast this car runs!'
d. Vergüenza por lo tan para poco que hemos sido (*El Diario.es* 02/06/2014)
'We should be ashamed of how unimportant we have been!'

---

6. Quoted from http://www.spaniards.es/foros/2009/04/14/oslo-nos-espera-un-sitio-donde-dormir-help

As seen in (27a), the definite article agrees with the noun; for all other cases, the neuter article *lo* is picked up. The possibility exists that the neuter determiner *lo* alone covers the degree information provided by the quantified phrase as a whole, since neuter pronouns may be arguments and adjuncts:

(28) a. ¡Lo que me ha dicho!
    'The things s/he has said to me!'
  b. ¡Lo que es María!
    'What a person M. is!'
  c. ¡Lo que corre este coche!
    'How fast this car runs!'

It is important to keep in mind that some high or extreme value must necessarily be interpreted in (27) and (28), even if optional modifiers are absent. There is, thus, no appreciable difference between the two variants in (29):

(29) No sabes lo (mucho) que te lo agradezco.
    'You can't imagine how much I appreciate this.'

The main properties of DADEs are pointed out in most general descriptions of Spanish exclamatives (Alonso-Cortés, 1999a, 1999b; RAE-ASALE, 2009, § 42.16; see also Casas, 2005; González Calvo, 1984–1988), as well as in the previous grammatical tradition summarized therein. Root DADEs are only exclamative, but their subordinate counterparts may be propositional complements selected by predicates taking indirect questions (as in [30a], not addressed here), or indirect exclamatives, as in (30b). They are rejected by predicates that select for neither one, as in (30c):[7]

(30) a. Eso depende de lo bien que se porte.
    'That depends on how well s/he behaves.'
  b. Es curioso lo bien que se porta.
    'It is curious how well s/he behaves.'
  c. *Creo lo bien que se porta.
    'I believe how well s/he behaves.'

---

7. Factive non-wh-readings are also possible, but they will not be considered here:
  (i) De {lo que bien que trabaja/*qué bien trabaja} se deduce que la contratarán enseguida.
    'One may deduce that she will be hired soon from the fact that she works so well'

DADEs do not exactly contain wh-phrases, but some A' degree operator on extreme degrees/amounts must be an essential part of their syntactic structure, as argued by Gutiérrez-Rexach (1996, 1999, 2001, 2008). In fact, this operator licenses parasitic gaps, as Torrego (1988) observed:

(31) ¡Los libros que ha devuelto sin haber leído!
'How many books s/he has returned without reading!'

The interpretation of DADEs is subject to categorial variables. DADEs built out of count nouns receive qualitative readings, as in (32a). DADEs built out of mass and plural nouns are ambiguous between qualitative and quantitative interpretations. That is, (32b) is about some noteworthy brand or variety of champagne, or rather about some extremely high amount of champagne:

(32) a. ¡La noche que he pasado!
'What a rough night I've had!'
b. ¡El champán que bebe Juan!
'The champagne that J. (usually) drinks!'

On this ambiguity see Grosu and Landman (1998), Neelman et al. (2004), and Szczegielniak (2012). The variant with "*la de* +N" selects for quantitative readings only. According to Torrego (1988), other quantitative readings require verb internal complements, that is, those of transitive or unaccusative verbs. Consequently, only the qualitative reading (i.e., the one referring to people of a certain kind) is available in (33), with a subject DP:

(33) ¡La gente que te preocupa!
'The people that worry you!'

One must add that the distinction between qualitative and quantitative readings of nominal DADEs may simply be impossible to draw in certain cases, namely whenever extreme properties of nominals are contextually interpreted in relation to high amounts, as happens in (34a). The difficulty to tell the interpretation of *cómo* 'how' and *cuánto* 'how much' exclamatives apart in certain cases provides a similar situation, as noted in § 6.1, below. Similar factors exclude qualitative readings, and favor quantitative ones, in a number of DADEs involving abstract mass nouns, as *razón* 'reason' in (34b):

(34) a. No me explico el frío que hace.
'I can't explain why it's so cold.'

b. ¡La razón que tenía mi abuela!
      'How right my grandmother was!'

As regards the syntactic analysis of DADEs, most proposals attempt to relate them to the patterns in (20), even if C° must be always overt in DADEs, as opposed to wh-exclamatives. Brucart (1994, p. 155) and Masullo (2012) suggest a variety of (21a) in which *lo fuertes* in (35) is placed at Spec/CP.

(35) ¡Lo fuertes que son!
     'How strong they are!'

Zanuttini and Portner's (2003) analysis of the Paduan equivalent of (35) is like (21c), except for the fact that an operator, FACT, heads CP1. Gutiérrez-Rexach (2008) extends the structure in (21d) to DADEs, so that *lo* and *fuertes* are separated in different projections, the former being placed at ForceP. Other extensions of Kayne's (1994) anti-symmetric analysis of relatives to DADEs include Grosu and Landman (1998) and Kaneko (2008), the latter for French.

5.2. FOCAL AND POLARITY EXCLAMATIVES

We saw that, strictly speaking, focus movement is not bound to primary exclamatives. In fact, it is possible inside relative clauses, as in (36a), which (arguably) involve no ForceP (but see [58] below). Focus preposing may also be a cyclic movement, as in (36b), as opposed to exclamative wh-preposing (§ 6.4), and it does not have to be associated with degree quantification, as shown in (36c):

(36) a. Un libro que a mucha gente habría hecho pensar.
        'A book that would have made many people think.'
     b. Un poco más de paciencia me parece a mí que necesitas tú.
        'A bit of patience is what it seems to me you need.'
     c. Este elijo.
        'I choose this one.'

But other factors make focalized exclamatives behave as primary exclamatives, according to the classification in (5). First, quantifiers such as *mucho* 'much' or *poco* 'little,' together with exclamative adjectives such as those in (16), give rise to rhetorical and ironic readings that cannot be reduce to simple cases of focus preposing:

(37) a. ¡Mucho te interesa a ti la sintaxis!
'You are not very into syntax, are you?'
b. ¡Menudo explorador estás tú hecho!
'You look like such a good explorer!'

Many more examples of this pattern are provided in Casas (2005), Hernanz (2001, 2006), and Andueza (2011). These are rhetorical exclamatives because they introduce evaluations almost exactly opposed to the ones they express. One way to account for this fact, following Andueza (2011) and Andueza and Gutiérrez-Rexach (2011), is to suppose that reversed interpretations associated with irony are triggered by a negative operator with scope over the degree phrase. From a different perspective, Escandell Vidal and Leonetti (2014) associate these effects to those of the so-called *verum focus*. In their view, rhetorical exclamatives crucially hinge on the magnifying effect of emphasis, more specifically the hyperbolic meaning triggered by the propositional scope of *verum focus*. Interestingly, ironic interpretations in standard wh-exclamatives may be subject to some calculus, as in *¡Qué oportuno ha sido tu comentario!* 'How timely your comment was!,' so that the speaker's intended inference might fail or be missed.

There is also a close link between rhetorical exclamatives, as those in (37), and the "doubly filled COMP effects" characteristic of wh-exclamatives, as in the ones we saw in (19). As in that pattern, overt C° may be optionally present with preposed exclamative adjectives, as well as phrases built out of *bueno* 'good,' *bien* 'well,' *mucho* 'much,' *poco* 'little,' and similar degree expressions:

(38) a. ¡Menudo sinvergüenza (que) está hecho!
'What a crook he is!'
b. ¡Poco (que) te gusta a ti el chocolate!
'No doubt you like chocolate!'
c. ¡En buenos líos (que) me metes!
'You always get into such a big trouble!'
d. ¡Vaya cosas (que) dices!
'What absurd things you say!'

Hernanz and Rigau (2006) locate these instances of *que* as heads of a FocusP. Notice that this projection cannot be identified with the one typically associated with focus movement, since the latter requires C° to be empty:

(39) a. ¡Eso mismo (*que) pienso yo!
'That's exactly what I think!'
b. ¡Un buen helado (*que) me tomaría yo ahora!
'I could go for a good ice-cream now.'

As opposed to the patterns in (38)-(39), C° must be overt in two exclamative types:

1) Evidential exclamatives.
2) Emphatic polarity exclamatives.

Evidential exclamatives are constructed with modal adverbs and adjectives. See Rodríguez Ramalle (2008a, 2008b, 2008c, 2011), Andueza (2011), and Andueza and Gutiérrez-Rexach (2011):

(40) a. ¡Naturalmente que tienes razón!
'Of course you are right!'
b. ¡Claro que ella lo sabía!
'Of course she knew!'

This exclamative type is somehow paradoxical: on the one hand, it cannot be reduced to a binomial exclamative (§ 5.4.), as Rodríguez Ramalle has convincingly argued. On the other hand, evidential words in (40) seem to be predicates of propositional arguments. In fact, Andueza and Gutiérrez-Rexach (2011) argued that evidential exclamatives crucially hinge on the idea that the speaker explicitly rejects possible doubts of their propositional content. As regards their syntactic analysis, perhaps the predicative relation may be established within a low small clause, before the evidential items reach ForceP—the place where Hernanz and Rigau (2006) locate them.

"Emphatic polarity exclamatives" is the label that Batllori and Hernanz (2009, 2013) give to exclamatives formed with a left peripheral emphatic particle, such as *sí* 'yes' and *bien* 'well' (see also Hernanz, 2007).

(41) a. ¡Sí que tiene María prisa!
'M. sure is in a hurry!'
b. ¡Bien que te has divertido!
'No doubt, you've had fun!'

Some emphatic particles allow for focal interpretations when associated with IP or VP in Spanish. For example, *sí* behaves as a contrastive focus marker (Martínez Álvarez, 1997; González Rodríguez, 2007b, 2009), and *bien* is a manner adverb.

Exclamatives in 2) require V-preposing, as all focus movement structures do in Spanish, and they are not compatible with negation, whether expletive or not (§ 6.6), or subordination (6.5). Crucially, emphatic polarity exclamatives are also subject to the effect that RAE-ASALE (2009, § 42.15ñ-p) calls *cuantificación a distancia* 'quantification at a distance' (QD). This refers to the fact that degree expressions contained in emphatic polarity exclamatives reject *in situ* quantifiers, since the initial emphatic particle (or maybe the null operator in its specifier) provide that information.

(42) a. ¡Sí que tiene María (*mucha) prisa!
  'Of course M. is in a real hurry!'
 b. ¡Bien que te has divertido (*bastante)!
  'You have sure had a real good time!'

QD effects may be captured either by overt movement of these emphatic particles from low degree projections (which amounts to taking them as proper degree quantifiers) or by associating them with operators binding degree variables at some distance in local environments. Battlori and Hernanz (2013) argue that, besides focus, force, and degree projections, a polarity projection must be involved in these cases, arguably below focus phrase.[8]

---

8. In any case, there is no consensus on what exclamative particles compose this paradigm. *Ya* seems to be a good candidate, but it does not exhibit QD effects, as shown in (ia). *Vaya* is another potential candidate. It is subject to these effects (as observed in RAE-ASALE, 2009, § 42.15ñ), but it is also compatible with expletive negation, as in (ib):

(i) a. ¡Ya quisiera yo ser muy rico!
   'No doubt I'd like to be very rich!'
  b. ¡Vaya que no has tenido suerte!
   'You sure have been lucky!'
  c. ¡Mira que Juan es tonto!
   'J. is so dumb!'

Mira displays QD effects and does not reject expletive negation, but it does not require V- preposing, perhaps because it is not an emphatic particle but a mirative one (Sánchez López, 2014b; see also Ocampo, 2009; Gutiérrez-Rexach & Andueza, this volume).

5.3. MATRIX COMPLEMENTIZER EXCLAMATIVES

A large number of papers, written from various formal and functional perspectives, address non-wh matrix exclamatives headed by the complementizers *que* 'that' and unstressed *si* 'that, if' in Spanish (not to be confused with stressed *sí*). Matrix complementizer exclamatives (MCE, hereafter) may fit within so-called *embedded root phenomena* (Heycock, 2006) or *insubordination structures* (Evans, 2007). These cover particular interpretations of subordinate sentences when used in main contexts. Some specific connection of the head complementizer with the appropriate Force or Mood projections seems to be necessary, since these sentences may express reports, quotations, evaluations, and replies in rather subtle ways, as well as some forms of degree quantification in a restricted number of cases.

Non-exclamative sentences headed by matrix C will not be addressed here. The simplest formal classification of MCEs is as follows (a "*que* + *si*" option might be added, but it will not be considered here, since it seems to be compositional):

(43) a. *Que* + indicative.
 b. *Que* + subjunctive.
 c. *Si* + indicative.
 d. *Si* + subjunctive.

Type (43a) corresponds to sentences such as (44), often called "reportative" or "quotative" (Etxepare, 2007, 2008, 2010):

(44) ¡Que son las diez!
 'Hey, it's ten o'clock already!'

Even so, these general meanings allow for a wide range of related interpretations, going from mere notification to reminding or warning. Reportative *que* is considered to be an evidential marker in Rodríguez Ramalle (2008a, 2008b) and Demonte and Soriano (2013). The latter authors argue that the pattern in (43a) may correspond to either an echoic structure or a quotative one, with a number of syntactic differences. Porroche (1998a, 1998b) argues that it has also an argumentative value, since it may be used by the speaker in order to emphasize the contextual relevance of the exclamative's propositional content, not necessarily its novelty, as in (45a):

(45) a. ¡Que ha venido Marta!
   'Martha is finally here!'
   b. Vamos, que no quieres venir.
   'So, it's just that you don't want to come.'

Gras (2013, 2016) suggests that (45b) exhibits a "connective interpretation," which might be considered a variety of the quotative reading in which the speaker introduces a personal reformulation of a preceding discourse. On these and other aspects on the pattern in (43a) see also Pons (2003), Casas (2005), Biezma (2007), and Rodríguez Ramalle (2007a, 2011).

The MCE type in (43b) allows for four variants: (1) an evaluative one, with rising final intonation, as in (46a); (2) a quotative or echoic reading, reporting someone else's instructions or commands, as in (46b); (3) an optative or desiderative interpretation, as in (46c); and (4) a directive reading, as in (46d):

(46) a. ¡Que tenga yo que aguantar esto!
   'I can't believe I have to put up with this!'
   b. ¡Que no tardes!
   '(Remember,) Don't you be late!'
   c. ¡Que te diviertas!
   'Have a good time!'
   d. ¡Que pasen!
   'Let them come in!'

Compound tenses are allowed in the first three types. As pointed out by Sánchez López (2015a, 2015b) only the type in (46a) is factive, since it expresses the speaker's feeling (almost always negative) on a present or past attested fact. Although desirable on theoretical grounds, it is hard to subsume (46c) and (46d) into a single optative interpretation. On this issue and some other aspects of the readings distinguished in (46), see Dumitrescu (1998), Garrido Medina (1999), Sansiñena, Cornillie, and De Smet (2013), and Sansiñena, De Smet, and Cornillie (2015). Sánchez López (this volume) argues that hypotheses that postulate a hidden main predicate of propositional attitude face a number of difficulties to overcome.

Type (43c) may be subdivided in two varieties. The first one is exemplified in (47):

(47) a. ¡Si estoy callado!
   'But I am quiet!'

b. ¡Si es una maravilla!
'But this is awesome!"

This variety introduces a justification in a reply or a possible (counter) argumentative reinforcement of the speaker's position (Contreras, 1960; Porroche, 1998a, 1998b; Schwenter, 1996, 1999, 2012; Montolío, 1999a, 1999b). Sánchez López (2015a, 2015b) argues that it may involve scalarity as well, since by uttering (47b) the speaker rejects all possible alternatives located below some implicit point. This suggests an extension of Zanuttini and Portner's (2003) widening process to situations (somehow as in the *declarative exclamatives* above), even if the sentence contains no wh-word.

The second variety of the pattern in (43c) involves QD, interpreted as explained above:

(48) a. ¡Si será Juan tonto!
'J. is so dumb!'
b. ¡Si habrá escrito libros este hombre!
'He's sure written tons of books!'

That is, adjectives in this pattern reject overt degree modifiers (* ... *muy tonto!*, in [48a]), and nominals must be bare (*... *muchos libros* in [48b]). Hernanz (2012) argues that in these sentences a null operator acting as a specifier of a FocusP headed by *si* binds a null degree or amount quantifier in its base position. Another feature, which she calls *irrealis*, is argued to be located in ForceP in order to provide the modal information (epistemic future or conditional) encoded in the verb's inflexional morphology:

(49) [$_{\text{ForceP}}$ [+irrealis] Op$_i$ ... [$_{\text{FocusP}}$ Op$_j$ *si* [$_{\text{FinP}}$ Juan será$_i$ [$_{\text{Deg}}$ [e$_j$ tonto]]]]

One may add that the degree features associated with the null operator binding the degree variable seem to be shared by *tan(to)* 'so much,' since they are able to trigger consecutive degree complements headed by *que* 'that,' as in (50a). Grande Rodríguez and Grande Alija (2004) argue that wh-exclamatives have this very property, as in their example (50b):

(50) a. ¡Si será Juan tonto que no se da cuenta de que le están tomando el pelo!
'Juan must be so dumb to not realize that people are pulling his leg!'

b. ¡Qué bien lo haría, que hasta le dieron un premio!
'S/he did it so well that s/he was even given a prize!'

Finally, type (43d) is an optative pattern (therefore, it may be placed in group 5.6 as well), restricted to imperfect or pluperfect of the subjunctive mood. These are sometimes called "conditional exclamatives":

(51) ¡Si yo fuera rico!
'If I were a rich man!'

Biezma (2011a, 2011b) argues that the structure in (51) is conditional, even if it contains no overt apodosis, a fact that strongly associates this pattern with that of suspended exclamatives (§ 5.6). In any case, conditional exclamatives do not fit in the pattern in (43c), as Sánchez López (this volume) argues, which introduces an asymmetry triggered by mood inflections.

Conditional exclamatives are also characterized in some languages by admitting the modifier ONLY in a non-restrictive interpretation (Rifkin, 2000), as in Eng. *If I only had time.* Spanish prefers *tan solo* (lit. "so much only") in these contexts. Grosz (2011) argues that *only* locates the prepositional content in the lowest point of a supposed set of possible wishes; as a consequence, these become exclamative conditionals of minimum requirement. Interestingly, Sp. *tan solo* alternates with *al menos* 'at least' and *(tan) siquiera* 'if . . . even' in this pattern.

Since both *que* and *si* may give rise to optative interpretations in subjunctive MCEs, the natural question is how to tell them apart. Sánchez López (2015a, 2015b, this volume) argues that optative *que* expresses a feasible desire, therefore an eventuality that is not real but is compatible with the actual state of things; optative *si*, on the contrary, introduces a non-feasible or impossible desire. From a formal point of view, she argues (this volume) that both *que* and *si* are heads of a ForceP projection (whose specifier bears the exclamative operator) taking a subjunctive modal head.

5.4. BINOMIAL EXCLAMATIVES

Binomial exclamatives (BEs) may also be called "two-membered" (Sp. *bimembres*). They are further called "verbless clauses," as in Gutiérrez-Rexach and González-Rivera (2013, 2014) or Munaro (2006). BEs are predicational exclamatives containing a subject and a predicate. They may be subdivided into various groups, illustrated in (52):

(52) a. ¡Un poco aburrido, tu amigo!
'A little boring, this friend of yours!'
b. ¡A la horca con ellos!
'Send them to the gallows!'
c. ¡Las patatas, que se queman!
'The potatoes! They're burning!'
d. ¡Las maletas, junto al sofá!
'The suitcases next to the sofa!'

As can be seen in (52), predicates precede subjects in types (52a) to (52c), but follow them in the rest. Type (52a) is the most studied of all BEs. As regards Spanish, see Bosque (1984a), Carbonero Cano (1990), Alonso-Cortés (1999a, 1999b), Hernanz and Suñer (1999), Casas (2005), González-Rivera (2011), and Gutiérrez-Rexach and González-Rivera (2013, 2014). On Italian, see Munaro (2006) and Benincà (1995); on French, see Henry (1953/1977), Vinet (1991), and Obenauer (1994); on Portuguese, see Sibaldo (2013).

Predicates in BEs of the type in (52a) may contain qualifying adjectives, indefinites DPs and wh-APs, as well as DPs built out of elatives and evaluative nouns, in Milner's (1978) sense, such as *desastre* 'disaster' or *maravilla* 'wonder.' Some PPs are also possible predicates in this pattern, as in *De no perdérsela, esta película* 'A must, that film!' (Munaro, 2006). All of them must be individual level predicates. The possible subjects of these BEs are DPs (whether wh- or not) and CPs, including infinitivals, as in *¡Qué bien poder hablar de ello!* 'How nice, to be able to talk about that!'[9]

The predication expressed in BEs of the type in (52a) involves a deictic interpretation bound to present time. As regards the syntactic analysis of these sentences, Sibaldo (2013) argues for Portuguese that they are root TP

---

9. Focal exclamatives bear a relationship to binomial exclamatives, but they are different structures. As indicated above, mood selection (subjunctive in [ib]) is crucial in binomial exclamatives with sentential subjects:

(i) a. ¡Muy bien que hiciste! [FOCAL EXCLAMATIVE]
'You sure did well!'
b. ¡Muy bien, que hagas la compra! [BINOMIAL EXCLAMATIVE]
'It's great you are able to do the shopping!'

Evidential exclamatives are also related to BEs, as pointed out after (40).

phrases that behave as free small clauses. Gutiérrez-Rexach and González-Rivera (2013, 2014) claim that preposing of the predicate is triggered by a strong affective feature, which is checked at a focus projection.[10]

Example (52b) illustrates a discontinuous *a . . . con. . . .* 'to . . . with . . .' optative reading. It is made up of a goal predicative PP (Hernanz & Suñer, 1999, p. 557) and a PP containing the predicational subject denoting the entity that the speaker wants to end up in some particular place.

Type (52c) corresponds to so-called "tetic exclamatives" (Kaneko, 2008, and references therein). These exclamatives express a non-standard (i.e., remarkable, unexpected, or worth noticing) present situation by associating a definite subject and a sentential predicate. This subject-predicate association is similar to the one found in so-called "pseudo-relatives," as in *Lo vi que huía* 'I saw him running away.'

Type (52d) resembles optative exclamatives (§ 5.6), since it introduces a location in which someone or something must be located according to the speaker's orders.

5.5. SUSPENDED EXCLAMATIVES

Suspended exclamatives (SEs) exhibit final rising intonation. Some of them look like comparative and consecutive sentences lacking *que*-codas. Casas (2005, 2006) calls them *exclamativas truncadas* 'truncated exclamatives,' and Masullo (2012, this volume) names them "covert exclamatives." SEs include *in situ* exclamative phrases built of five possible degree words: *tan(to)* 'so much/many,' *tal* 'so much,' *un(o)* 'a,' *cada* 'each,' and *más* 'more.' Here are some examples:

(53) a. ¡Eres {tan/más} tonto . . . !
'You are so dumb . . . !'
b. ¡Había tal barullo . . . !
'There was such a racket . . . !'
c ¡Juan dice unas tonterías . . . !
'J. says such nonsense . . . !'

---

10. Apparently, sentences such as *¡Maldita la gracia que me hace salir ahora de casa!* 'It's no fun to have to go out now!' belong to this pattern, but, strangely enough, the adjective *maldito* 'curse' seems to be able to precede a DP headed by an article, as in [. . .] *nadie se iba a enterar de maldita la cosa* (J. Sanchís Sinisterra, *Lope de Aguirre, traidor,* CREA). Perhaps this structure involves a syntactic amalgam, in Lakoff's (1974) sense.

d. ¡Se ve por ahí cada cosa . . . !
'One sees so many weird things out there . . . !'

A null sixth degree quantifier may be added to these five options, according to Di Tullio (2004) and Masullo (this volume). In this variant, *de* precedes APs, DPs, and AdvPs and blocks any other possible overt quantifier:

(54) a. ¡Llegó de (*muy) cansado . . . !
'S/he arrived so very tired . . . !'
b. ¡Sabe de (*tantas) cosas . . . !
'S/he knows so many things . . . !'

Di Tullio (2004) suggests that a null quantifier immediately precedes the *de* PP in these cases and also that the immobilized indefinite article *una* (as in *¡Leyó una de libros . . . !* 'S/he read so many books . . . !') might occupy its place. Masullo (this volume) argues that the null quantifier or extreme degree, which takes *de* PPs as complements, is bound by an operator at the higher FocusP. He further shows that this binding process is subject to islands effects.

Even if consecutive *que*-codas are licensed in all these variants, as they are in (50), Casas (2005, pp. 72ff., pp. 109ff) and Di Tullio (2004) argue that SEs do not reduce to equality comparatives or consecutive structures. SEs exhibit other interesting properties. Krueger (1960) constitutes an in-depth description of Spanish and Catalan SEs from both diachronic and synchronic perspectives. See also Alonso-Cortés (1999a, § 62.2).

5.6. OPTATIVE EXCLAMATIVES

Optative sentences are a group of exclamatives that express vivid desires, then propositional attitudes on non-veridical or non-attested situations. Most refer to present or past states of affairs, the latter through compound tenses. Propositions denoting the situations being desired are not necessarily extreme (unlike the degree values associated with most exclamative sentences), but they are salient, prominent, or non-standard in the speaker's personal view. Spanish optatives may be subdivided into three groups (Sánchez López, this volume):

(55) a. Optatives with *quién* 'who.'
b. Optatives with initial particles.
c. Verb initial optatives.

Quién optatives (55a) are constructed with an imperfect or subjunctive pluperfect. As Sánchez López (2014a, this volume) remarks, *quién* agrees with the verb in 3rd person features, but the sentence necessarily encodes a desire of the speaker on a counterfactive situation:

(56) a. ¡Quién fuera millonario!
    'Wish I were a millionaire!'
 b. ¡Quién hubiera estado allí!
    'Who would've been there!'

In her analysis, first-person features are linked to the intensional operator (after Grosz, 2011) expressing ilocutionary force, whereas third-person features are provided by *quién* and reflected by the verb. Grosz (2011) argues that these optative utterances incorporate a mood head responsible for their counterfactive reading, as well as (arguably) their inflectional mood in some languages.

The initial optative particles to which (55b) refers are marked in italics in the examples in (57):

(57) a. ¡*Si* yo fuera rico!
    'If I were a rich man.'
 b. ¡*Que* tengas suerte!
    'Luck be with you!'
 c. ¡*Así* se muera!
    'May s/he drop dead!'
 d. ¡*Ojalá* (que) termine pronto la crisis!
    'Wish the crisis would end soon!'

We have already seen the patterns in (57a) (=[43d]) and (57b) (=[43b]). *Así* 'May, I wish' is mostly restricted to curses; it forces V-preposing, unlike the other items in (57). *Ojalá* 'I wish' has the interesting property of being able to appear in subordinate clauses (RAE-ASALE, § 32.5q; Alonso-Cortés, 2011), as in (58a). Although *ojalá* may be an interjection in other contexts, it seems to be a modal adverb when heading an optative utterance (Alonso-Cortés, 2011; Sánchez López, this volume), but also when used in answers or replies. It is controversial whether illocutionary force holds in subordinate clauses, but examples such (58b) suggest that it might do so in certain cases:

(58) a. Una película que ojalá te guste
'A film that I hope you like.'
b. El libro que te prometo leer.
'The book that I promise you to read.'

As other optatives, the ones in (55b) are not counterfactive, unless constructed in subjunctive imperfect or pluperfect. The speaker who says ¡*Ojalá haya aprobado!* 'I hope I've passed' is not presupposing that s/he has failed, but only expressing a vivid desire for this situation not to be true. In Sánchez López's analysis (this volume), *ojalá* is moved to Spec/ForceP from a modal head. The optional complementizer that it allows for, as seen in (57d), is similar to those examined in (19) or (38).

Verb inicial optatives (55c) present at least two varieties. In the first one, counterfactive pluperfects are used in recriminations, as in (59a), or in comments or remarks on missed opportunities, as in (59b):

(59) a. ¡Te hubieras fijado! [American Spanish]
'You should have paid attention!'
b. ¡Te hubieras divertido!
'You would've had fun!'
c. ¡Haberte fijado!
'You should have paid attention!'

A variant of (59a) containing infinitive compound tenses, as in (59c), was argued to be an imperative in Bosque (1980b). This analysis was supported and developed by Vicente (2010) and Van Olmen (2014), and criticized by Biezma (2008, 2010), who takes all the patterns in (59) to be variants of *si* conditional counterfactuals. Counterfactive optatives with compound tenses allow for the pattern in (59a) as well, as in ¡*Que se hubiera fijado!* 'S/he should have paid attention!'

The second variety of (55c) corresponds to so-called "jussive mood," also called "optative subjunctive" in the Spanish grammatical tradition after Bello (1847/1964).

(60) a. ¡Tenga usted un buen día!
'Have a nice day'!
b. ¡Haya paz!
'Let there be peace!'

b. Supóngase una situación en la que . . .
 'Let us suppose a situation in which . . .'

On the grammatical properties of this pattern, see Sánchez López (this volume) and references therein.

6. Are Exclamatives Defective Structures? Syntactic and Semantic Constraints on Exclamatives

A number of constraints suggest that exclamative sentences are defective constructions. These constraints certainly exist, but they may be proven to be natural results of the defining characteristics of these utterances; namely, the denotation of extreme degrees, the widening process that wh-exclamative variables are subject to, the specific illocutionary force required by root exclamatives, and (arguably) factivity. The crossing of these features with the grammatical requirement of some syntactic structures, such as clefts, negative islands, and multiple questions, provides a plausible explanation for most of the restrictions found. Here is a sketchy presentation of the ways in which this interaction might take place.

6.1. FEWER EXCLAMATIVE WH-WORDS IN A DIFFERENT DISTRIBUTION

Most wh-interrogative words have exclamative counterparts. Exceptions include *quién* 'who,' *cuándo* 'when,' and *por qué* 'why.' According to Castroviejo (2006), Rett (2008), Andueza (2011), and Andueza and Gutiérrez-Rexach (2010, 2011), wh-exclamative operators are associated with degree variables, and these wh-words provide none. As a consequence, (61b) cannot be a legitimate wh-exclamation in which the speaker expresses his or her amazement at the hearer's weird mealtimes. On the non-existence of this pattern, see also Casas (2005, pp. 71ff.):

(61) a. ¡Cuánto comes!
     'How much you eat!'
  b. *¡Cuándo comes!
     'When you eat!'
  c. ¡A qué horas comes!
     'How strange your mealtimes are!'

d. *¡Quién es Juan! [rhetorical question reading disregarded]
   'Who is J.!'

Notice that (61c) represents no exception, since *qué horas* is a qualitative DP, not a wh-adverb. One may find apparent exceptions to this generalization and also some (arguably) true ones. Apparent exceptions include rhetorical questions, often written between exclamative orthographic symbols. In this particular reading, (61d) is grammatical, as indicated, and so are the sentences in (62):

(62) a. ¡Quién me iba a decir a mí que estaría hoy aquí!
   'Who could have told me that I would be here today!'
   b. ¡Por qué no te callas!
   'Why don't you shut up!'
   c. ¡Adónde vamos a llegar!
   'How far are we going with this?'

See Castroviejo (2006) for similar examples. These rhetorical questions lack an intended answer, but they do not become exclamative utterances as a consequence of this (Escandell-Vidal, 1984, 1989; Gutiérrez-Rexach, 1998; Alonso-Cortés, 1999a, 1999b). Other possible apparent exceptions include optatives, fully compatible with *quién,* as seen in (56). This might follow from the fact that the subject *quién* in counterfactual optatives is exceptionally licensed through the person features provided by an exclamative operator, according to Sánchez López (2014a, 2016, this volume).

True exceptions include sentences such as (63). For similar examples, see Michaelis and Lambrecht (1996), Michelis (2001), Casas (2005, p. 71), and Sánchez López (2014a).

(63) a. Pero ¡quién viene a verme!
   'But look who's coming to see me!'
   b. Es curioso quién protesta ahora.
   'It's funny who is complaining now!'

Notice that if no wh-indirect exclamative is present in (63b), there is no place for this structure in the grammar, since this sentence contains no indirect question. In any case, the potential exclusion of *quién/ quiénes* 'who' from the paradigm of exclamatives needs some clarification, since paraphrases of these items with nouns such as *personas* 'persons,' *individuos* 'individuals,' or *gente* 'people' constitute possible wh-exclamative phrases. One may argue that this paradox is similar to the contrast in (61b–61c). It relies on the fact that interrogative *quién* or *qué gente* attempt to identify a variable in a certain context, whereas their exclamative counterparts search for no one. Qualitative exclamative wh-phrases such as *qué individuos* or *qué gente* provide a set of implicit non-standard properties for those nouns. The range of the variable bound by *quién* is "person," but this sublexical information is (apparently) not accessible for the syntax (maybe for reasons related to lexical integrity), and no set of extreme properties is built for exclamative *quién*.

But another option exists. We may also suppose that individuals may be ranked in scales according to contextually salient properties (on this view, see Michaelis & Lambrecht, 1996; Michaelis, 2001; Sánchez Lopez, 2014a). This option provides a place for (63b), since *quién* is allowed in the paradigm of wh-exclamatives. It must be restricted, in any case, and may be parametrized, since, as Nouwen and Chernilovskaya (2013) show, remarkable differences among languages exist as regards these uses.

Lexical restrictions extend to other wh-exclamative words. The wh-adverb *cuánto* 'how much/many' is the only wh-word that admits the superlative suffix *-ísimo* (*cuantísimo* 'how very much'), again restricted to exclamatives (a fact that nicely fits in Zanuttini and Portner's widening theory). It is also the only bare wh-exclamative accepting the doubly filled COMP analyzed in § 5.1.1:

(64) a. ¡Cómo (*que) canta!
'How s/he sings!
b. ¡Cuánto (que) trabaja!
'How much s/he works!

The contrasts between exclamative *cómo* and *cuánto* may be addressed from various perspectives. Rett (2009) argues that *how* questions may ask about either manner or evaluation, as in *How does Buck ride his horse?* Manner-*how* roughly means "in what specific manner," and evaluation-*how* equals "how well." On the contrary, exclamative-*how* only allows for the second reading. See also Wiese (2003) and Gutiérrez-Rexach and Andueza (this volume) on this difference.

We might add that "how" and "how much" exclamatives do not seem to be able to differentiate these two interpretations in some situations: if extreme manners of doing something exist, then the pragmatic scales relevant to identify them may not be distinguished from the values provided by adverbs denoting highest or lowest grades for event evaluation according to properness or standardness. In Bosque (1984a, 1984b) it is observed that *cómo* 'how' and *cuánto* 'how much' may be interchangeable in some exclamatives, whether direct or indirect, but not in interrogatives:

(65) a. ¡{Cómo/cuánto} te gusta el arroz! [*synonymous*]
  'How much you like rice!'
 b. ¿{Cómo/cuánto} te gusta el arroz? [*non-synonymous*]
  '{How/How much} do you like rice?'

It is suggested there that root exclamations about manners, such as ¡*Qué manera de llover!* 'What a way to rain!,' come close to exclamations about amounts or degrees. The pattern in (65a) is mainly restricted to change of state and psychological verbs (see Rodríguez Espiñeira, 1996, § 4r for corpus examples), as well as measure verbs (*costar* 'cost,' *pesar* 'weight,' *durar* 'last'), even if *medir* 'measure' is an exception.

Wh-APs exclamatives with *qué* are restricted as well. Besides lacking counterparts in questions, they are rejected in "P + Adj" PPs functioning as secondary predicates in exclamative wh-phrases, as Casas (2005, p. 54) observed:

(66) a. Lo tienen por muy tonto.
  'They consider him rather dumb.'
 b. *¡Por qué tonto lo tienen!
  'How dumb he is considered!'

(67) a. Pasaba por sumamente lista.
  'She passed for a very smart girl.'
 b. *¡Por qué lista pasaba!
  'How smart for a girl she was taken to be!'

6.2. NO CLEFTS

This constraint is not attested in the literature: wh-interrogative phrases may be clefted, but their exclamative counterparts may not:

(68) a. ¿Qué piso es el que te has comprado?
  'Which apartment is the one you've bought?'
 b. *¡Qué piso es el que te has comprado!
  '*Which apartment is the one you've bought!'

Potential counterexamples may be interpreted as rhetorical questions, therefore not real exceptions:

(69) ¡Qué es lo que has hecho!
'What have you done!'

One might be tempted to argue that the asymmetry in (68) is related to the illocutionary properties of questions, but this is not correct, since (68a) might be embedded under, say, *Sé muy bien* . . . 'I know quite well . . .' The key to the asymmetry in (68) should rather be found in the crash of the two different tasks that the wh-phrase must simultaneously perform in the exclamative cleft sentence. It must (1) pick up an item from a set of alternatives, as all foci do in clefts (Krifka, 2007; and much related work), and (2) be placed within an enlarged or widened interval (Zanutini & Portner, 2003) characterized by some implicit standard scale.

One of these two tasks will be unaccomplished in (68b). Since the variables to be bound are quite different, in either of these two processes there will be an operator unable to properly bind its variable. Notice that there are two wh-operators in (68a): one is provided by the free relative, and the other one corresponds to the focal wh-DP *qué piso*. We may safely argue that the first one does not play any role in the asymmetry in (68). An argument in support of this conclusion is the fact that so-called "*que*-galicado" sentences, present in most varieties of American Spanish (Brucart, 1994; Di Tullio & Kailuweit, 2012), lack free relatives. Interestingly, they reject wh-exclamatives as well. Foci are preposed in these structures approximately as they are in clefts, and identification of a variable in a set of alternatives is identical in them as well:

(70) a. ¿Cuánta plata fue que se robó? [American Spanish]
   'How much money did s/he steal?'
b. *¡Cuánta plata fue que se robó! [All dialects]
   'How much money s/he stole!'

6.3. NO *IN SITU* NOR MULTIPLE WH-EXCLAMATIVES

Unlike their interrogative counterparts, exclamatives cannot be multiple:

(71) a. ¿Qué libros has enviado a qué clientes?
   'Which books did you send to which clients?'

b. *¡Qué libros has enviado a qué clientes!
'*Which books you sent to which clients!'

A natural account of this asymmetry relies on the fact that operator-variable pairs may be satisfied in answers (RAE-ASALE, 2009, § 22.2h), but no answers are required (or even possible) in exclamatives. The non-existence of *in situ* exclamatives is also related to the absence of dialogues in which variables could be bound. In fact, the dialogue in (72), quoted from RAE-ASALE (2009, § 22.2h), provides a potential counterexample, since it includes an exclamative sentence in an answer:

(72) —¿Sabes que Pascual se ha comprado tres pisos en tres ciudades?
'¡Did you happen to know that P. has bought three apartments in three towns?'
—Sí, ¡y qué pisos en qué ciudades!
Lit. 'Yes, and what apartments in what towns!'

On the other hand, the fact that multiple exclamatives are possible in Japanese (Ono, 2004) suggests that their anomaly does not stand on a fundamental semantic conflict.

6.4. NO CYCLICITY

Villalba (2008b, 2016) observes that cyclic movement of wh-interrogative phrases is rejected. Here is a simple contrast:

(73) a. ¿Qué estupideces te han dicho que escribe hoy Juan en la prensa?
'What silly things did they tell you that J. has written in today's paper?'
b. ¡Qué estupideces (*te han dicho que) escribe hoy Juan en la prensa!
'What silly things (*they tell you) that J. has written in today's paper!'

Few explanations of this asymmetry are given in the literature. I suggest that it is probably related to the fact that so-called "brigde verbs" have been repeatedly associated with parenthetical expressions (Dehé & Kavalova, 2007; Schneider, Glikman, & Avanzi, 2015 and references therein), and parentheticals are incompatible with exclamatives:

(74) a. ¿Cuántos coches, según los cálculos, caben aquí?
'How many cars, according to calculations, could fit in here?'
b. *¡Cuántos coches, según los cálculos, caben aquí!
'*How many cars, according to calculations, could fit in here!'

In any case, some potential counterexamples of this constraint may be found. Many native speakers accept (75a), with a wh-AP preposed through cyclic movement. As regards (75b), it is from a literary translation:

(75) a. ¡Qué contenta dice tu madre que está la niña con su regalo!
Lit. 'How happy your mother says the girl is with her gift!'
b. ¡[...] qué tarde parece que has visto lo acertado!
'How late it seems you have seen the right thing!' (From Sophocles, *Antigona,* translation into Spanish, Google Books)

6.5. RESTRICTIONS ON EMBEDDING

Whereas predicates taking indirect questions are numerous, and belong to many semantic classes (nine in the typology in RAE-ASALE, 2009, § 43.7j for Spanish), those taking indirect exclamatives are much more restricted (Bosque, 1984a; Alonso-Cortés, 1999a, pp. 4011ff.). They include some verbs of speech, a few perception verbs that also take indirect questions, such as *ver* 'find out,' *mostrar* 'show,' or *revelar* 'reveal,' and a larger number of emotional factives. Non-factive emotional predicates, as *temer* 'fear,' are excluded (Gutiérrez-Rexach & Andueza, this volume). Here are some clear examples of indirect exclamatives in Spanish (DADEs are included, as advanced in [30]):

(76) a. Ya veo cuánta gente está de acuerdo contigo.
'I can see how many people agree with you.'
b. Es sorprendente lo fuertes que son.
'It is surprising how strong they are.'
c. Es una vergüenza cómo tratan aquí a la gente.
'It is shame how people are treated here.'

A much-studied issue, as regards similar lists of predicates, is the fact that those related to emotional notions are rejected in embedded questions. Apparent counterexamples may be reduced to fixed or lexicalized expressions and semi-idioms. This rejection is related to the incompatibly of factive predicates with an open variable that must be identified in wh-questions.

On this topic, see Abels (2004, 2007), Sæbø (2010), Chernilovskaya (2010, 2011), Andueza and Gutiérrez-Rexach (2012), and Gutiérrez-Rexach and Andueza (2016, this volume).

It is not obvious whether or not total (i.e., non-wh) embedded exclamatives exist. Apparently, they do not:

(77) Es curioso {cómo/*si} se las arregla para salirse con la suya.
'It is amazing {how/whether} s/he manages to get away with it.'

But a few potential counterexamples exist, as argued by Girón (2014). They include sentences such as (78):

(78) a. Ahora verás si aprovecha. (Cervantes, *Quijote*; from Girón, 2014, p. 46)
'You will now see what it's good for.'
b. Dígame usted si no tengo razón.
'You will now see what it's good for.'
c. Figúrate tú si será grande la casa.
'Just imagine how big the house must be.'

Example (78a) is unclear, since it allows for a disjunctive ... *o no* ('... or not') coda, and disjunctive codas are incompatible with exclamatives as a natural consequence of the illocutionary nature of exclamative speech acts. Other potential counterexamples suggested by Girón, such as those headed by *mira* or *fíjate*, are dubious as well, since these expressions seem to behave as mirative particles (Sánchez López, 2014b) rather than transitive verbs (in fact, *fijarse* is an intransitive verb: *Fíjate si corre este coche* 'See how much this car runs' > **Fíjatelo* 'See it'). In a similar vein, the fact that *no sabes* 'you can't imagine' allows for indirect exclamatives does not contradict the fact that *saber* rejects them. Nevertheless, Girón is right in arguing that a number of predicates taking indirect exclamatives may historically come from grammaticalization processes on perception verbs.[11]

Indirect exclamatives are also defective in that they reject infinitives:

(79) Es {misterioso/*sorprendente} cómo encontrarlo.
'It is {mysterious/amazing} how to find him/it.'

---

11. Interestingly, QD effects apply in (78), which suggests that a degree operator similar to Hernanz's (2012) might be at work. See Gutiérrez-Rexach and Andueza (this volume) on other aspects of the relationship between perception and emotive verbs as regards indirect exclamatives.

This may be derived from the fact that wh-infinitive questions are always prospective. If a null modal head is responsible for their presence in questions, whether main or subordinate (RAE-ASALE, 2009, § 43.7w), it follows that it will be unavailable for exclamatives.

Other grammatical restrictions on embedded exclamatives exist. Gutiérrez-Rexach and Andueza (this volume) show that qualitative exclamatives cannot be embedded. One of the relevant conditions they fail to meet, according to their analysis, is the inability of the subordinate sentence to maintain the capacity of illocutionary operators as licensers of grounded knowledge:

(80) a. ¡Qué dibujos hace María!
'What amazing drawings M. does!'
b. *Es increíble qué dibujos hace María.
'It's incredible what amazing drawings M. does.'

Other constraints on indirect exclamatives are related to mood. Factive emotive predicates select for the subjunctive mood, but embedded exclamatives (whether DADEs or not) are exceptions:

(81) a. Me sorprende que {*son/sean} tan fuertes.
'It amazes me that they are so strong.'
b. Me sorprende lo fuertes que {son/*sean}.
'It amazes me how strong they are.'
c. Me sorprende cómo {son/*sean} de fuertes.
'It amazes me how strong they are.'

The relationship between (81b) and (81c) may be interpreted as an argument in favor of the wh-nature of the null operators in DADEs (Gutiérrez-Rexach, 1999, 2001, 2008). But notice that the reduction of (81b) to (81c) does not quite explain the anomaly of the subjunctive in the latter, since indirect questions allow for this pattern with some verbs (e.g., *depender* 'depend'; see Bosque, 2012).

In spite of these and some other asymmetries,[12] exclamatives and interrogatives are alike in a number of respects, as pointed out in the literature

---

12. Bosque (1984a) argues that indirect exclamatives are rejected in nominal and adjectival complements (*La vergüenza de cómo tratan aquí a la gente* 'The shame of how people are treated here'), but Casas (2005, p. 42) quotes some potential counterexamples in literary texts, such as [. . .] *la noticia de cuán pronto había pacificado la ciudad* [. . .] *llegó pronto a Fernando* 'News

(D'Avis, 2002; Gutierrez-Rexach, 1996; Abels, 2004, 2005; Groenendijk & Stokhof, 1982; among others). For example, concealed exclamations (CEs) (see Grimshaw, 1979; Schwager, 2009; Portner & Zanuttini, 2005; Gutiérrez-Rexach & Andueza, this volume) parallel concealed questions (CQs). The former are DP complements, interpreted as CPs, which receive the extreme value interpretation characteristic of indirect exclamatives. That is, no extreme height is explicitly attributed to a building in (82):

(82) It's amazing the height of that building.

(82) contains no subordinate clause, but the DP in that sentence (a CE) is approximately interpreted as "how tall that building is."

But even if some consensus exists on the idea that CEs denote kinds or individual types, as CQs do, the process necessary to obtain their exact meaning is not so obvious. There is no doubt that (83a), with a CQ, means "I didn't know what his/her profession was."

(83) a. Yo no sabía su profesión.
    'I did not know his/her profession.'
  b. Me extrañó su profesión.
    'I was weirded out by his/her profession.'

In a parallel way, one might argue that (83b), with a CE, means "It surprised me how-x (x = an extreme property pragmatically accurate for professions) his profession was," but a simpler paraphrase, involving internal predication in a complement of the noun "fact," might be more accurate: "The fact that his/her profession was the one it was surprised me." Notice that no extreme degree is exactly predicated of a profession in (83b). If this is on the right track, at least some CEs may diverge from their interrogative counterparts in more fundamental respects.

6.6. RESTRICTIONS ON NEGATION

Negation in exclamative sentences may be interpretable (i-neg) or uninterpretable (u-neg), the latter often called "expletive." If neither option is

---

about how rapidly s/he had pacified the town soon arrived to F.' (M. Fernández Álvarez, *Isabel la Católica*).

possible, negation is excluded (e-neg), and an ungrammatical sentence is obtained. Here are the three possibilities:

(84) a. ¡Cuántas cosas importantes no ha dicho el orador! (I-NEG)
'How many important things the speaker has not said!'
b. ¡Cuántos recuerdos no le vendrían a la cabeza! (U-NEG)
'How many memories would come to his/her head!'
c. ¡Qué fuerte (*no) es María! (E-NEG)
'How strong M. is (*not)!'

Villalba (2004) argues that e-neg results from the negation's incapability of taking scope over the degree operator, as a consequence of exclamatives's being factive structures. The interpretation of (84c) is meaningless, since it implies that "there is no degree d, such that d is maximal in the scale of strength and such that María is strong to degree d." Since potential arguments against the factivity of root exclamatives exist (§ 2), an alternative might be worked out that does not crucially depend on that notion. In fact, Espinal's (1997, 2000) analysis of e-neg in exclamatives is grounded on specificity rather than factivity. Notice that there is a relationship between e-neg in exclamatives and typical effects of so-called "negative islands" (Abrusán 2014, ch. 3 and references therein). The anomaly of sentences such as *How much does John not weight? is repaired if the QP is able to become specific by denoting a particular amount or degree recoverable from context, as in How much did John not weigh and how much should he have weighed? But this resource is unavailable for exclamatives, just as it is for clefts or multiple exclamatives, since there is no possible variable to be contextually identified in either of these constructions. As expected, specific amount wh-exclamatives provide i-neg contexts, as in (84a). The fact that qualitative wh-DPs reduce to sets of extreme properties (§ 4.1) explains e-neg in (85):

(85) *¡Qué coche no tiene Juan!
'*What a car J. does not have!'

González Rodríguez (2007a, 2008, 2009) claims that elatives are positive polarity items not licensed via movement to functional projections (in this volume she extends this treatment to adverbs such as *extremadamente* 'extremely'). She argues that e-neg effects are derived from the elative's inability to be interpreted under the scope of negation as a consequence of their upper endpoint orientation.

Other phrases, not conditioned by this restriction, are compatible with i-neg contexts in wh-exclamatives. Masullo (2012) relates the e-neg in (84c) to the unavailability of low scope (that is, internal or non-clausal predicate-bound) negation of elatives, as in *El cine no está carísimo* 'The movies is not extremely expensive,' as well as their incompatibility with imperatives and other speech acts (on related phenomena, see also Bosque, 2001, 2002; González Rodríguez, 2006, this volume). A potential problem of Masullo's (2012) analysis of e-neg in these expressions (in which elatives must locally move to the specifier of a Focus projection to check an exclamative feature) might be its excessive power, since it predicts no elatives in relative clauses, DP sentential complements, and other syntactic islands.

There is no consensus on whether or not other e-neg effects in exclamatives must be excluded as a result of scope relations. For example, the question remains whether or not factivity is the key factor accounting for e-neg in predicates selecting for embedded exclamatives—first observed by Elliott (1974) for English—as in (86):

(86) (*No) es curioso cómo se las arregla para salir adelante (E-NEG)
'It is (*not) curious how s/he manages to get by.'

The issue may, again, be addressed from either a syntactic or a semantic perspective. According to the former, one might say that a wh-phrase denoting an extreme value cannot be interpreted under the scope of a modal operator. According to the latter—adopted by Villalba (2004) and Octavio de Toledo and Sánchez López (2009)—(86) is meaningless if *no* is included (metalinguistic negation being disregarded) because the main clause explicitly denies the strangeness or non-standardness of some presupposed extreme value on manners, denoted in the embedded clause. Other, somehow intermediate, approaches exist. According to Zanuttini and Portner (2003), the phenomenon in (86) results from negation preventing the necessary widening process in the subordinate clause. Gutiérrez-Rexach (1996) regards (86) as a selectional problem, since negation would exclude the negative matrix predicate from the class of factive emotives.

Let us briefly consider u-neg in exclamatives now. U-neg is triggered by (epistemic) conditional inflection, as in (84b), or epistemic futures, as in

(87), which constitute a subset of intensional or non-veridical environments—in Giannakidou's (1998) sense:

(87) ¡Que de excusas no habrás buscado para evitar hacer los deberes!
'How many excuses you sure have looked for to avoid doing your homework!'

Other potential intensional candidates, such as imperatives, questions, or "if" condicionals, display incompatibilities with exclamatives related to illocutionary force.[13]

Negation in rhetorical exclamatives allows for some varieties. The type in (88a) may be considered i-neg, rather than u-neg, since ironic effects in these cases mostly result from a calculation process that depends on contextual factors (Escandell-Vidal & Leonetti, 2014):

(88) a. ¡No corre este tío ni nada!
'This guy sure runs fast!'
b. ¡Poco te gusta comer! (from Andueza & Gutiérrez-Rexach, 2010, p. 21)
'How little you like eating!'

Antonymic readings or some quantifiers, as in (88b), are derived from a covert negative element with narrow scope over a degree phrase in Andueza and Gutierrez-Rexach (2010).[14]

---

13. Apparently, y/n questions are able to induce u-neg, as opposed to non-wh-exclamatives:

(i) a. ¿No tendrás cambio de 50 euros? (u-neg)
'Could you change a 50 euro bill for me?'
b. ¡No tendrás cambio de 50 euros! (i-neg)
'You will end up with no change for 50 euro bills!'

But this asymmetry may lie in the role of negation in polite rhetorical questions (see RAE-ASALE, 2009, § 43.10k), implying that (ia) is not a proper instance of u-neg. As for u-neg in *vaya si* exclamative structures, as in (ii), it does not require intensional contexts. As Tirado (2015a) argues, this type of u-neg is restricted to contexts of rebuttal:

(ii) A esa gente, vaya si no les gusta. (R. Rey, *Lo que soñó Sebastián*, CREA)
'These people, of course they like it.'

14. The negative interpretation of *qué* in some wh-exclamatives, as in ¡Qué va a venir ese! 'No doubt he will not come!'—Di Tullio's (2008) example—is most probably rhetorical as well. In fact, *qué* might be a reduction of *para qué* in these constructions. See also Rojas (1985) on very similar patterns.

7. This Volume

All authors invited to this compilation have previously published several pieces on Spanish exclamative constructions from some theoretical point of view. Most of the fundamental issues addressed in this overview are dealt with in the coming chapters: exclamative operators, both wh- and degree, are discussed in all of them, and so is the specific nature of illocutionary force in exclamative utterances. Special attention is given to exclamatives in negative (chapters 4, 5, and 6) and embedded (chapter 7) contexts, but also to factivity (chapter 5), elative items (chapters 4 and 6), and optatives (chapter 3).

In chapter 2, "*Más*-Support," Luis Sáez argues that the semantic composition of Sp. non-comparative *más* (as in ¡Qué libro mas curioso! 'What a curious book!') is partially similar to that of Zanuttini and Portner's (2003) null exclamative operator. He argues that this false comparative quantifier is licensed by this operator. In a process similar to *do*-support for T° or *that/for*-support for C°, *más* is interpreted as a support item, inserted in order to satisfy the affixal requirements of an abstract morpheme.

Chapter 3, by Cristina Sánchez López, is entitled "Optative Exclamatives in Spanish." Sánchez López deals with exclamatives that express the speaker's desires toward some state of affairs. These structures, always displaying subjunctive morphology, combine two factors. One, she argues, is a generalized exclamative operator EXC—as in Gutiérrez Rexach (2001) analysis—related to the emotion toward the status of the modified proposition on a contextually provided scale. The other factor is a mood head (encoding factuality, counterfactuality, and other similar values), that determines tense and mood, as well as the content of the C° initial head.

In chaper 4, entitled "Exclamatives in (Argentinian) Spanish and Their Next of Kin," Pascual J. Masullo analyzes the relationship between a series of covert exclamatives (CEs)—that is, exclamative sentences containing no overt wh-word—with overt wh-exclamatives (OEs). Showing they are subject to similar constraints, he argues that, while CEs contain an empty operator binding an extreme degree expression *in situ,* in OEs the wh-word conflates both the operator and extreme degree feature at once. He also analyzes new elatives in Argentinian Spanish in detail, arguing that, although associated with an extreme degree feature, they need not to be used in exclamative patterns.

In chapter 5, "At-Issue Material in Spanish Degree Exclamatives: An Experimental Study," Xavier Villalba deals with the notion of high degree in exclamative sentences, and specifically the question whether it should be analyzed as a presupposition (Gutiérrez-Rexach, 1999) or as a conventional implicature (Zanuttini & Portner, 2003). He carries out two experiments and he concludes that when speakers react negatively to wh-exclamatives, they tend to cancel the ascription of the relevant property rather than the high degree to which it is attributed. He argues that the relationship between wh-exclamatives and their propositional contents fits within the notion of projective meaning, as understood in Tonhauser, Beaver, Roberts, and Simons (2013), more properly than within that of presupposed knowledge.

Raquel González Rodríguez deals with the grammatical differences between exclamative wh-phrases and extreme degree modifiers in Spanish in chapter 6, "Exclamative Sentences and Extreme Degree Quantification." She points out a number of differences between wh-exclamative phrases and elatives, in spite of the fact that both are polarity items. These differences are related to their (in)compatibility with downward-entailing and anti-morphic operators. She argues that adverbs denoting extreme degree, as in *extremadamente* 'extremely,' close open scales, in Kennedy and McNally's (2005a) sense, and suggests a link between exclamative wh-phrases and modal adverbs denoting surprise.

In chapter 7, entitled "Embedded Exclamatives and the Ingredients of Grounded Belief," Javier Gutiérrez-Rexach and Patricia Andueza analyze the semantic properties of predicate-taking embedded exclamatives and argue that they are factive-emotive because they select for facts. They also claim that the meaning of main clause and embedded exclamatives does not change, and that evidential predicates can embed exclamatives expressions. Grounded belief is argued to be an underlying factor for several classes of embedded exclamatives, although other elements, such as factivity, degree reference, or evidential content, also play a crucial role in them.

Más-Support

Luis Sáez

1. Introduction

This chapter focuses on the properties and distribution of Spanish *más* 'more' in exclamative environments. The study of *más* is usually undertaken in connection with the analysis of (pseudo-) comparative constructions (RAE-ASALE, 2009, p. 45), so it is commonly described as a quantifier either comparing magnitudes (degrees of tallness in [1a]) or adding entities to a previously stated set (of books in [1b]); discourse reasons may allow the non-pronunciation of the sequence introduced by *que* in these constructions (hereafter, the "*que*-sequence"), generally regarded as a complement selected by *más* (Bresnan, 1973):

(1)   a. Juan es más alto (que Luis).
       Juan is more tall than Luis
       'Juan is taller (than Luis).'

This work has been financed by the Spanish Ministerio de Economía y Competitividad (research project: "Las construcciones exclamativas en español y sus relaciones con otras modalidades oracionales"; reference number: FFI2012-34974), and by grant UCM-930590 from the Complutense University (Madrid). I deeply thank Ignacio Bosque for having given me the opportunity to participate in this volume, as well as having provided me with many fruitful comments that have considerably improved this work. All the shortcomings still remaining are my own.

b. Juan compr-ó más libros (que *Niebla*).
Juan buy-PAST.3SG. more books than *Niebla*.
'John bought more books (than *Niebla*).'

The sequences *más* + adjective/noun of (1a, 1b) may show up in exclamative environments as well (cf. [2a, 2b]), but only if suspension intonation is added and both the *que*-sequence and the comparison/additive reading are missing; instead, unexpectedness/surprise will be entailed (Rett, 2008) motivated by a property related to a degree/amount (of tallness/books), which might lead to suspicion that *más* simply encodes surprise in these particular cases:

(2) a. ¡Juan es **más** alto (*que Luis) . . . !
'Juan is so tall!'
b. ¡Juan compró **más** libros (*que *Niebla*) . . . !
'Juan bought so very many books!'

Accordingly, it might be tempting to consider the word *qué* 'what' in examples like (3) (now incompatible with suspension intonation) to be the wh-correlate of this putative "surprise-*más*"; it would predict that *qué* and *más* may not co-occur, which at first glance seems to be borne out by the ungrammaticality of (4) (derived from inserting *más* in [3]):

(3) ¡**Qué** alto es Juan!
what tall is Juan
'How tall Juan is!'

(4) *¡**Qué más** alto es Juan!
*'How much taller Juan is!'

However, such prediction conflicts with examples like (5), where *interesantes* 'interesting' postnominally modifies a noun *libros* 'books,' whose projection unproblematically contains both *más* and *qué*:

(5) ¡**Qué** libros **más** interesantes compr-ó!
what books more interesting buy-PAST.3SG
'What interesting books (s)he bought!'

The point of examples like (5) is that, under a reading strictly relating the surprise to the degree of the property "interesting," it is *qué* rather than *más* conveying such surprise; in fact, in (6), a semantically identical variant of (5) with prenominal *interesantes, más* does not even show up, which, on the one hand, evidences the spurious semantics of *más* in (5) (and, presumably, in [2]) and, on the other hand, allows one to conclude that the conflict between *más* and *qué* in (6) (and, presumably, in [4]) cannot be due to their both being variants of a single "surprise-operator:"

(6) ¡**Qué** (***más**) interesantes libros compró!
'What interesting books s/he bought!'

The non-relevance of *más* for the surprise reading in (5)/(2) does not conflict with the fact—already observed by Castroviejo (2006) for Catalan and to be explained in § 3.3—that *más* is unavoidable in these examples under the relevant interpretation.[1] This is illustrated by (7a), the *más*-less correlate of (5), where the surprise conveyed by *qué* must focus on the kind of books, rather than on the property "interesting" (thus giving rise to a pragmatically odd interpretation like "what a sort of interesting books s/he bought!"); this is also the case in (7b), where adjectives are not even present:

(7) a. ¡Qué libros interesantes compró!
   'What books which are interesting s/he bought!'
   b. ¡Qué libros   compró!
   'What books s/he bought!'

As for (2) or, for instance, (8) (the semantically identical non-wh correlate of [5]), assuming the non-relevance of *más* for the surprise interpretation leads

---

1. As pointed out to me by Ignacio Bosque (personal communication), in these contexts it is not even possible to replace *más* with other apparently similar degree quantifiers/adverbs, like *sumamente* 'extremely':

   (i) *¡Qué libros **sumamente** interesantes compró!
       what books extremely   interesting buy-PAST.3SG
       'What extremely interesting books s/he bought!'

In this chapter I will show this is due to the fact that *más* is not an actual degree quantifier here, but rather a dummy item whose insertion is necessary under certain conditions (with postnominal adjective and prenominal *qué*, always under the relevant interpretation) in order to support an abstract morpheme related to exclamative constructions. It is worth pointing out that the ungrammaticality of (i) cannot be the result of an alleged incompatibility between the items *sumamente* and *qué*, since they unproblematically co-occur in (ii):

   (ii) ¡Qué sumamente interesante!
       'How extremely   interesting!'

one to suspect that the latter is conveyed by a covert operator (represented as "Op") whose plausible phonological manifestation is a suspension intonation otherwise only possible (and mandatory) in this sort of example—unlike what happens with the covert operator sometimes attributed in the literature to so-called "nominal exclamative": *¡Las cervezas que bebes!* 'The many beers you drink!'; cf. Torrego (1988):

(8) ¡Compr-ó   unos libros **Op** más interesantes . . . !
    buy-PAST.3SG a.PL books more interesting
    '(S)he bought such interesting books!'

In this chapter I will claim that *más* makes no semantic contribution to Spanish exclamatives. Instead, it is just a dummy item prompted by a morphological requirement to be satisfied in these environments and imposed by a null clitic-like morpheme I will introduce below.

The chapter is organized as follows. In § 1 I introduce Zanuttini and Portner's (2003) (hereafter, Z&P) proposal for the internal composition of Italian exclamative wh-phrases, a proposal I will roughly adopt in my approach to Spanish ones. For my purposes, the relevant feature of such a proposal will be the existence of a null morpheme playing a relevant role in certain instances of wh-exclamatives. In § 2 I will focus on the properties of Spanish exclamative phrases containing *más*. In § 3 I will mainly elaborate on the semantic and morphological properties of the above-mentioned null morpheme and try to explain why *más* is obligatory in certain contexts and impossible in others. The main proposal of the chapter will be made here: the null morpheme is a clitic-like element with particular morphological properties responsible for the presence of *más* in certain environments; *más* is a contentless support item post-syntactically inserted in order to support the null morpheme. In § 4 I summarize the chapter.

2. The Internal Makeup of Exclamative Phrases

Z&P propose that the fact that the distribution of certain wh-phrases is restricted to exclamative environments derives from their exhibiting a particular overt/covert "exclamative-only" ("E-only") morpheme. For instance, according to Z&P, the fact that the English wh-phrases in (9a, 9b) (in bold type) may appear in interrogative sentences, while the ones in (10a, 10b) are restricted to exclamative environments (cf. [10c, 10d]), is due to the absence/ presence of *very,* an E-only morpheme:

(9) a. **How many books** did you buy?
    b. **How tall** are you?

(10) a. How very many books you bought!
     b. How very tall you are!
     c. *How very many books did you buy?
     d. *How very tall you are?

Z&P propose that the exclamative noun phrases in (11a, 11b) consist of the sequence of components in (11c), where "measure" refers to the relevant measure units used for quantification ([+count] with *many* or [-count] with *much*), and "sortal" refers to the sort of things being measured, a set of books or a mass of work in these particular cases:

(11) a. How   very   many   books!
     b. How   very   much   work!
     c. WH   E-ONLY   MEASURE SORTAL

Presumably, exclamative APs like the one in (12a) also exhibit the structural slot (represented as "Ø") corresponding to the measure component; in fact, when the adjective is replaced by a pro-form *so,* as in (12b), the measure slot is filled with *much* (as was the case in [11b]), which Corver (1997) considers to be a functional dummy quantifier in these cases:[2]

(12) a. How very Ø   tall!
     b. How very much so!

---

2. In certain varieties of American Spanish, examples like (i) (from Mexican) are attested, where *mucho* 'very much' immediately precedes *muy* 'very' just as *very* precedes *much* in (12b). Then, as suggested to me by Ignacio Bosque (personal communication), perhaps this *muy* might also be regarded as an overt manifestation of the measure slot in the adjectival domain in these varieties of Spanish (due to space constraints, a full analysis of these interesting cases must be left for future work):

   (i) La Asamblea fue **mucho**   muy positiva. (*Proceso,* 29-9-2006, CREA)
        the meeting   was very-much very fruitful
        'The meeting was very fruitful.'

Adopting the so-called "functional head hypothesis" (Abney, 1987; Corver, 1991), Corver (1997) puts forth the adjectival extended projection in (13) (the "split degree system hypothesis"), where the dummy quantifier *much* is externally merged as Q (the leftmost items would probably be merged as part of the Deg[ree] layer or other layers higher than QP):

(13)

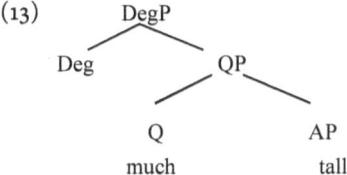

Therefore, I propose that Z&P's measure component, commonly lexicalized as *much/many* in English, is also located in Q in an extended projection shared by APs and NPs:

(14) [$_{DegP}$ Deg [$_{QP}$ [$_Q$ much/many] [$_{AP/NP}$ {tall/books/work}]]]

The measure component is also present in interrogative wh-phrases like the ones in (15a, 15b), where *many/much* does not entail the "higher-than-a-standard-amount/degree" interpretation entailed by *many/much* in non-interrogative clauses like (16a, 16b) (Rett, 2008, p. 13):

(15) a. How many books?
b. How much work?

(16) a. He bought many books.
b. Much work is necessary.

Instances of *much* like the ones in (16) led Corver to propose two different sorts of *much*: an adjecival (contentful) *much* contributing a degree argument (higher than a standard degree) and a dummy (contentless) *much*. By contrast, Solt (2010) argues that there is only one *much*, always contentless; the semantic entailment in (16) (the "higher-than-a-standard-degree/amount" interpretation) is actually contributed by another element that, being phonologically null, demands the presence of *much* as a mere "signal"; in other words, *much* is always a support item.

According to Solt (following Schwarzschild, 2006), the actual contentful element externally merged as Q is a measure function eventually providing a scalar interval (a set of degrees); as for the "higher-than-a-standard-degree/amount" interpretation in (16), she argues it is contributed to by a further contentful element, namely, a null "positive" operator (von Stechow, 2006). I will assume Solt's proposal of a null positive operator and will further claim it must be externally merged as the head of a functional projection higher than Q. Such functional projection, though, cannot be the DegP layer expected from a configuration like (13)–(14); rather, it is conceptually closer to the one proposed by Pastor (2008) for Spanish APs like those in (17) (in bold type):

(17) a. El es **muy alt-o.**
 he is very tall-MASC.SG
 'He is very tall.'
 b. El es **muy poco alt-o.**
 he is very little tall-MASC.SG
 'He is very short.'

According to Pastor, (17a, 17b) contain a functional projection encoding the upward/downward (positive/negative) orientation (from a contextual standard) for a particular degree; this degree is expressed by *muy*, which belongs to the DegP layer. I will propose that the orientation functional projection, which I will call the orientation phrase (OrP), is a sort of "degree polarity" layer, its clausal correlate being, for instance, Laka's (1990) sigma phrase. The head Or projects the scalar interval introduced by QP (Solt, 2010) into the positive/negative area of the scale by hosting a positive/negative operator. After insertion of *muy* at the DegP level, the interpretation "much under the standard of tallness" is obtained in (17b), where *poco* 'little' is the negative operator downwardly orientating the scale;[3] by contrast, the interpretation "much over the standard of tallness" is obtained in (17a), where a null positive operator replaces *poco*.

OrP may exist irrespective of the presence of *muy*, as shown both by (18a)/(18b), to be (respectively) interpreted as "his tallness is located in the

---

 3. In fact, Heim (2006) translates English *little* as expressing negation, and Kennedy and McNally (2005b) conceive it as a "scale adjuster" that inverts the polarity of the adjective it modifies (for Catalan *poc*, cf. also Castroviejo, 2006, p. 153).

positive/negative area of the scale" (with no further specifications), and by the above-introduced (16a, 16b), where, as claimed by Solt, the "higher-than-the-standard-amount" interpretation results from the null positive operator, not from *many/much*; on the other hand, it is worth insisting that OrP should not be identified with QP, since, as illustrated by (19), *poco* may not take part of interrogative wh-phrases, which, as was already shown in (15) for English, clearly exhibit a QP:

(18) a. El es **alto.**
    'He is tall.'
  b. Es **poco** alto.
    he-is little tall
    'He is short.'

(19) ¿Cuánt-o-s   (*poc-o-s)   libro-s?
    how.many-MASC-PL few-MASC-PL book-s
    'How many (*few) books?'

As a result of all these considerations, I propose (16)–(18) and (11)–(12) share a configuration like the one in (20), where English *very* is understood as an upward Or, the overt reverse of Spanish *poco*; consequently, *very*, unlike Spanish *muy* (cf. [21]), will be both compatible with elements located in DegP—as already observed by Corver (1997) by referring to the English translation of (21)—and incompatible with interrogatives (recall [10c, 10d]). As a matter of fact, Corver points out that, unlike APs containing true degree heads, APs containing *very* do not move to the left of the article *a* in indefinite noun phrases (see the contrast in [22], where the APs are in bold type):

(20)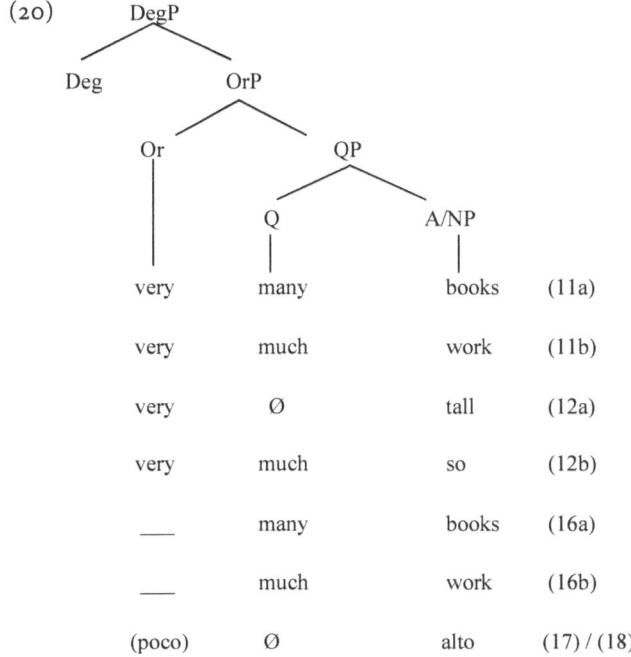

(21) John es tan (*muy) inteligente que resolve-rá   el problema.
     John is so   very intelligent that solve-FUT.3SG the problem
     'John is **so very** intelligent that he will solve this problem.'

(22) a. **{how/so/too/that} big** a man
     b. ***very big** a man

Corver further observes that, as shown by (11b), *very* may co-occur with *much*. This is a problem for his theory, according to which non-degree quantifiers must fill some position in the QP layer (the only alternative to DegP in his configuration [13]); however, quantifiers located there (like *extremely*) may not co-occur with *much*, as in *extremely (*much) so*, since *much* is inserted only when the QP layer is empty (a side effect of the account Corver offers for the facts at issue; see further below). The configuration I propose in (20) predicts all the facts observed by Corver: on the one hand, the facts in (21) and (22) are predicted, since *very* is not a degree head; on the other hand, since *very* is merged outside the QP layer, it may co-occur with *much*.

The Italian correlate of (11a) is the NP in (23a), each of the components of which ([23b, 23c] according to Z&P) is overtly spelled-out; however, the

Italian correlate of (12a), the AP in (24a), involves a much more abstract representation, as shown in (24b, 24c) (where Z&P represent the abstract E-only morpheme by using a Greek *epsilon*):

(23) a. Che tant-i   libr-i!
        how so.many-MASC.PL book-MASC.PL
    b. che t-   anti   libri
    c. WH E-ONLY MEASURE SORTAL

(24) a. Che alt-o!
        how tall-MASC.SG
    b. Che ϵ   + ∅   alto
    c. WH E-ONLY + MEASURE SORTAL

As shown in (23b), Z&P claim that Italian *tanti* consists of an E-only morpheme *t-* and a measure component *-anti*. The Spanish exclamative correlate of *tanti* is *tantos* (cf. [25a]), which, devoid of the plural morpheme *-s*, may precede pro-forms/copies of degree adjectives, as illustrated in (25b):

(25) a. ¡Tengo tanto-s   libros...!
        I.have so.many-PL books
        'I have so many books...!'
    b. Alto, ¡lo es tanto   alto...!
        tall, it is so.much tall
        '(S)he is so tall!'

A segmentation of Spanish *tanto* like the one proposed by Z&P for Italian *tanti* in (23b) would raise several problems. For instance, assuming that a configuration like (20) is true and, as has been argued above, Spanish *poco* is merged as Or, (26a) suggests that the morphology of Spanish *tanto* should be addressed under either a morpho-phonological hypothesis (which I will call "Hypothesis A") or a syntactic one ("Hypothesis B"), both of which are in conflict with Z&P and briefly presented below (which hypothesis is the right one is a question requiring much deeper research; for now, the relevant thing is that none of them is compatible with Z&P's proposal):

(26) a. ¡Él es tan poco alto!
        he is so little tall
        'He is so short!'

b. ¡Él es {tan/*tanto} alto!
   'He is so tall'

HYPOTHESIS A

According to a morpho-phonological approach, there would be a basic lexical item, *tanto*, (the one in [25]) base-generated in Deg (higher than Or), and *tan* would merely be the truncated manifestation of *tanto* triggered by a morpho-phonological rule when *tanto* immediately precedes an overt adverb (as in [26a]) or an adjective (as in [26b]). This account can be extended to pairs like *muy* 'very'/*mucho* 'very much' and *cuán* 'how'/*cuánto* 'how much' (among others), illustrated in (27a, 27b) and (28a, 28b), respectively:

(27) a. Es   **muy** alt-o.
        he/it.is very tall-MASC.SG
     b. Alt-o,   lo   es   **mucho**   alto
        tall-MASC.SG, it.CL it/he.is very.much
        'He/it is very tall.'

(28) a. ¡**Cuán** alt-o   es!
        how   tall-MASC.SG. he/it.is
     b. Alt-o,   ¡**cuánto** alto   lo   es!
        Tall-MASC.SG how.much   it.CL it/he is
        'How tall it/he is!'

Similar truncation rules exist for cases like (29b), where an adjective *tercero* 'third' (see [29a]) becomes *tercer* when immediately preceding a noun:

(29) a. El capítulo tercero.
        'the third chapter.'
     b. El **tercer(*-o)** capítulo.
        'the third chapter.'

HYPOTHESIS B

According to a syntactic hypothesis, *tanto* might result from merging *tan-* and *-to* (rather than *t-* and *-anto*, Z&P's proposal for Italian *tanto*). *Tan-* would be generated in Deg as an item potentially independent of *-to,* since *tan-* may show up when *-to* is missing; if *poco* is missing, such independence would manifest itself whenever the degree adjective is not replaced by a copy or a pro-form, as illustrated in (26b) above.

An advantage of this hypothesis is that the contrast between (25b), with a copy of *alto,* and (26b), with overt *alto,* may be related to the one between (12b) with a pro-form of *tall* and (12a) with *tall;* the latter contrast is repeated below as (30a, b) for convenience:

(30) a. How very Ø tall!
b. How very much so!

Recall that Corver (1997) argues that the item *much* in (30b) is a functional dummy quantifier that (for reasons not concerning us here) must be merged as the head of an empty QP layer whenever the degree adjective has been replaced by a copy/pro-form (cf. [13]). Following Corver's intuition for English data, Hypothesis B might derive the contrast between (25b) and (26b) in a parallel way: *-to* is a functional dummy item merged in the head position of an empty QP whenever the degree adjective has been replaced by a copy. Since *–to* is not a free morpheme, a Morphological Merger (Halle & Marantz, 1993) must eventually take place between *-to* and *tan;* the process is represented with the symbol "+" in the configuration (31) (where I consider *tan* to be a degree element; see further below):

(31) [$_{DegP}$ [$_{Deg}$ tan + [$_{OrP}$ [$_{QP}$ [$_Q$ -to] [$_{AP}$ ~~alto~~]]]]

Androutsopoulou and Español-Echevarría (2006) (hereafter, A&E) develop a syntactic hypothesis too, but they offer an account for the alternation *tan/tanto* very different from the one I have just sketched. According to them, a Spanish null MUCH, correlate of the English functional dummy quantifier *much,* will be externally merged as Q in a Corver-style extended adjectival projection under the proper conditions (i.e., in cases like [25b], [27b], and [28b]; see the configuration in [32]); according to Kayne (2005), null elements like MUCH must be licensed by an overt [+N] item (adjectival *tanto* is [+N]; *tan* is not), which A&E locate in the Spec of QP:

(32) [$_{DegP}$ [$_{QP}$ tanto [$_Q$ MUCH] [$_{AP}$ ~~alto~~]]]

Notice that, under this proposal, the regular morphological link exhibited by the pairs *cuán/cuánto, muy/mucho,* and *tan/tanto* cannot be the result of a particular operation; according to A&E (footnote 9), the first member of each pair would quite simply historically derive from the second one. Instead, under a syntactic hypothesis like the one I just sketched, such a regular morphological pattern could be understood as the result of an operation, a morphological merger (Halle & Marantz, 1993), as illustrated above in (31); of course, this implies that no null MUCH is necessary for the cases at issue.

Let us now return to the Italian data addressed by Z&P, more concretely to the ones in (24), repeated below as (33) for convenience. Recall that, for cases like (33a), Z&P propose a much more abstract representation than the one corresponding to cases with *tanti* (cf. [33b, 33c]); this time, the "E-only" and "measure" semantic components are spelled-out as the covert morphemes "ε" and "Ø" (again, I assume Ø is externally merged as Q in a configuration like the one in [31] above):

(33) a. Che alt-o!
 how tall-MASC.SG
 b. Che ε + Ø alto.
 c. WH E-ONLY + MEASURE SORTAL

The Spanish correlate of (33a) is (34a), from which (34b) departs only in having *poco* externally merged as Or:

(34) a. ¡Qué alt-o!
 how tall-MASC.SG
 'How tall!'
 b. ¡Qué poco alt-o!
 how little tall-MASC.SG
 'How short!'

Since I said that Ø and *poco* are externally merged as Q and Or respectively, ε should be externally merged as Deg, just as was the case with Italian *t-* (assuming Z&P's segmentation of *tanti*) or Spanish *tan* (assuming the above-sketched syntactic hypothesis for Spanish *tanto*); on the other hand, the wh-component of the wh-phrase, i.e. *qué*, should be located in the Spec of DegP (or even higher) since, as evidenced by Italian exclamatives like the one in (23a), it is linearized to the left of Deg (cf. the structure in [35]):

(35) [$_{DegP}$ qué [$_{Deg}$ ϵ [$_{OrP}$ (poco) [$_{QP}$ [$_Q$ Ø] [$_{AP}$ alto]]]]

Finally, as the sequences introduced in (34) cannot ever shift from exclamative to interrogative force (cf. [36]), I have to conclude that *qué* must always be the specifier of an ϵ externally merged as Deg:

(36) *¿Qué alt-o?
      how tall-MASC.SG
      'How tall?'

The hypothesis that *qué* must be the specifier of an ϵ externally merged as Deg explains the mandatory exclamative interpretation of a noun phrase like the one in (37a); this *qué*, which co-occurs with the preposition *de*, should not be identified with the one in (37b) (the difference is clearly evidenced by the English translation) since the latter is externally merged as Det and, as we will see below, the preposition *de* heads a QP, that is, a functional projection that can be dominated by DegP, but not by DetP (QP is a function providing a set of degrees or a scalar interval, rather than a set of entities):

(37) a. ¡Qué de libros!
       what of books
       'How very many books!'
   b. ¿Qué (*de) libros?
       which of books
       'Which books?'

I will assume that *de* is the Spanish correlate of English *much/many*. As happens with *much/many* in assertive/exclamative environments where *very* is missing (cf. [16a, 16b]), *de* necessarily entails upward orientation in (37a). Likewise, I assume that, under a configuration parallel to the one in (20) (cf. [38a]), *de* raises from Q to Or, probably attracted by an upward-orientation feature located in Or; this correctly predicts that *poco* and *de* cannot co-occur (cf. [38b]):

(38) a.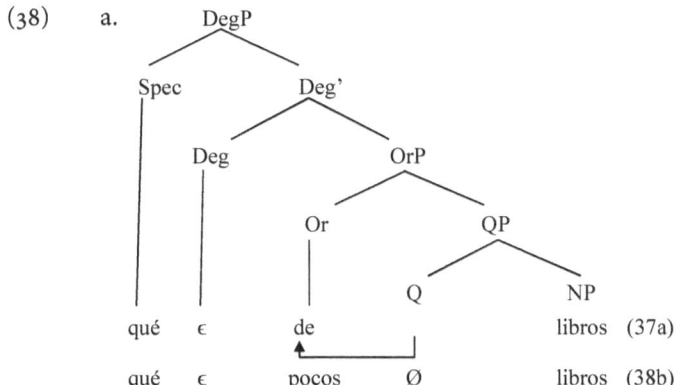

b. ¡Qué (*de) pocos libros!
   what   few   books
   'How few books!'

According to the hypothesis that *qué* must be the specifier of an ε externally merged as Deg, the exclamative *qué* in a noun phrase like the one in (39a) should be located in the Spec of an ε as well; the related configuration offered in (39b) accommodates the English translation, with the indefinite article *a* located in Deg, in accordance with Z&P's proposal that it may perform as an E-only morpheme too[4] (then, perhaps the Spanish noun phrase *¡vaya un libro!*, also exhibiting an indefinite article, can be accommodated in the same way):[5]

(39) a. ¡Qué libro!
       what book
       'What a book!'
   b. [$_{DegP}$ qué/what/vaya [$_{Deg}$ ε/a/un] [$_{OrP}$ [$_{Or}$ Ø] [$_{NP}$ libro/book/libro]]]

---

4. "It is natural to suppose that *a* represents the phrase's E-only nature, since it is the extra element not present in the interrogatives" (Z&P, 2003, p. 75). However, as was illustrated with *very*, in this chapter I am not assuming that "being compatible with exclamatives and not with interrogatives" automatically means "being an E-only morpheme located in Deg," therefore much further research needs to be done in order to elucidate whether or not *a* is located in Deg. I have to leave this question for future work.

5. However, it is important to point out that *¡Vaya un libro!* clearly implies that the book is not a good one, which is not entailed either by *What a book!* or the Spanish variant *¡Vaya libro!*, lacking the indefinite article; this suggests that the presence of the Spanish indefinite article in these constructions is related to a downward entailing operator located in OrP (see further below for the "speaker-oriented positive/negative evaluation" conveyed by OrP in these particular configurations). Again, due to space constraints, I will leave this question for future work.

In these sorts of noun phrases, Or does not convey upward/downward orientation with respect to a standard magnitude (QP is missing here), but rather "speaker-oriented positive/negative evaluation" of a property expressed by the noun itself; it is easy to evoke here the AP functional projection Abney (1987) puts forth for DPs like the one in (40a) (cf. the configuration in [40b]), where DP/AP are the correlates of the functional projections DegP/OrP in (39b):

(40) a. Un buen/mal libro.
'A good/bad book.'
b. [$_{DP}$ [$_D$ un [$_{AP}$ [$_A$ buen/mal [$_{NP}$ libro]]]

Since Spanish exclamative *qué* must be the Spec of an ϵ, we can now derive the ungrammaticality of Spanish exclamatives with a bare wh-phrase *qué* (cf. [41]) from the fact that ϵ must select an OrP, and Or must select either a QP (as in [35]/[38]) or an NP (as in [39]), both absent in (41):

(41) *¡Qué hizo!
lit: 'What he/she did!'

3. On Exclamative Phrases Containing *Más*

Recall that, upon examination of Spanish examples (2) to (8), repeated below as (42a–42g), I concluded in the introduction that the surprise component of exclamatives is conveyed either by *qué* in wh-sentences (cf. [42c, 42d, 42e]) or by a null operator (Op) in non-wh ones (cf. [42a, 42b, 42g]). Notice that (42c) is the wh-correlate of (42a), (42d, 42e) are the wh-correlates of (42g), and the wh-correlate of (42b) is the freshly introduced (42h) (containing the wh-phrase in [37a]). Finally, the non-wh correlate of (42f) is (42i) (freshly introduced as well; suspension intonation mandatory):

(42) a. ¡Juan es **Op** más alto . . . ! (2a)
'Juan is so tall!'
b. ¡Juan compró **Op** más libros . . . ! (2b)
'Juan bought so very many books!'
c. ¡**Qué** (*más) alto es Juan! (3)–(4)
'How tall is Juan!'
d. ¡**Qué** libros más interesantes compró! (5)
'What interesting books (s)he bought!'
e. ¡**Qué** (*más) interesantes libros compró! (6)

'What interesting books (s)he bought!'
f. ¡**Qué** libros (interesantes) compró! (7a, 7b)
'What books which are interesting (s)he bought!'
g. ¡Compró unos libros **Op** más interesantes . . . ! (8)
'(S)he bought such interesting books!'
h. ¡**Qué** de libros compró Juan!
'How very many books Juan bought!'
i. ¡Compró **Op** unos libros . . . !
'(S)he bought such books!'

In order to obtain the non-wh exclamative phrases listed in (42a, 42b), it is first necessary to substitute Op for the wh-word in the trees (35) and (38a) (cf. [43]); the position occupied by the word *más* immediately following Op is Deg, as suggested by the fact that it precedes *poco* (the head of OrP) in the counterparts of these non-wh phrases with *poco* (cf. [44]):

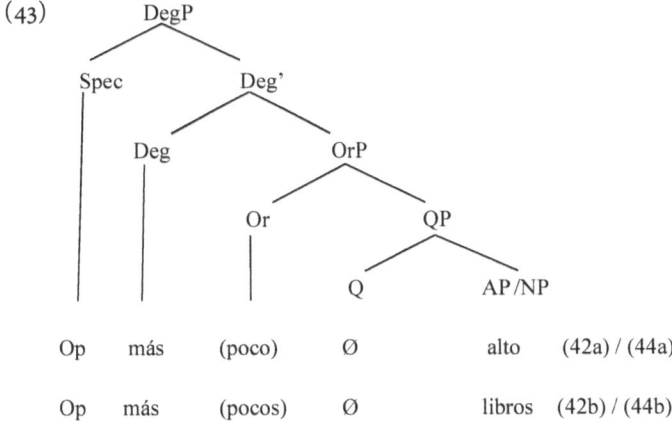

(44) a. ¡Juan es **Op** más poco alto . . . !
'Juan is so short!'
b. ¡Juan compró **Op** más pocos libros . . . !
'Juan bought so few books!'

A configuration like (43) also underlies adjectival noun modifiers like *más interesantes* in (42g), which I locate (following Cinque [1994]) in the specifier of a functional projection (here YP) extending the main DP spine (cf. [45]); leftward NP-movement (see the arrow) derives the eventual word order in (42g)—further Kayne (1994)-style leftward movements of YP and then DP to the specifier of DP-external functional projections will be independently needed in order to derive discontinuous exclamative phrases like the one in bold type in (46):

(45)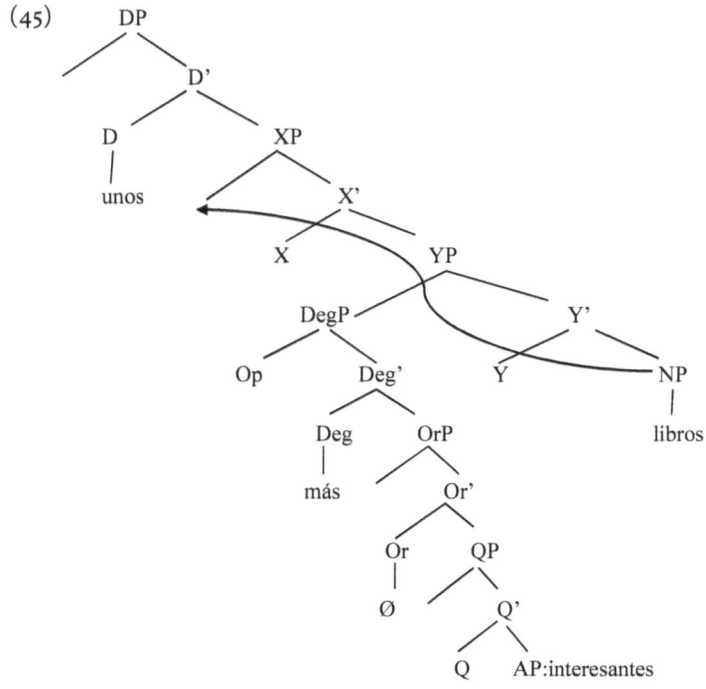

(46) ¡Compró   unos libros ayer   más interesantes . . . !
     buy-PAST.3SG a.PL books yesterday more interesting
     'Yesterday, (s)he bought such interesting books!'

By contrast, there are reasons to suspect that no Op is present in the adjectival sequence *más interesantes* of (42d). First, I said in the introduction that suspension intonation is a phonological effect related to the presence of the surprise null operators; crucially, such intonation arises in (42a, 42b, 42g), but is missing in (42d). Second, the DP dominating the adjectival sequence already contains a surprise wh-operator, *qué*, clearly related to the degree of the property "interesting", which suggests that *qué* has been base-generated in the specifier of DegP to be later displaced to a higher position; then, the actual configuration for the nominal in (42d) will be something like (47), where I assume *qué* raises to Spec-DP:

(47)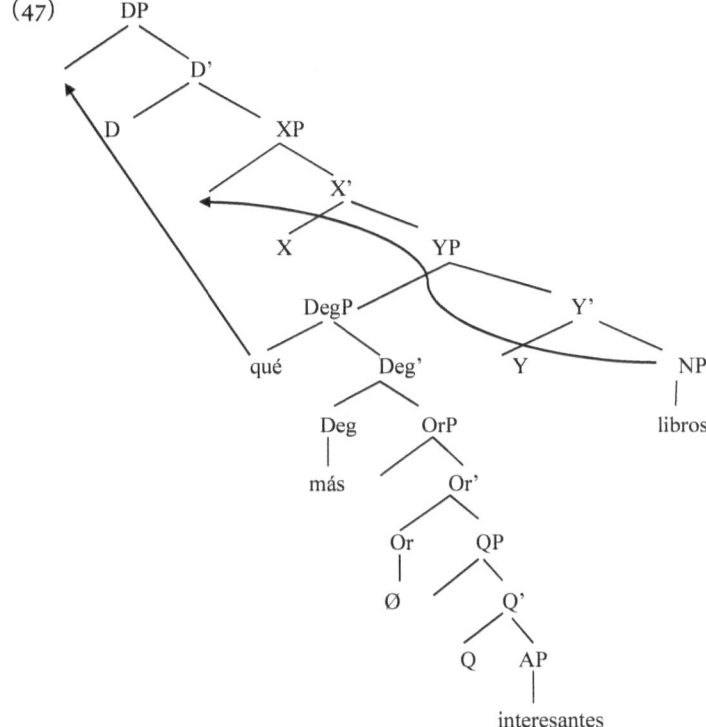

One advantage of the proposal that *qué* obtains its eventual prenominal position after movement from the specifier of the postnominal DegP is that it predicts that a typical barrier for movement cannot intervene between the two specifiers. Such prediction is borne out, as shown by the ungrammaticality of (48a), where a relative clause (between brackets) includes the DegP and excludes the Spec-DP; by contrast, in (48b), with a null surprise operator in Spec-DegP (notice the suspension intonation) and no syntactic movement to Spec-DP, the barrier status of the relative clause configuration is innocuous:

(48) a. *¡Qué libro [que parece más interesante]!
       what book that seems so   interesting
      'The book seems to be so interesting . . . !'
    b. ¡Un libro que parecía más interesante . . . !
       a   book that seemed so   interesting
      'A book that seemed to be so interesting . . . !'

A second advantage of the above proposal, where a movement originating in Spec-DegP targets Spec-DP, is that it predicts that the latter position must c-command the former one, since movement operates under c-command. Again, the prediction is borne out, as shown by the ungrammaticality of (49), where DegP is external to the DP containing the position hosting *qué*:

(49) *¡Qué libro era más interesante!
     what book was so interesting
     'The book was so interesting . . . !'

Another correct prediction of the movement proposal is that it should be possible to find cases where the wh-word *qué* pied pipes the whole DegP, instead of moving by itself. The existence of such cases seems to be illustrated by examples like (42e) (=[6]; repeated below as [50a] for convenience), where both *qué* and the adjective *interesantes* become prenominal and whose configuration I offer in (50b):

(50) a. **¡Qué** (*más) interesantes libros compró!
     'What interesting books (s)he bought!'

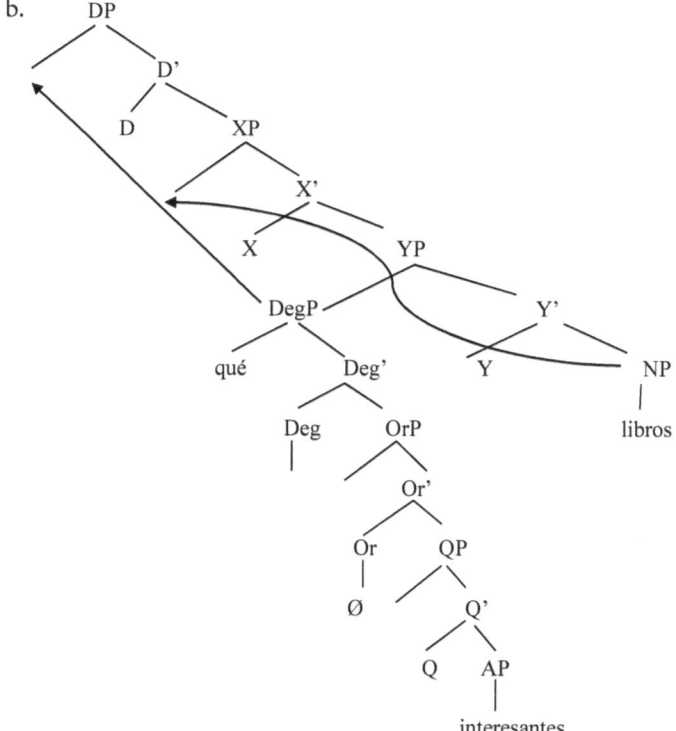

In fact, when the wh-operator *qué* is substituted by the alternative E-only wh-operator *cuán* 'how' (only found in literary style), the pied-piping strategy is mandatory, as illustrated by the contrast in (51):

(51) a. ¡**Cuán** interesantes libros compró!
'What interesting books (s)he bought!'
b. *¡**Cuán** libros (más) interesantes compró!'

I can derive this fact from either the morpho-phonological or the syntactic approach to (28a, 28b) sketched above, according to which *cuán(to)* is a sort of wh-counterpart of the overt E-only Spanish morpheme *tan* (notice the morphological parallelism *t-an/cu-án*); this amounts to saying that *cuán* (or pretruncated *cuánto*) should be externally merged as a head Deg (not as a specifier of DegP) and, consequently, will be unable to move by itself to the Spec of DP.

If it is true that the only difference between (42g) and (50a) relies on the absence/presence of pied-piping, an intriguing question arising now is why *más* must show up in (42g) and cannot do so in (50a) (notice the asterisk preceding *más* in [50a]). On the other hand, as I concluded in the introduction, the movement hypothesis for *qué* entails that *más* is not a non-wh surprise operator; moreover, *más* has no comparative/additive meaning in exclamative environments. All these facts raise the further question of what *más* is in these environments. A proper answer to this should also provide a solution for the puzzling distribution of *más* just described, which is the purpose of the next section.

4. *Más* as a Last-Resort Item

In § 1 I proposed that the E-only null morpheme ε introduced by Z&P as a component of exclamative wh-phrases is externally merged under Deg. In this section I will elaborate on the proper semantic and morphological nature of this morpheme in order to elucidate the questions arising at the end of § 2.

4.1. SEMANTIC PROPERTIES OF THE ε-MORPHEME

Z&P consider the ε-morpheme to be part of some exclamative wh-phrases; I will rather consider it to be an obligatory component of every exclamative (non-)wh-phrase. Moreover, I will also consider it to be the source of "presupposition"/"factivity," a commonly assumed semantic ingredient for exclamatives (Elliot, 1974; Z&P; Castroviejo, 2006; Andueza & Gutiérrez-Rexach, 2011), or, perhaps, "evaluativity" (Neeleman, van de Koot, & Doetjes, 2004), also called "comparative presupposition" in Kiefer (1978), which suggests that evaluativity and presupposition/factivity might be in a way not totally unrelated concepts.

According to Rett (2008, p. 155), "a sentence is evaluative if the degrees it makes reference to are restricted such that they must exceed a contextual standard." The examples (52a) and (52b), for instance, differ in evaluativity; the synthetic comparative in (52a) (with *longer* instead of *more long*) compares the degree of length of a table and the degree of length of a door and, crucially, it does not entail that the door is long; instead, the analytic comparative in (52b) (with *more long*) entails that the door is actually long (an "evaluation"), that is, it exceeds a contextual standard, and a comparison is established between two degrees of deviation from the standard, one corresponding to the door and the other to the table:

(52) a. The door is longer than the table.
b. The door is more long than the table.

According to Rett (2008), where evaluativity is encoded by an abstract operator (EVAL), wh-exclamatives ("degree exclamatives") always focus on a degree exceeding a contextual standard (for the relevance of degree in exclamatives, cf. Villalba, 2003; Castroviejo, 2006; an "extreme degree" is invoked in Gutiérrez-Rexach, 1996; Andueza & Gutiérrez-Rexach, 2011). Furthermore, Rett argues that such degree is a variable bound by an "illocutionary force operator" (the "Degree E-FORCE" operator) responsible for the "surprise" component of exclamatives (for an illocutionary exclamative operator including a null emotive predicate, cf. Gutiérrez-Rexach, 1996).

I can incorporate Rett's concepts into my configurational approach by proposing that the Degree E-FORCE operator is base-generated in the Spec-DegP in the above-introduced configuration (43) (that is, it corresponds to the Op/wh-word discussed thus far, a degree operator, according to Gutiérrez-Rexach, 1999). On the other hand, Deg hosts the degree variable. Finally, EVAL can now be considered to be the equivalent of Z&P's ε-morpheme, externally merged in Deg (alongside the degree variable) and obligatorily selecting OrP (interestingly, evaluativity is referred to as "orientedness" in Seuren, 1984). Such a configurational mapping of the semantic components of degree-exclamatives will allow us to understand why the analytic form in the comparative (52b) is the one conveying the evaluative reading.

I propose that the synthetic comparative (52a) lacks ε and, consequently, the functional projection OrP selected by EVAL; by contrast, both ε and OrP are present in the analytic comparative (52b). It is commonly assumed that synthetic comparative forms result from incorporation of the adjective into Deg under some version of Abney's (1987) functional head hypothesis (although, for a post-syntactic, "local dislocation" approach, see Embick & Noyer, 2001). For instance, assuming a configuration like (13), the derivation of *longer* can be represented as in (53) (the root *long-* incorporates into Q, and *long-*+Q incorporates into Deg, thus meeting the comparative suffix *-er*):

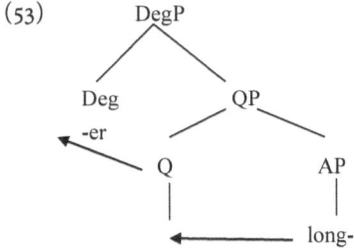

(53)

I propose that in (52b) the incorporation of *long-* into Deg is blocked by the intervention of OrP. Since *-er* is an affix, the support of a dummy "much" is needed, and the combination of "much" and *-er* gives rise to *more* (Bresnan, 1973). Intuitively, the reason why OrP blocks the incorporation of the adjective into Deg is that Or imposes a contextual standard, and Deg establishes an excess with respect to it, without being directly connected with the adjective—moreover, recall that the clausal correlate of OrP is Laka's (1990) sigma phrase, which also blocks V-to-C movement in Spanish imperatives (cf. Rivero, 1994).

Matushansky (2013, p. 15) speculates a similar idea when dealing with the analytic form attested to is monosyllabic "low scalarity" adjectives like *French* in (54) under coerced comparative interpretation; a functional projection forcing coercion intervenes between the adjective and Deg and, at the same time, blocks incorporation—*much*-support under Deg will follow, giving rise to *more* (Bresnan, 1973). As emphasized by Matushansky, such a coercion head should be stipulated to appear only when Deg is present, which is also the case with Or under my approach to degree exclamatives:

(54) Becky is more French (*Frencher) than Napoleon.

Synthetic comparatives also exist in Spanish: *mejor* 'better,' *peor* 'worse,' *mayor* 'bigger,' *menor* 'smaller'; as in English, their analytical variants are semantically more restricted. Thus, while (55a) can be felicitously answered by somebody asked to choose between two different sorts of deaths, (55b) would be pragmatically odd (EVAL = ε conveys an interpretation according to which some death is good):

(55) a. Esta muerte es mejor que esa.
       'This death is better than that one.'
    b. #Esta muerte es más buena que esa.
       'This death is better that that one.'

However, synthetic forms are not possible in exclamative environments, as illustrated in (56); crucially, Spanish synthetic forms are also suppletive forms, which means that, under a Distributed Morphology framework (Halle & Marantz, 1993), assumed here, they should be obtained after a syntactic process of incorporation/affix hopping (Matushansky, 2013) and never under a post-syntactic process like local dislocation (see § 3.2) relating linearly adjacent late-inserted exponents—and proposed by Embick and Noyer (2001) and Embick (2007) for non-suppletive synthetic forms in English:

(56) ¡Esta película es {más   buena /*mejor} ... !
     this film   is more good / better
     'This film is so good!'

I claim that, for cases like (56), it is Or (once more) that blocks the incorporation process required by the synthetic form.

It is worth pointing out that, perhaps, the only suppletive form allowed in exclamative environments is *menos* 'less' (cf. [57]); if, on the one hand, we assume that *menos*—like *less* = -er + *little*, according to Bresnan (1973) (cf. also Heim, 2006)—results from combining *más* and *poco* (*menos* and *más poco* are semantically identical and, moreover, the sequence *menos poco* is not attested: *_Juan es menos poco alto que Luis_ 'lit: Juan is less little tall than Luis'), and, on the other hand, it is true that *poco* is externally merged as Or (as claimed above), then *menos* can be considered to be a late-inserted exponent for a complex head obtained via unproblematic (local) incorporation of Or into Deg (according to Bresnan, *more* is also a suppletive form resulting from *-er* + *many/much*; however *many/much* are rather externally merged as Q and are unrelated to Or, as was argued in § 1 when dealing with [11], [12b], and [15]):

(57) ¡Esta persona es {menos/ más poco} eficiente . . . !
      this person is less   more little efficient
      'This person is so inefficient . . . !'

Once the semantic nature of the EVAL = ϵ-morpheme has been clarified, I will focus on its morphological properties.

4.2. MORPHOLOGICAL PROPERTIES OF THE ϵ-MORPHEME

I propose that ϵ is a clitic-like item that, in degree exclamatives, needs support from an overt exclamative operator to its left; such an operator is *qué* in (42c, 42e, 42f, 42h), repeated below as (58a, 58b, 58c, 58d) for convenience:

(58) a. ¡**Qué** alto es Juan!
      'How tall is Juan!'
   b. ¡**Qué** interesantes libros compró!
      'What interesting books (s)he bought!'
   c. ¡**Qué** libros (interesantes) compró!
      'What interesting books (s)he bought!'
   d. ¡**Qué** de libros compró Juan!
      'How very many books Juan bought!'

As the operator *qué* may move by itself to Spec-DP in an example like (42d) (repeated below as [59] for convenience; cf. the configuration in [47]), I concluded in § 2 that it is base-generated in Spec-DegP as a maximal projection, that is, it does not head a functional projection extending an AP/NP; as a consequence, neither incorporation of ϵ (=Deg) into *qué* nor Affix Hopping of *qué* to ϵ can be the proper way for ϵ to obtain support from *qué* in (58):

(59) ¡**Qué** libros más interesantes compró!
      What interesting books (s)he bought!'

I propose that ϵ obtains support through the above-mentioned post-syntactic process called "local dislocation" (Embick & Noyer, 2001; Embick, 2007), which, after linearization and vocabulary insertion, merges two adjacent exponents triggering either inversion or (string-vacuous) "leaning." In the case of (58), I assume that ε leans into an overt operator *qué* right to its left.

In this regard, the contrast between the interpretation of (58b) and the interpretation of (60a) is particularly interesting; both show a prenominal adjective but, in (60a), adjacency between *qué* and a hypothetical ε heading an AP-related DegP would be broken by an intervening number phrase hosting *dos* 'two' (cf. [60c]); I correctly predict that, with the leaning of ε into *qué* being impossible, no ε is available in such a position, and *qué* must convey here a surprise reading related to the positive/negative evaluation of the property introduced by the noun *libros* (as in [58c]; cf [60b]):

(60) a. ¡Qué dos interesantes libros!
 what two interesting books
 'How interesting those two books are!'

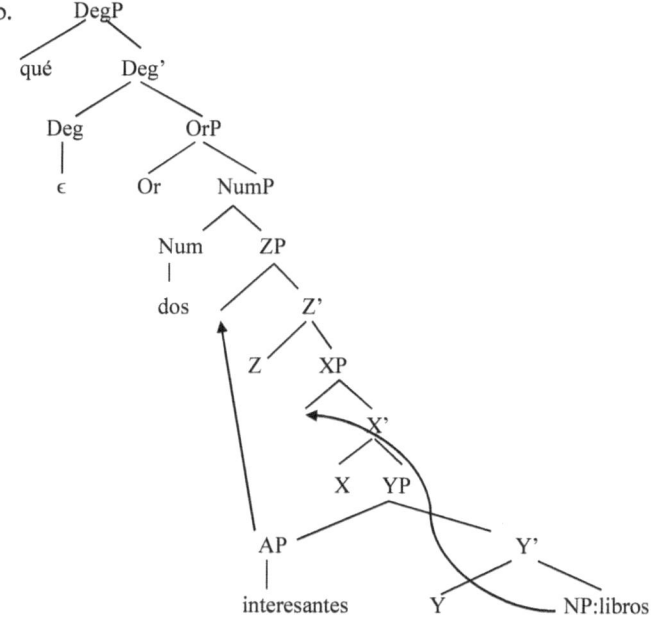

c.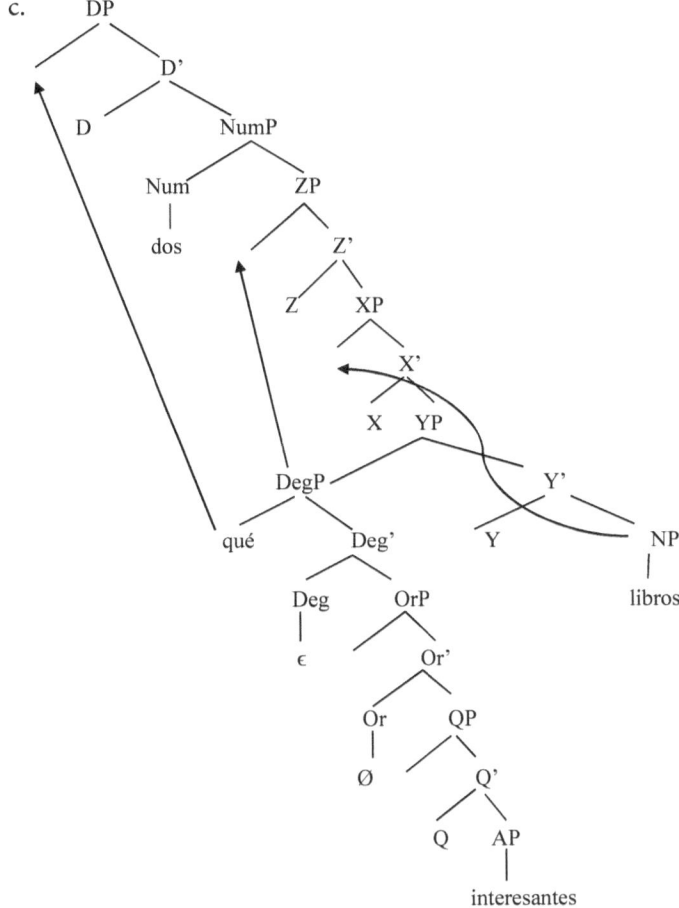

As for (45a, 45b, 45g, 45i) (repeated below as [61a, 61b, 61c, 61d] for convenience) the operator is abstract (non-overt), while in (59) it is overt but it has been displaced to a position non-adjacent to ε (no pied-piping of AP has taken place):

(61) a. ¡Juan es **Op** más alto ...!
'Juan is so tall!'
b. ¡Juan compró **Op** más libros ...!
'Juan bought so very many books!'

c. ¡Compró unos libros **Op** más interesantes ... !
   '(S)he bought such interesting books!'
d. ¡Compró **Op** unos libros ... !
   '(S)he bought such books!'

It is interesting that all these cases disallowing leaning of ϵ into *qué* are rescued by the presence of the comparative quantifier *más* (or the indefinite article *unos*). In the next section I show that this is not an accidental fact.

4.3. *MÁS*-SUPPORT

As said previously, (61a, 61b, 61c, 61d) do not offer a configuration where ϵ can lean into an overt exclamative operator; nevertheless, these examples are grammatical. I propose this is so because leaning takes place into the item *más* (or *unos*) adjacent to ϵ in all these cases. It is also interesting that *más* cannot be present when leaning is satisfied by an overt exclamative operator (cf. [58]). I conclude *más* is a last-resort item post-syntactically inserted in order to support ϵ whenever *qué* is not available for leaning.

The proposal that *más* 'more' might be a support element is not new—see the processing-based approach in Mondorf (2009). On the other hand, it should be expected, since related elements like *many* have also been reinterpreted as support elements in the literature (cf. Corver [1997] and, particularly, Solt [2010], who claims that *many* is always a dummy support item). Moreover, the semantic characterization of comparative *more* as a (generalized) quantifier element selecting a degree or a degree property is unclear. For instance, Matushansky proposes that the item selecting the *que*-sequence in comparative constructions is a null element located in the specifier of the DegP headed by *more*. The reason is that the comparative quantifier compares two degree properties; one is denoted by the comparative clause, and the other is denoted by the main clause once the comparative quantifier undergoes quantifier raising by itself at LF, a movement that cannot be performed by *more*—a head selecting an AP, according to Abney (1987).

In the same vein, Ishii (1991), focusing on comparatives like (62) with multiple *more* (Chomsky, 1981), proposes that *more* is just a marker of variables simultaneously ("unselectively") bound by an abstract adverb of quantification (Lewis, 1975) and that it is the adverb that actually selects the only degree denoted by the *que*-sequence, otherwise unable to perform as a complement of multiple *more*:

(62) Más estudiantes compraron más libros de lo esperado.
'More students bought more books than expected.'

Ishii's proposal on *more* is based on Heim's (1982) focusing on indefinites; according to Heim, indefinites are not quantifiers either, but rather they mark the position of variables unselectively bound by an abstract operator. In this regard, it should be emphasized that the characterization made in this chapter for *más* as a support item might also be desirable for indefinite articles like the one in (61d) (*¡Compró Op* **unos** *libros . . . !*), where the null operator has replaced the overt one present in the configuration (58c) and, as a consequence, the insertion of the indefinite article as a support element for ϵ seems to be required.

To conclude, it is worth mentioning that *más* freely alternates with the contentless preposition *de* 'of' in some contexts, as illustrated in (63) (Masullo, 1999); this alternation constitutes a further argument in favor of considering *más* as just a contentless support item in the data dealt with in this chapter:

(63) ¡Ese libro es Op {más/ **de**} interesante . . . !
'That book is so interesting . . . !'

5. Conclusion

In this chapter I have proposed that Spanish *más* is a contentless, dummy support item post-syntactically inserted in order to satisfy the morphological requirements posed by a null E-only morpheme arising in certain exclamative environments. This morpheme encodes the factivity semantic component commonly attributed to exclamatives and needs to (post-syntactically) lean into an overt exclamative operator linearly adjacent to it. When the operator is null or independently displaced, *más*-support is required as a last resort strategy in order to satisfy the leaning requirement of the morpheme.

Optative Exclamatives in Spanish

Cristina Sánchez López

1. Introduction

Optative sentences are main clauses that express a vivid wish, hope, or desire without using a verb of wish, hope, or desire. They express the speaker's desire about an actual or future situation, but they also are able to express a desire about a past situation and convey a contra-factual reading. They are prosodically marked by exaggerated acoustic intensity (wide ranging peaks and troughs) and orthographically indicated by exclamation marks «¡!». This property makes optatives look like exclamative sentences, but this is not the only common point between both kinds of clauses, since optatives and exclamatives are two varieties of non-declarative speech acts.

Exclamatives have aroused the interest of linguists in the past ten years, but the study of optatives from a formal view is recent. This chapter is devoted to presenting an analysis of Spanish optatives with two main objectives: one is to describe and explain the syntactic and semantic properties of Spanish optatives; the other one is to determine which properties optatives share with exclamatives and what exactly sets them apart.

This investigation has benefited from grant FFI2012-34974 from the Spanish Ministerio de Economía y Competitividad.

There is a large variety of optative sentences in Spanish.[1] I will focus on the three types that are fully productive: (1) optatives introduced by *ojalá*, (2) optatives introduced by conjunctions such as *que* 'that' and *si* 'if', and (3) optatives introduced by the wh-word *quién* 'who':

(1) ¡Ojalá haya paz entre los hombres!
 OJALÁ have$_{subj}$ peace among the men
 'Let there be peace among men!'

(2) a. ¡Que la suerte te acompañe!
 that the luck you$_{ac}$ accompanies$_{subj}$'
 'May luck be with you!'
 b. ¡Si hubierais encontrado un trabajo!
 if you.had$_{subj}$ found a job!
 'If only you had found a job!'

(3) ¡Quién fuera millonario!
 Who were$_{subj}$ millionaire
 'If only I were a millionaire!'

I will start by analyzing the optatives exemplified in (1) and (2). I will show that these are main sentences with a complex left periphery and will propose an analysis that combines two main ideas. First optatives contain a generalized

---

1. Sentences with a subjunctive verb such as the ones in (i)–(iv) are considered volitives or desideratives by grammarians:

 (i) ¡Pleitos tengas y los ganes!
  lawsuits you.have$_{subj}$ and them$_{ac}$ you.gain$_{subj}$
  'If you have lawsuits, I hope you win them!'
 (ii) ¡Dios te bendiga!
  God you$_{ac}$ bless
  'God bless you!'
 (iii) Sea el conjunto de los números naturales.
  is$_{subj}$ the set of the numbers natural
  'Let X be the set of natural numbers.'
 (iv) Agítese antes de usar.
  stir$_{subj}$-it$_{refl}$ before of using
  'Stir before using.'

These sentences fall beyond the scope of this chapter. Optatives in (i) and (ii) are formulas or semi-lexicalized expressions whose syntactic pattern is not fully productive (cf. Porto Dapena 1991, 77). The more productive patterns—that is "jussives" of (iii) and "exhortatives" of (iv)— usually lack exclamatory force and fall somewhere in between proper optatives and imperatives (Merin & Nicolaeva, 2008, p. 50).

exclamation operator EX (as proposed for exclamatives by Gutiérrez-Rexach, 1996), that serves to express an emotion toward the status of the modified proposition on a contextually provided scale. The optative reading arises if the context provides a scale of the speaker's preferences, as understood by Grosz (2011). Second, optatives have a mood head that encodes a semantic feature of anti-factivity. The way this mood feature is checked determines the different lexical realization of C. With this analysis in mind, it will be possible to show which properties optatives share with exclamatives and which properties differ.

The last section of the chapter is devoted to the optative sentences in (3). This syntactic type is not as common as those in (1) and (2). I will propose a restriction on optatives headed by a wh-word that follows from the semantics of these sentences and will try to explain how Spanish *quién*-optatives, contrary to expectations, escape this restriction and turn out to be fully grammatical.

2. Optative Sentences: The EX-Operator and the Left Periphery

The two main properties of optative sentences in (1) and (2) are the obligatory presence of lexical material in the left periphery—the conjunctions *que* and *si* or the expression *ojalá*—and the obligatory subjunctive morphology in the verb. I will propose that the optative meaning is the result of the compositional contribution of these two elements. Optatives project a MoodP with an uninterpretable "anti-factive" feature associated with the morphological subjunctive mood; in addition, they contain an EX-operator in ForceP, which is responsible for the exclamatory force of the sentence, as well as for the desirability effect. The different ways in which the uninterpretable feature in mood is checked give rise to the different realizations of C like *que, si,* or *ojalá*. In this section, I will develop my proposal about the left periphery of optative sentences. The contribution of mood to the meaning of the sentences will be analyzed in greater detail in section 3.

2.1. *QUE*-OPTATIVES AND *SI*-OPTATIVES

Spanish optatives may be introduced by a complementizer in two different forms: the conjunction *que* 'that,' as in (4a), and the conjunction *si* 'if,' optionally followed by the adverbial expression *al menos* 'at least,' as in (4b). In both cases, the conjunction is obligatory:

(4) a. ¡Que la suerte te acompañe!
    that the luck you$_{ac}$ accompanies$_{subj}$
    'May luck be with you!'
   b. ¡Si al menos hubieses estado allí!
    If at least you.had$_{subj}$ been there
    'If only you had been there!'

Optatives differ from polar exclamatives in (5) both in semantic and syntactic properties. As it is well-known, exclamatives express the speaker's surprise about the fact denoted by the proposition. They may be introduced by a conjunction, but this particle is usually absent:

(5) a. ¡(Que) la suerte te acompaña!
    that the luck you$_{ac}$ accompanies$_{ind}$
    'I am surprised that you are lucky!'
   b. ¡(Si) estás aquí!
    if you.are here
    'Oh, you are here!'

Optative sentences look like embedded or subordinated clauses in that they are introduced by a subordinating conjunction, but they both occur without an overt matrix clause. This phenomenon is known as "insubordination" (Evans, 2007) and has been explained through a process of reconstruction of the omitted clause. This analysis, called the D(eletion)-hypothesis, defends the presence of an abstract or elided embedding verb. For Spanish, Spaulding (1934), Bustos Kleiman (1974), Rivero (1977), and Porto Dapena (1991) argue that these sentences are only apparently main clauses. In fact, they argue that they are really subordinated clauses that depend on a silent main verb selecting the subjunctive mood in the embedded clause. An alternative analysis, the I(ndependence)-hypothesis (Grosz, 2011), does not involve deletion of the matrix clause. I will defend the latter hypothesis and will argue that optatives are constituents of the category CP.

According to the D-hypothesis, Spanish *que*-optatives result from the ellipsis of an attitude predicate such as *querer* 'want,' *desear* 'desire,' or *esperar* 'hope.' This analysis presents, at least, two empirical problems. Firstly, it predicts that the optative sentence in (6a), whose subject is first-person singular, would derive from the ungrammatical sentence in (6b), since volition verbs, as other verbs selecting the subjunctive mood, display an "obviation effect" that prevents subjunctive complements if the matrix and the subordinate subjects are co-referent. The D-analysis predicts that the optative must take the form in (6c); this sentence is grammatical, but its meaning is not optative (cf. Grohmann & Etxeparre, 2003):

(6) a. ¡Que yo gane el premio!
   That I win$_{subj}$ the prize
   'If only I won the prize!'
 b. *Quiero que yo gane el premio.
   I.want that I win$_{subj}$ the prize
   'I want to win the prize!'
 c. ¡Ganar yo el premio! Eso sería fantástico.
   Win$_{inf}$ I the prize that would.be fantastic
   'Me win the prize?! That would be fantastic.'

Secondly, the subjunctive verb in *que*-optatives must be in present or present perfect tense (7a); other tense forms (like past and pluperfect) make the sentence ungrammatical, as shown in (7b). However, nothing prevents these verbal forms from occurring in a subordinate clause depending on a volition matrix verb, as shown in (7c). The D-hypothesis wrongly predicts that (7b) should be grammatical, unless a specific condition on tenses restricts the ellipsis of the matrix predicate. As it obvious, such a condition would not be far from being an ad hoc stipulation:

(7) a. ¡Que {llegue/ haya llegado} ya María!
   That {arrives$_{subj}$ has$_{subj}$ arrived} yet M.
   'I want María to arrive!'
 b. *¡Que {llegase/ hubiese llegado} ya María!
   That arrived$_{subj}$ had$_{subj}$ arrived yet M.
   'I wish that María {arrived/had arrived} {already/by now}.'
 c. Yo quería que {llegase/ hubiese llegado } ya María.
   I wanted that arrived$_{subj}$ had$_{subj}$ arrived yet M.
   'I wished that María {arrived/had arrived} {already/by now}.'

The D-hypothesis has been proposed for *si*-optatives in some other languages as well. Biezma (2011a, 2011b) considers English *if*-optatives as truly conditional sentences that differ from non-optative conditionals in the nature of the matrix clause. According to her, *if*-optatives include an elided matrix clause (the "consequent", in Biezma's terms). The elision of the matrix clause is possible because *if*-optatives have reverse topicality; that is, the *if*-clause is the focus and the main clause is the topic. According to Biezma's proposal, the schematic representation of the information structure of an if-optative would be the following (the example is hers):

(8) a. How would I have brought it about that I played in the NBA?
b. If only I had been taller, ~~I would have played in the NBA~~!

In order to derive the intuition of what is desired in the implied consequent, Biezma (2011a) argues that desirability arises in those contexts in which optative conditionals provide answers to a question of how to bring about some salient consequent. In her proposal, the "mention-some" nature of optatives is due to the presence of "only," which marks the modified statement as the strongest answer to the immediate question under discussion.

I will show that the D-hypothesis cannot be applied to Spanish *si*-optatives. In fact, Spanish provides a strong argument against the hypothesis, as Spanish conditionals admit both an indicative (9a) and a subjunctive verb (9b), but optatives require a subjunctive verb:

(9) a. Si tengo dinero, compraré un coche nuevo.
    if I.have$_{ind}$, money I.will.buy a car new
    'If I have some money, I will buy a new car.'
b. Si tuviera dinero, compararía un coche nuevo.
    if I.had$_{subj}$ money I.would.buy a car new
    'If I had some money, I would buy a new car.'

In the spirit of Biezma's (2011a) analysis, the elision of the matrix clause in (9a) would correctly derive a *si*-optative with the verb in the indicative mood under two conditions: a) the utterance is in a context that favors the inverse informative structure, and b) a scalar adverb marks the statement as the strongest answer to the preceding question. Although both conditions are satisfied in (10), the elision of the matrix clause does not produce an optative sentence. The answer in b cannot receive an optative reading and is not interpretable; it could be grammatical if interpreted as a cut off utterance with conditional meaning and suspended intonation, as in (10c):

(10) a. -¿Comprarás un coche nuevo?
    'Will you buy a new car?'
b. -#¡Si al menos tengo dinero!
    if at least I.have$_{ind}$ money

c. -Si tengo dinero...
    if I.have_ind money
    'If I have the money...'

I have provided empirical arguments that allow us to reject a D-analysis and support, instead, the I-analysis. This implies that Spanish optative sentences are main sentences of the category CP, introduced by a conjunction *que* 'that' and *si* 'if', and displaying a complex left periphery.

2.2. THE OPERATOR EX AND THE STRUCTURE OF THE LEFT PERIPHERY

In this section I will propose that the left periphery of optative sentences consists of an EX-operator that selects an overt conjunction in C and is responsible for their semantic and syntactic properties. The idea that exclamative sentences have an Exclamative operator was proposed by Gutiérrez-Rexach (1996, 2001), and it has been implemented in various forms in the studies of Castroviejo (2006) for Catalan, Jónsson (2010) for Icelandic, and Grosz (2011) for German, among others. Following Grosz (2011), I will extend the EX-operator analysis to optatives and will argue that optatives contain a generalized exclamation operator EX expressing an emotion toward the status of the modified proposition on a contextually provided scale; the optative reading arises if the context provides a scale of the speaker's preferences.

Being expressive speech acts, both exclamatives and optatives differ from declaratives, which are descriptive utterances. Expressive utterances reveal emotional or affective reactions that constitute over manifestations of emotional or affective behavior. On the contrary, descriptive statements are truth functional propositions bound to be true or false. Expressive utterances are either felicitous or infelicitous in a given context, but they cannot be true or false. They cannot be denied or confirmed either, in the same way in that an assertion can. The examples in (11) show that the listener may react to an optative utterance expressing his agreement, as in the b answer, but he or she might not confirm the truth value of the expressive utterance. As a consequence, the c answer is not adequate:

(11) a. ¡Que venga Pepe!
        'If only Pepe came!'
     b. Yo también lo deseo.
        'Yes, I wish so too.'

c. #Es {verdad/falso} que tú quieres que venga Pepe.
'It is {true/false} that you wish Pepe would come.'

Interestingly, declarative statements with a verb of desire can be denied or confirmed by the listener, as the examples in (12) clearly prove. This supports the idea that they are declarative sentences, but not expressive utterances. The different behavior of optative and declarative sentences with verbs of desire provides an additional argument against a D-analysis for optatives:

(12) a. Yo deseo que venga Pepe.
'I want Pepe to come.'
b. Es {verdad/falso} que tú deseas eso.
'It is {true/false} that you want that.'

The fact that optative utterances are inherently emotive and evaluative is confirmed by the observation that the perceived emotion/evaluation cannot be easily cancelled. The unexpected inference conveyed by exclamatives cannot be cancelled, as the examples in (13) show; similarly, the implication of desirability (attributed to the speaker) cannot be cancelled in optatives either, as can be seen in (14):

(13) a. Me sorprende que haya venido Pepe, aunque en el fondo me lo esperaba.
'I am surprised that Pepe has come, although deep down I expected it.'
b. #¡Ha venido Pepe, aunque en el fondo me lo esperaba!
'Pepe has come, although deep down I expected it!'

(14) a. Deseo que sea despedido, aunque eso no importa mucho.
'I wish he was fired, although it does not matter much.'
b. #¡Ojalá sea despedido, aunque eso no importa mucho!
'If only he was fired! Although that does not matter much.'

The expressive nature of exclamatives and optatives is due to the presence of an EX operator that combines with a truth conditional statement (i.e., a proposition) and turns it into a felicity-conditional expression of an emotion. Both in exclamatives and optatives, the emotion is connected to a scale, since EX takes a scalar argument and quantifies over scalar alternatives. I take the formulations below from Grosz (2011):

(15) a. An utterance of EX(ø) conveys that the speaker at the point of utterance has an emotion ε (or at least an evaluative attitude ε) toward ø. By uttering an utterance of EX(ø), the speaker intends to express an emotion ε, rather than describe ε.
b. EX: For any scale S and proposition p, interpreted in relation to a context c and assignment function g, an utterance EX(S)(p) is felicitous if: $\forall q\ [\text{THRESHOLD}(c) >_s q \rightarrow p >_s q]$

That is to say: EX expresses an emotion that captures the fact that *p* is higher on a (speaker-related) scale S than all contextually relevant alternatives *q* below a contextual threshold, where THRESHOLD(c) is a function from a context into a set of worlds/a proposition that counts as high with respect to a relevant scale S. If S refers to a scale that models the speaker's surprise, we get an exclamative reading. If S refers to a scale that models the speaker's preferences (i.e., a bouletic scale), we get an optative reading.

This account is consistent with the idea that desirability is the result of the comparison of a proposition and salient alternatives. Villalta (2007, 2008) discusses Heim's (1992) analysis of desire as a polar comparison of a proposition and its opposite. She concludes that desirability involves a comparison of a situation such that a proposition *p* is more preferable to the speaker than all contextually salient alternatives. Villalta's view provides an explanation for the fact that we can wish something that is not optimal. The desired situation is not necessarily the best possible case, but it is a case desirable enough as to be satisfactory in some relevant sense. This is why someone may utter a sentence like (16) considering that his or her actual job forces him or her to work 60 hours a week:

(16) ¡Ojalá tuviera que trabajar cuarenta horas a la semana!
OJALÁ I.had$_{subj}$ to work forty hours to the week!
'If only I only had to work 40 hours a week!'

Associating the expressive interpretation of a sentence with an exclamatory operator entails that there has to be a syntactic projection hosting this constituent expressing force. In line with the cartographic approach that takes CPs to involve a fine-grained structure encoding topic, focus, and force constituents, I will assume that EX is syntactically merged in the specifier of ForceP (Rizzi, 1997; Gutiérrez-Rexach, 2001). I will propose that an overt conjunction *que* 'that' or *si* 'if' merges to satisfy the mood feature entailed in optative sentences. C has an interpretable feature that attracts the uninterpretable feature [mood], in MoodP, associated with subjunctive morphology.

The fact that exclamatives do not necessarily contain an overt conjunction reflects the absence of a parallel uninterpretable feature in MoodP, since the verb displays indicative morphology.

(17)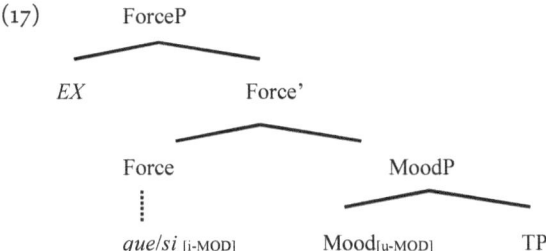

The role of MoodP on the semantic properties of optatives will be pursued in section 3. In the following section, I will propose that the analysis in (17) can be extended to Spanish *ojalá*-optatives.

2.3. *OJALÁ (QUE)*-OPTATIVES

The most common exclamative sentences with optative meaning in Spanish are introduced by the word *ojalá*, for which English 'I wish' is just an approximate translation. *Ojalá*-optative sentences admit an optional *que*, as shown in (18):

(18) ¡Ojalá (que) tu vida sea larga y feliz!
 OJALÁ that your life is$_{subj}$ long and happy
 'I wish you a long and happy life!'

The grammatical categorization of *ojalá* is a controversial issue. I will consider it to be a modal adverb, such as *quizás* 'maybe' or *acaso* 'perhaps'. All these particles show a very similar distribution, and all have the capacity to select a verb in the subjunctive mood.[2] Like modal adverbs, *ojalá* can be used

---

2. I agree with Alonso-Cortés (2011, p. 27) that *ojalá* is not an interjection because it has a constant meaning, whereas interjections can convey different pragmatically dependent senses. However, Alonso-Cortés (2011, p. 26) considers *ojalá* not to be an adverb because it cannot be coordinated with another adverb (**Ojalá y seguramente* 'OJALÁ and sure') and because it does not admit quantifiers (cf. **Muy ojalá que Juan venga* 'Very OJALÁ that Juan comes'). In my opinion, the ungrammaticality of the coordinate phrase above can be due to a semantic incompatibility (a similar incompatibility arises in **seguramente y probablemente* 'sure and probably').

as an answer (19a) and is able to occupy incidental positions in the middle or the end of the sequence (19b, 19c):

(19) a. -¿Terminarás   tu   trabajo a tiempo?
   you.will.finish$_{ind}$ your work   at time
   'Will you finish your work on time?'
   -{Ojalá/quizás}
   {OJALÁ/maybe}
   '{I hope/maybe}'
   b. Mañana   todo   habrá   acabado, {ojalá/quizás}.
   Tomorrow everything will.have$_{ind}$ finished, OJALÁ maybe
   'Everything will be done tomorrow, I hope/perhaps.'
   c. Todos nuestros problemas se resolverán, {ojalá/quizás}, muy pronto.
   All   our   problems will.be.solved OJALÁ/ maybe very soon
   'Our problems will, {I hope/perhaps}, soon be solved.'

As with other modal adverbs, *ojalá* selects for a verb in a subjunctive mood under a government relation; the subjunctive is not possible if *ojalá* does not c-command the verb:

(20) a. Ojalá {*llegas/   llegues}   a tiempo.
   OJALÁ {you.arrive$_{ind}$/you.arrive$_{subj}$}on time
   'I hope you arrive on time.'
   b. {Llegarás/   *llegues}   a tiempo, ojalá.
   you.will.arrive$_{ind}$/you.arrive$_{subj}$ on time, OJALÁ
   'You will arrive on time, I hope.'

I will propose that *ojalá*-optatives contain an EX operator in the same way as optatives with *que* and *si*. However, the adverb *ojalá* merges in the position of the specifier of MoodP and checks the uninterpretable feature of mood *in situ*. Afterward, it is displaced to Force in order to check the exclamatory feature of EX. As such, *ojalá*-optatives do not involve the obligatory realization of C as the conjunctions *que/si*. Movement of *ojalá* to Force guarantees

---

On the other hand, gradability is not a necessary property of all adverbs. I conclude, therefore, that his arguments against *ojalá* as an adverb are not sound.

the realization of overt adequate lexical material in the CP layer under ForceP. The structure of an *ojalá*-optative without *que* would be as follows:

(21) [~ForceP~ EX *ojalá* [~MoodP~ ~ojalá~~[i-mood]~ [~Mood [u-mood]~]]]]

Optional *que* after *ojalá* is homonymous with the conjunction *que* of *que*-optatives, but they differ both in their optionality and in their relation with the morphological mood of the verb. The *que* heading *que*-optatives is obligatory. As we will see below, this complementizer has an effect on the tense and the mood of the predicate, since it selects a verb in present or present perfect, but rejects past or pluperfect (22):

(22) ¡Que {llegue/ haya llegado/ *llegara/ *hubiera llegado}!
That s/he.arrives$_{subj}$ he.has$_{subj}$ arrived he.arrived$_{subj}$ he.had$_{subj}$ arrived
'I wish he {had arrived}!'

Contrarily, the *que* after *ojalá* is optional, and, thus, it cannot be considered responsible for the mood features of the verb. In addition, the presence of the optional *que* seems to be unconstrained by the tense of the verb. Demonte and Fernández Soriano (2009) suppose that *que* is not possible with a pluperfect, but the truth is that all the combinations of subjunctive tenses with *ojalá que* are documented: not only present tense (as in [18] above), but also perfect (23a), past (23b), and pluperfect (23c):

(23) a. ¡Ojalá que haya secado mi chompa!
OJALÁ that had$_{subj}$ dried my jersey
'If only my jersey had dried out!'
(C. Vega, *Ipacankure*, Perú, CREA)
b. ¡Ojalá que estuviera dormido!
OJALÁ that s/he.were$_{subj}$ asleep
'If only he was asleep!'
(J. A. Lira, *Medicina andina*, Perú, CREA)
c. ¡Ojalá que nunca hubiera crecido, ni conocido a Pedro!
OJALÁ that never s/he.had$_{subj}$ grown nor known to Pedro
'If only he had never grown up, nor known Pedro!'
(L. Esquivel, *Como agua para chocolate*, México, CREA)

In order to explain the special behavior of both *que*'s, I will propose that the *que* following *ojalá* is related to the *que* that optionally follows some focused elements in exclamative sentences, such as the ones exemplified in (24):

(24) a. ¡Qué guapa (que) es María!
  what pretty that is María
  'How pretty Mary is!'
 b. ¡Bien (que) me habías engañado!
  well that me$_{ac}$ you.had cheated
  'You sure cheated me!'

I will assume, following Gutiérrez-Rexach (2008), that the optional presence of *que* is related to the activation of the focus layer in C. This explains that the difference between *ojalá*-optatives and *ojalá que*-optatives lies in the focal or emphatic import of the latter. Consequently, the analysis of an *ojalá que*-optative would be as follows:[3]

(25) [$_{ForceP}$ EX *ojalá* [$_{FocusP}$ [$_{Focus}$ *que* [$_{MoodP}$ <s>*ojalá*</s>$_{[i\text{-mood}]}$ [$_{Mood\,[u\text{-mood}]}$ [$_{TP}$ ......]]]]]]

According to this proposal, *ojalá*-optatives contain an EX-operator in the same way as *que*-optatives and *si*-optatives; the operator shifts the propositional content of the utterance into the expressive domain. This analysis differs from Grozs (2011, pp. 185–190), who supposes that *ojalá*-optatives belong to a special kind of optatives, *adv*-optatives. This variety is supposed to contain an idiosyncratic speech act adverbial, but not an EX-operator. Grosz's main argument is that *ojalá*-optatives are embeddable, whereas EX-optatives are not. The following examples, adapted from Grosz (2011, p. 186), show that a quantifier is able to bind to an *ojalá*-optative from a super-ordinated clause (26a). Wh-movement is possible as well from within an embedded *ojalá*-clause (26b):

(26) a. Cada bruja$_1$ dice que ojalá su$_1$ escoba estuviera aquí.
  each witch says that ojalá her broom were here
  'Each of the witches says that she wished her broom were here.'

---

3. Considering that the optional *que* in *ojalá*-optatives is the same focus-related element that optionally occurs in exclamatives supports Gutiérrez-Rexach's (2008) observation that *que* is not the overt realization of factivity, contrary to the proposal by Zanuttini and Portner (2003).

b. ¿Qué dijo Juan que ojalá hubieras comprado?
   What said Juan that ojalá you.had bought
   'What did Juan say that he wished you had bought?'

However, as Grosz (2011) notes himself, *ojalá*-optatives are problematic under a verb of speech other than *decir* 'to say,' as well as ungrammatical under a wish verb (27a). To these arguments, one may add that they cannot depend on a predicate of desire, as shown in (27b):[4]

(27) a. Cada bruja {dice/??piensa/??insiste en/??espera/??desea/*quiere}
       each witch says thinks insists on waits hopes wants
       que ojalá su escoba estuviera aquí.
       that OJALÁ her broom were here
       'Each witch {says/thinks/insists/hopes/waits for/wishes/wants} her broom is here.'
   b. *Es deseable que ojalá todas las escobas estuvieran aquí.
      It.is desirable that OJALÁ all the brooms were here
      'One would desire all brooms to be here.'

On the other hand, *ojalá que*-optatives are not embeddable, as the example in (28a) shows; extraction is not possible in (28b), either:

(28) a. *Cada bruja₁ dice que ojalá que su₁ escoba estuviera aquí.
       each witch says that ojalá that her broom were here
       'Each of the witches says that she wished her broom were here.'
   b. *¿Qué dijo Juan que ojalá que hubieras comprado?
      What said Juan that ojalá that you.had bought
      'What did Juan say that he wished you had bought?'

More arguments may be found; if *ojalá*-optatives were embeddable, the sentence in (29) would be expected to be grammatical with the meaning "each of the witches says that she does not desire that her broom were here," but this is not the case:

(29) *Cada bruja niega que ojalá su escoba estuviera aquí.
     each witch denies that OJALÁ her broom were here
     'Each of the witches denies that her broom was here.'

---

4. The English translation in (27b) expresses the expected but not available reading of the Spanish example. This is also the case for examples (28) and (29) below.

Finally, Grosz (2011) argues that volitional adverbs operate on the propositional level. This means that, when *ojalá* is embedded, the wish expressed does not seem to be a wish on the part of the speaker, but rather a wish on the part of the person referred to by the matrix subject. Nevertheless, this is not all true, since *ojalá* is able to refer to the speaker's desire in the embedded context as well. The example in (30) shows that *ojalá* refers to the speaker's desire if it is inside a relative clause because the only available reading of the utterance is the one in (30b):

(30) María escribió un libro que ojalá   no hubiera   escrito.
     M.   wrote   a   book that OJALÁ not she.had$_{subj}$ written
     a. #'Mary wrote a book and she wishes she had never written it.'
     b. 'Mary wrote a book and the speaker wishes that she had never written it.'

To summarize, the data above suggest that the fact that *ojalá* is able to modify an embedded sentence cannot be considered a conclusive argument against analyzing *ojalá*-optatives as root sentences with an EX-operator. It is necessary to investigate which kind of embedded sentences allows *ojalá* to occur. At a glance, it seems that only restrictive relative clauses and clauses depending on speech verbs do so. In any case, I have to leave this issue open for space limitations. I will confine myself to arguing that in these cases *ojalá* merges in the specifier of a MoodP, but the numeration does not have an EX-operator and it remains in situ. As opposed to this, there are empirical arguments for considering that in main sentences, *ojalá* merges in the specifier of MoodP and moves to the ForceP inside a complex left periphery; if the focus layer of this complex left periphery is activated, Focus merges as an optional *que*.

3. Mood and Tense in Optatives

The use of subjunctive morphology in optative sentences is related to two semantic features. On one hand, the grammatical role of mood is to overtly mark the sort of model in which a proposition must be interpreted (Giannakidou, 1997; Quer, 1998). The operator EX forces the proposition to be evaluated according to a scale. If the scale models the speaker's preferences (i.e., a bouletic scale), we get an optative reading. If the scale models the speaker's surprise (i.e., an inverse prior likelihood scale), we get an exclamative reading. Optative and exclamative sentences clearly illustrate that the shift from subjunctive mood to indicative mood signals a shift in the model of evaluation for the proposition.

On the other hand, I propose that the subjunctive is related to the semantic feature of anti-factivity. It is widely assumed that exclamative sentences involve a factive feature, which explains that the proposition denotes a fact (see Zanuttini & Portner, 2003, and the references therein). I will show that optatives are characterized by the semantic property of anti-factivity, in the sense that they express a desire about an event that cannot be interpreted as a fact. This property goes beyond the intuitive idea that people usually desire something that is not actually happening. This is proven by the contrast between optative and declarative sentences with a verb of desire. Descriptive sentences containing these predicates are compatible with a context in which the factual nature of the desire is expressed. This happens in the examples in (31):

(31) a. Yo quiero que tú seas   el   jefe y   por eso lo eres.
        I   want   that you is$_{subj}$ the boss and by that it$_{ac}$ you.are
        'I want you to be the boss, and that is why you are.'
     b. Esperaba que hubiera venido Pepe, como de hecho ha   venido
        I.hoped   that had$_{subj}$ come   Pepe as   of fact he.has come
        'I was hoping Pepe had come, as he in fact did.'
     c. Deseo que me ames,   y   soy feliz porque sé   que
        me amas.
        I.wish that me$_{ac}$ you.love$_{subj}$ and I.am happy because I.know that me$_{ac}$ you.love
        'I want you to love me, and I am happy because I know you love me.'

Contrarily, optative sentences are anomalous in a context in which the factual nature of the desire is entailed:

(32) a. ¡Ojalá tú   seas el   jefe! #Y   por eso lo eres.
        OJALÁ you is$_{subj}$ the boss   and by that it$_{ac}$ you.are
        'If only you were the boss! And that is why you are.'
     b. ¡Que haya   venido Pepe . . . , #como de hecho ha venido!
        That has$_{subj}$ come Pepe,   as   of fact   he.has come
        'If only Pepe had come, as he in fact did.'

c. ¡Si al menos tú   me amaras! #Y   soy feliz   porque sé
   que me amas
   if at least   you me$_{ac}$ loved$_{subj}$ and I.am happy because I.know
   that me$_{ac}$ you.love
   'If only you loved me! And I am happy because I know that you love me.'

I propose that the anti-factivity feature of optatives merges as an uninterpretable feature in MoodP. This feature is checked in two different ways: it can be checked by an interpretable feature mood in C (in this case, C merges as an overt conjunction *que/si*), or by spec-head agreement with the lexical adverb *ojalá*. I will show that the way in which this feature is checked has syntactic and semantic consequences.

The Spanish paradigm of subjunctive mood consists of four tenses: present (*ame* 'I love'), past (*amara/amase* 'I loved'), (present)-perfect (*haya amado* 'I have loved'), and pluperfect (*hubiera/hubiese amado* 'I had loved'). The data presented so far show that both *que*-optatives and *si*-optatives require verbs with certain tense features: the verb in *que*-optatives may display present or perfect morphology, but not past or pluperfect (cf. [22] repeated in [33a]); the verb in *si*-optatives is in the past or pluperfect tense, but it rejects present and perfect, as shown in (33b).

(33) a. ¡Que ella {llegue/   haya llegado/*llegara/*   hubiera llegado} ya!
    That she   arrives$_{subj}$ has$_{subj}$ arrived arrived$_{subj}$ had$_{subj}$ arrived yet
    'I wish she {had arrived} {already/by now}.'
   b. ¡Si al menos yo {*sea/   *haya   sido/ fuera/ hubiera sido} millonario!
    If at least   I   am$_{subj}$ have$_{subj}$ been was$_{subj}$ had$_{subj}$ been millionaire
    'If only I {were/had been} a millionaire!'

Ojalá-optatives don't have tense restrictions, as shown in the examples in (23) above. Table 1 summarizes the tense restrictions of optative sentences. The table shows that there is a relationship between the way mood is checked and the restrictions on the tense of the subjunctive verb. When checking takes place in C, it has consequences on the lexical realization in C. In the

Table 3.1.
Tense Restrictions in Spanish Optative Sentences

	Present	Perfect	Past	Pluperfect
Ojalá-optatives	✓	✓	✓	✓
Que-optatives	✓	✓	*	*
Si-optatives	*	*	✓	✓

following, I will show that this is due to the semantic specification of the feature of anti-factivity.

Grammarians have noted that tense features in optative sentences are not exclusively related to temporal anchoring, but also to the interpretation of the event as a feasible or unfeasible desire (cf. Bello, 1847/1964, § 692; Gili Gaya, 1961, § 40; Ridruejo, 1983; among others). When combined with present tense, the desired situation is a present stage or a future event (34a); when combined with a present perfect tense, the desired situation consists of the present or future results of an event, which can be accomplished at any time (34b). In both cases, the desire is supposed to be feasible. The sentences in (34) express a feasible desire, that is, an eventuality that is not real but is compatible with the actual state of things.

(34) a. ¡Ojalá llueva {*ayer/ hoy/ mañana}!
   OJALÁ it.rains$_{subj}$ yesterday/today/tomorrow
   'I wish it would rain {today/tomorrow}!'
b. ¡Ojalá haya terminado la huelga {??ayer/ hoy/ mañana}!
   OJALÁ has$_{subj}$ finished the strike yesterday/today/tomorrow
   'I hope the strike will be finished {today/tomorrow}!'

When combined with a past tense, optatives express that the desired situation is simultaneous or subsequent to the time of the utterance (35a). When combined with the pluperfect, the desired situation described by optatives consists on the present or future results of an event, which can be accomplished at any time (35b). In both cases, optatives express a non-feasible or impossible desire, that is, an eventuality that is not real and is not compatible with the actual state of things:

(35) a. ¡Ojalá estuviera lloviendo {ahora/mañana}!
    OJALÁ was$_{subj}$ raining now/ tomorrow
    'If only it was raining {right now/tomorrow}!'
   b. ¡Ojalá hubiese terminado {ya/ mañana} el artículo!
    OJALÁ had$_{subj}$ finished already/tomorrow the paper
    'If only I had finished my paper {yet/tomorrow}!'

Only the pluperfect can anchor the desired situation in the past. In that case, both the aoristic (36a) and resultative/perfect reading (36b) are possible for the pluperfect:

(36) a. ¡Ojalá su esposa hubiera ido ayer a la fiesta!
    OJALÁ his wife had$_{subj}$ gone yesterday to the party
    'If only his wife had gone yesterday to the party!'
   b. ¡Ojalá hubiera terminado el trabajo ayer!
    OJALÁ had$_{subj}$ finished the paper yesterday
    'If only I had finished my paper yesterday!'

The temporal anchoring of the pluperfect provides the contra-factual reading. The sentences in (35) and (36) express a non-feasible or impossible desire, that is, an eventuality that is not real and is not compatible with the actual state of things (Ridruejo, 1999, p. 3217; Rojo, 1974; Rojo & Veiga, 1999, pp. 2918–2919).

Table 2 sums up all the possible interpretations of the subjunctive tenses in optative sentences. In all these cases, the subjunctive refers to an antifactive situation. The combination of the morphological tense of the verb and the temporal anchoring of the non-factual event gives rise to two different readings related to the speaker's attitude. Optatives with a present or present perfect tense are interpreted as feasible desires, which is consistent with Laca's (2010, p. 198) idea that "the present is a deictic tense, always anchored with regard to Utt-time." Optatives with a past or pluperfect tense are interpreted as non-feasible desires, as contra-factivity is a special case of non-feasibility. Tense selection is, then, associated with the modal base to which the proposition is evaluated: optatives with present and perfect tense provide a non-realistic modal base (Iatridou 2000), that is, a non-unitary domain of words of evaluation including the real world (w_o); on the other hand, optatives with past and pluperfect provide a non-realistic modal base, which excludes the real world. This explains that only optatives with a past tense are compatible with a contra-factual reading, as example (37) shows:

Table 3.2.
Interpretations of Subjunctive Tenses in Optatives

	Event in the past	Event in present or future	Past result of an event	Present or future result of an event
Ojalá + present$_{subj}$ / *Que* + present$_{subj}$	*	Feasible	*	*
Ojalá + perfect$_{subj}$ / *Que* + perfect$_{subj}$	*	*	*	Feasible
Ojalá + past$_{subj}$ / *Si* + past$_{subj}$	*	Non-feasible	*	*
Ojalá + pluperfect$_{subj}$ / *Si* + pluperfect$_{subj}$	Contra-factive	*	Contra-factive	Non-feasible

(37) No llueve, pero ¡ojalá {*esté/ estuviera} lloviendo ahora mismo!
Not it.rains$_{ind}$, but OJALÁ it.is$_{subj}$ / it.was$_{subj}$ raining now right
'It is not raining, but ... if only it were raining right now!'

Finally, it is important to recall that the merging of C in optatives is related to the interpretation of the anti-factive feature of mood. C merges as *que* if the anti-factive feature has a "feasible" reading, since this conjunction is only allowed with present and perfect tenses. On the other hand, C merges as *si* if the anti-factive feature has a contra-factive or non-feasible reading, since *si* is only compatible with preterite and pluperfect tenses. The fact that *ojalá*-optatives are compatible with all tenses supports the idea that the adverb can lexically check the anti-factive feature of mood without resorting to C.

4. Wh-Words in Optative Sentences

In previous sections, it has been shown that exclamatives and optatives have some common properties: they are expressive sentences without a truth value that express the speaker's emotion about a proposition, and they contain an EX-operator that selects a scalar argument and quantifies over scalar alternatives. However, they differ in the type of scale involved (a preference scale for optatives but an inverse prior likelihood scale for exclamatives). They differ as well in the factual nature of the proposition (which is factual for exclamatives but anti-factual for optatives). In this section, I will show that they also differ in the possibility of containing a wh-word.

4.1. WH-OPTATIVES DO NOT EXIST...

It is known that predicates of desire, wish, or hope cannot take wh-sentences as arguments, as shown in (38):

(38) a. *I hope who comes.
    b. *She wishes where he goes on holidays.
    c. *It is desirable when he lives.

As expected, wh-optatives are not possible, either. The subjunctive morphology excludes an exclamative reading in the Spanish examples in (39), so that, only the optative reading is available. But even so, the sentences in (39) are ungrammatical. The English translation expresses the expected, but not available, reading of the Spanish examples:[5]

(39) a. *¡Dónde esté yo ahora!
       Where is$_{subj}$ I   now
       'If only I were in such a place now!'
    b. *¡Cuán interesante haya sido el artículo que he   escrito!
       How interesting has$_{subj}$ been the paper   that I.have written
       'If only the paper I wrote were very interesting!'
    c. *¡Cuántos   países   visitase   durante mis vacaciones!
       How-many countries I.visited$_{subj}$ during my holidays
       'If only I visited many countries during my holidays!'

Wh-exclamatives are, instead, perfectly grammatical:

(40) a. ¡Dónde estoy yo ahora!
       Where am$_{ind}$ I   now!
       'It is amazing where I am now!'
    b. ¡Cuán interesante ha   sido el   artículo que he   escrito!
       How interesting has$_{ind}$ been the paper   that I.have written
       'How interesting the paper I have written is!'

---

5. To the best of my knowledge, sentences with this pattern are ungrammatical in German and English and other Romance languages as well.

c. ¡Cuántos   países   visité   durante mis vacaciones!
How-many countries I.visited$_{ind}$ during my holidays
'How many countries I have visited during my holidays!'

I propose that the ungrammaticality of the examples in (38) and (39) is due to the intensional anchoring of the proposition involved in optatives. Assuming that propositions are anchored to worlds, and worlds are anchored to individuals, I consider that both exclamatives and optatives are modalized propositions anchored to the speaker's world. As we have seen above, EX contributes the speaker's emotion about a proposition, so that the world in which the proposition must be evaluated is a world, or set of worlds, introduced by the speaker.

Optatives and exclamatives differ, however, with regards to this world or set of worlds. Since EX in optatives is associated with the world the speaker considers desirable, it naturally follows that optative-EX is a "strong intensional operator"—in McCawley's (1981) terms. It introduces a set of worlds that the speaker takes to be possible alternatives to his or her real world. The content of the proposition is anchored in each one of these worlds, and the proposition is true in them. As expected, the optative EX operator is nonveridical. As other strong intensional predicates do, it does not guarantee the truth of the proposition in the embedded model (see Giannakidou, 1995; Quer, 1998).

As opposed to optative operators, EX in exclamatives is a "weak intensional operator" and introduces a single world in the context where the proposition is true. This explains that the proposition under the exclamative EX operator is not only a veridical proposition, but it actually denotes a fact. According to this, EX in exclamatives is a veridical operator because the truth of its complements is implied or entailed in the model it introduces.

Going back to the examples in (39)–(40), I assume that a wh-clause denotes basically a set of propositions *p* true in the world *w*. That means that clauses with a wh-word denote the set of all possible true propositions of the form *p(x)*, *x* being all the possible values for the wh-variable in the world of evaluation.[6] According to this, wh-words are grammatical under the scope of an exclamative EX-operator because the proposition is evaluated in a single world that coincides with the world of the speaker's knowledge. The proposition is, then, veridical. The exclamative reading involves the presupposition

---

6. This is the classic analysis of Hamblin (1973) and Karttunen (1977) for interrogatives, which Gutiérrez-Rexach (1996), Abels (2004), D'Avis (2002), and Zanuttini and Portner (2003), among others, extend to exclamatives.

that the wh-variable instantiates. As a consequence, it has a single value that is known by the speaker.[7]

To the contrary, wh-words are ungrammatical under the scope of an optative EX-operator because the proposition is evaluated in a set of worlds that coincides with the desires and wishes of the speaker. The denotation of the wh-optative would be the set of all possible true propositions $p(x)$, where x is the wh-variable. Nevertheless, since the proposition is under the scope of a non-veridical operator, it is not possible to guarantee the truth of the proposition, what makes the utterance uninterpretable.

4.2. . . . EXCEPT FOR SPANISH *QUIÉN*-OPTATIVES

Contrary to what we would expect, Spanish wh-optatives with the pronoun *quién* 'who' are grammatical. They are, actually, an extremely common productive pattern of optative sentences in both Spanish and other Ibero-Romance languages (see Sánchez López, 2016). Let me enumerate their most relevant syntactic and semantic properties.

Quién is a pronoun that is marked with singular and third-person features [+human], which the verb displays in subject-verb agreement.[8] Somehow paradoxically, *quién*-optatives express the speaker's desire, that is, they are interpreted as having a first-person singular, as shown in the gloss of (3), which I repeat here as (41):

(41) ¡Quién fuera   millonario!
     Who   were$_{subj}$ millionaire
     'If only I were a millionaire!'

Quién must be the subject of the sentence. The sentence becomes ungrammatical (the optative reading being available) if *quién* is a direct

---

7. This is consistent with the factive content of exclamatives and also with the scalar interpretation of the proposition, since only one of all the possible values of x can satisfy the condition of being the highest in an inverse prior likelihood scale that models the speaker's surprise.

8. In the preterit subjunctive, first and third persons are homonymous. However, the agreement with a reflexive pronoun clearly shows that the verb in *quién*-optatives has third-person features:

   (i) ¡Quién pudiera   ir {se/   *me}   al   Caribe!
       Who   could$_{subj}$ go{himself$_{refl}$/myself$_{refl}$} to-the Caribbean
       'If only I were able to travel to the Caribbean sea!'

object (42a) or a prepositional complement (42b). The English glosses express the expected but impossible meaning of the utterance:[9]

(42) a. *¡A quién amara él!
To whom loved$_{subj}$ he
'If only he loved me!'
b. *¡Para quién hubieses trabajado en esa empresa!
For whom you.had$_{subj}$ worked in that company
'If only you had worked for me in that company!'

The interpretation of *quién* as a first-person singular, despite its morphological features, can be overtly explicit in context. In the following examples, the first person merges in the verb of the relative clause:

(43) a. ¡Quién tuviera el ansia de aventura que **tuve** siempre!
Who had$_{subj}$ the yearning of adventure that I.had ever
'If only I had the yearning for adventure that I always had!'
(J. Martín Recuerda, *El engañao*, España, 1981)
b. Quién hubiera podido comprarlos con el dinero
who had$_{subj}$ been-able buying-them$_{ac}$ with the money
que **gané** bailándole a los franceses en las tabernas de Cádiz.
that I.earned dancing-him$_{dat}$ to the Frenchmen in the taverns of Cádiz
'If only I was able to buy them with the money I earned dancing in the Cadiz taverns for the Frenchmen!' (J. Martín Recuerda, *Las arrecogías*, España, 1988)

The verb in *quién*-optatives must be in the subjunctive mood. Present and perfect tenses are not possible. The past has a "non-feasible" reading (43a), and the pluperfect, as expected, has a contra-factual reading (43b).

I will now explain how *quién*-optatives escape from the general restriction of wh-optatives. Considering the ungrammaticality of the examples in (38) and (39) above, the grammaticality of (41) is quite surprising. The EX-operator ought to make the proposition "to be a millionaire(x)" (where x is the wh-variable associated with *quien* 'who') true in the set of worlds

---

9. These sentences would be ungrammatical if *quién* 'who' refers to another person than the speaker as well.

compatible with the speaker's desire. But it is not possible to know whether this proposition is true in all these possible worlds, since the value of the wh-variable is not instantiated. In other words, the speaker cannot express an emotion about a proposition that contains a variable whose value is expected to be different in each of the worlds compatible with his desire.

The only way to save the derivation of a wh-optative would be to interpret the wh-variable as having a constant value instantiated by some special mechanism. I will argue that this is exactly what happens in *quién*-optatives. Since EX is necessarily associated with the speaker's emotion, I propose that it contains a first-person feature that guarantees that exclamatives and optatives do not express the surprise or the desire of another person other than the speaker.[10] EX enters the derivation with an interpretable first-person feature, yielding an expressive utterance that conveys the speaker's emotion about a proposition. I assume that the features of third-person and singular *quién* 'who' are uninterpretable (that is, they are default values for person and number), acquiring a value by agreement with INFL. Being a quantifier, *quién* 'who' is associated with a covert partitive phrase, which provides their quantification domain. This partitive phrase may acquire a person feature in the course of the derivation, via binding. I propose that EX binds the partitive complement of *quién*. By so doing, it restricts the quantifier domain to the set of individuals with the features [+human] [person:first], as shown in (44):

(44)

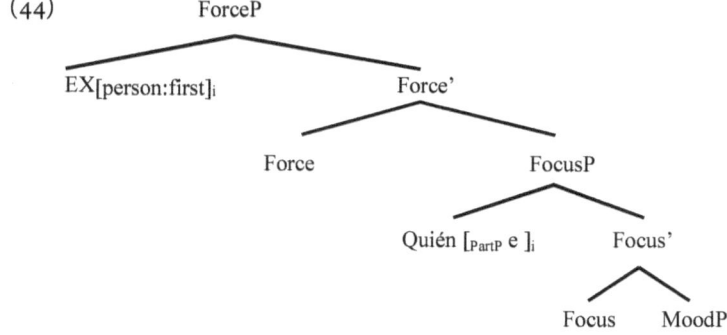

---

10. Similarly, Zanuttini, Pak, and Portner (2012) propose that jussive, hortative, and imperative sentences contain a jussive operator with second-person features. This is necessary to explain the mandatory reference to the addressee in these sentences.

My analysis ensures that a relation is established between the EX-operator and the subject, as opposed to some other argument. The examples in (41) crash because of the presence of a potential binder for *quién* (i.e, the subject or another argument). The binding of the partitive complement of *quién* 'who' by EX restricts the quantifier domain to the individuals with the feature [person:1], that is, the speaker. This saves the derivation of the wh-optatives because the proposition under the EX-operator contains a variable whose value is constant in all the possible worlds compatible with the speaker's desire. The sentence in (40), thus, is interpretable and expresses the speaker's emotion about the proposition "to be a millionaire(x) where x is the speaker."

5. Conclusion

Optatives are main sentences with a complex left periphery. As exclamative sentences, optatives have an EX-operator in ForceP. EX makes the sentence expressive, and it conveys the speaker's emotion about the content of a proposition. The composition of an exclamative or an optative meaning is made up from several ingredients that are responsible for the differences between optatives and exclamatives. In optatives, EX quantifies over scalar alternatives in reference to a bouletic scale that models the speaker's preferences. The proposition has an anti-factual feature that is encoded in a mood head whose content determines both morphological mood (subjunctive) and the expressions that overtly surface in the position of force. The uninterpretable feature in mood is checked in force and merges as the conjunction *que* 'that' if associated with a feasible reading, but merges as *si* 'if' when associated with a non-feasible or contra-factual reading. The uninterpretable feature of mood can be checked lexically by agreement with the adverb *ojalá*, so that all the possible readings for anti-factuality are available. *Ojalá* can move to ForceP and no conjunction is required; the sequence *ojalá que* is the result of the merge of an optional *que* 'that' in the focus head. Finally, I have proposed that the operator EX has strong intensional properties in optatives that are responsible for the ungrammaticality of wh-optatives. Contrary to what is expected, Spanish *quién*-optatives are possible because the identification of the first-person feature in EX with the wh-variable of *quién* makes the sentence interpretable.

Exclamatives in (Argentinian) Spanish and Their Next of Kin

Pascual José Masullo

Introduction

In this chapter I examine a wide range of constructions in Spanish (with a focus on the present-day Argentinian variety) which, although not full-fledged exclamatives on the surface, bear several degrees of resemblance to them, thus reinforcing the idea often put forth in the literature that exclamative constructions do not constitute a homogeneous phenomenon, as is generally assumed. In this respect, the chapter draws on Masullo (2012), even if some revisions, and a more complete and refined analysis, are proposed.

Firstly, I examine a class of well-established colloquial expressions and constructions (often loosely characterized as elative or emphatic), which, as I show, are bona fide exclamatives at LF, except that the expression denoting the EXTREME DEGREE feature that must be associated with this class of sentence (Zanuttini & Portner, 2003) is not an overt qu- (or wh-) expression, such as *qué* 'what,' *cómo* 'how,' or *cuánto* 'how much,' but rather a constituent that could otherwise be used non-exclamatively, such as partitive *de* 'of,' the indefinite article (*un* and variants), or a quantifier such as *cada* 'each.' These

---

This research was partly funded by grant 40-B-60/2010, Universidad Nacional de Río Negro, Argentina. I am thankful to Ignacio Bosque for a thorough review of this chapter, and for several valuable comments and suggestions. Needless to say, I am fully responsible for any remaining errors or shortcomings.

usually occur *in situ*, though, for independent reasons, they could be fronted as well, as will be shown in ensuing sections. Examples are provided below, contrasted with their overt equivalents:

(1) a. ¡El Nahuel Huapi es de bello!¹ (= ¡Qué bello (que) es el Nahuel Huapi!)
The Nahuel Huapi is of beautiful
'How beautiful the Nahuel Huapi is!' (cf. The Nahuel Huapi is so beautiful/ such a beautiful lake!)
b. ¡El niño es un vivaracho!² (= ¡Qué vivaracho (que) es el niño!)
The child is one smart
'How smart the child is!'
c. ¡El tipo dijo cada verdura!³ (= ¡Qué barbaridades (que) dijo el tipo!)
The guy said each vegetable
'What nonsense the guy talked!'

After showing that the above sentences are tantamount to overt wh-exclamatives at LF, I go on to discuss what I call "plain elatives," that is expressions of different kinds and categories associated with an EXTREME DEGREE feature, but which may only optionally be used in exclamative sentences. Some of these elatives are part of the stock pan-Hispanic vocabulary, though others are new developments in (Argentinian) Spanish. It is to the latter that I pay special attention in this study. In the examples below, the featured elatives (*se... todo* and *mal*) are equivalent to the counterparts in *-ísimo* also provided (the exclamation marks in parentheses indicate the optional exclamative illocutionary force of the sentences):

(2) a. (¡) Los chicos **se** comieron **todo** en la fiesta (!)
The children REFL ate ALL at the party
'The children ate an awful lot at the party(!)'

---

1. As will be pointed out below, these sentences entail an implicit consecutive or resultative clause.

2. This use of the indefinite article is not to be confused with the productive process of nominalizing (usually) negative adjectives, as in *El hombre es un irresponsable* 'The man is an irresponsible person.' As an exclamative, the indefinite article is not restricted in the same way, as is shown by a sentence like *¡Pedro puso una cara!* 'Peter put on such a face!' Naturally, a previously nominalized negative adjective can occur in the exclamative construction too: *¡EL hombre es un irresponsable!* 'How irresponsible the man is!'

3. Drawn from everyday spoken language, many of the examples given have a truly colloquial or slang flavor.

b. (¡) Los chicos comieron **muchísimo** en la fiesta (!)
   The children ate very much-ÍSIMO at the party
   'The children ate an awful lot at the party (!)'
c. (¡) Papá se enojó **mal** anoche (!)
   Father got-angry badly last night
   'Father got terribly angry last night (!)'
d. (¡) Papá se enojó **muchísimo** anoche (!)
   Father got-angry very much-ÍSIMO last night
   'Father got terribly angry last night (!)'

Although I present a host of examples of new elatives of this kind in (Argentinian) Spanish, I focus on *se... todo* and *mal*, as in (2a) and (2c) above, characterizing them both formally and semantically. I propose that, unlike the exclamatives in (1), they act as exclamatives only when bound by an empty exclamative operator, since they do not intrinsically possess an exclamative feature. I thus establish three kinds of kindred constructions, viz., wh-overt exclamatives, covert exclamatives, and optional exclamatives with plain elatives. While the first type has been satisfactorily studied and is quite well-understood, I believe the other two have not received adequate treatment so far. I therefore hope this study may pave the way for further future collaborative research.

2. Covert Exclamatives

In this section I deal with exclamatives containing partitive *de*, the indefinite article and the quantifier *cada*, as illustrated in (1) above. I characterize them as *covert* exclamatives on a par with covert interrogatives in languages like Chinese in which there is no explict wh-word in Spec (CP) (Huang, 1982) and in contrast with well-known overt wh-exclamatives (see Alonso-Cortés, 1999b; Contreras, 1999; Gutiérrez-Rexach, 2001; among several others). It is not my aim to provide an exhaustive list of covert exclamatives here. However, I must mention one more besides the three presented in section 1: the comparative quantifier *más* 'more' (with an implied consecutive clause), since it is quite frequently used, though always with a negative connotation (see section 5.5 in chapter 1 and references therein):

(3) ¡El tipo es **más** {terco/ egoísta/tacaño/antipático}!
    The guy is more {stubborn/selfish/ stingy/ unpleasant}!
    'The guy is so {stubborn/selfish/stingy/unpleasant}!'

Interestingly enough, (3) is interchangeable with (4) below, a combination of an overt and covert exclamative expression, which I will not attempt to analyze here:

(4) ¡Qué tipo más {terco/ egoísta/tacaño/antipático} (que es)!
What guy more {stubborn/selfish/ stingy/ unpleasant} (that is)!
'What a {stubborn/selfish/stingy/unpleasant guy} he is!'

Before spelling out my analysis, I must first point out some crucial similarities between covert and canonical wh-exclamatives by examining the formal properties and requirements they have in common, as well as some of the restrictions they are both subject to. Apart from sharing practically the same semantic, pragmatic, and prosodic properties, covert exclamatives cannot co-occur with other elements in Spec (CP) (or FocusP, in the sense of Rizzi, 1997), or other exclamatives and elatives (for more details, see Masullo, 2012):[4]

(5) a. *¿Qué lago es de bello?
'*{What/which} lake is so beautiful?' [unless *so* is anaphoric]
b. ¿Qué niño es un vivaracho?
'{What/which} child is so smart!
c. *¿Quién dijo cada barbaridad?
'Who talked such nonsense?'
d. *¡Cuántos lagos de Argentina y Chile son de lindos!
'How many Argentinian and Chilean lakes are so beautiful!'
(Cf. ¡Cuántos lagos de Argentina y Chile son lindos!)
e. *¡Cuántos niños son unos vivarachos hoy día!
'*How many children are so smart today!'
(Cf. ¡Cuántos niños son vivarachos hoy día!)
f. *¡Cuánta gente dice cada barbaridad!
'*How many people talk such nonsense!'
(Cf. ¡Cuánta gente dice barbaridades!)

By the same token, they cannot occur in jussive, dubitative, or desiderative sentences. Being true exclamatives, the clash is self-explanatory, that is, a sentence cannot be exclamative and jussive or desiderative, etc., all at once.

---

4. Naturally, some of these sentences are acceptable with a different reading, for example, as echo questions.

In other words, C (or Focus) cannot be associated with clashing features, e.g. EXCLAMATIVE and JUSSIVE:

(6) a. *¡{Sé/no seas} de bueno!
'{*Be/don't be} so good!'
b. *¡Tal vez el niño sea un vivaracho!
'*Maybe the child is so smart!'
c. *¡Que diga cada barbaridad el tipo!
'*Let the guy talk such nonsense!'

Likewise, as in the case of embedded wh-exclamatives (7a), they cannot be selected for by predicates that require an assertion, such as *sostener* 'claim, maintain,' *afirmar* 'assert,' etc.:

(7) a. *El educador afirmó cuántos analfabetos aún había.
'*The educator asserted how many illiterate people still remained.'
b. Los turistas todos sostienen que el Nahuel Huapi es de bello . . .
'Tourists all maintain that the Nahuel Huapi is so beautiful . . .'
c. *Afirmo que el tipo dijo cada barbaridad.
'I assert that the guy said such nonsense.'
d. *Reafirmo que los políticos son unos corruptos
'*I reasseart that politicians are so corrupt!'
(OK if *un* is not exclamative)

Naturally, this is not so with reportative verbs, which do not select for the content per se of the reported discourse, so that they can take as complements not only declarative, but also interrogative and exclamative embedded clauses introduced by *que* 'that':

(8) a. María dijo: "El Nahuel Huapi es de bello . . ." [direct discourse]
'Mary said: "The Nahuel Huapi is so beautiful!"'
b. Los turistas todos sostienen que el Nahuel Huapi es de bello . . .
'Tourists all maintain that the Nahuel Huapi is so beautiful . . .'
c. María exclamó que qué lindo era el lago.
'Mary exclaimed "how nice the lake was."'
d. María preguntó (que) cuándo terminaría el conflicto.
'Mary asked when the conflict would end.'

However, unlike wh-exclamatives, covert ones cannot be directly embedded as complements to verbs such as *mirar* 'look,' which typically select for an embedded exclamative clause, since they lack the "complementizer" feature of overt wh-elements (interrogative, relative, and exclamative) which allows direct syntactic subordination:

(9) a. ¡Mirá qué bello (que) es el Nahuel Huapi!⁵
    'Look how beautiful the Nahuel Huapi is!'
  b. *¡Mirá el Nahuel Huapi es de bello . . . !
    '*Look the Nahuel Huapi is so beautiful!'

Crucially, covert exclamatives are not unlike overt ones in that they cannot be (internally) negated,⁶ as the ungrammaticality of the following sentences confirms:

(10) a. *¡El Nahuel Huapi no es de bello!
    'The Nahuel Huapi is not so beautiful!'
  b. *¡El niño no es un vivaracho!
    'The child is not so smart!'
  c. *¡El tipo no dijo cada barbaridad!
    'The guy did not say such nonsense!'

Finally, as anticipated in footnote 3, it must be stressed that covert exclamatives behave very much like *tan(to/a(s))* 'so,' 'so much,' 'so many,' and *tal* 'such,' which are not colloquial, but stylistically neuter and pan-Hispanic (the same holds of their equivalents in English). Like these, *de* and *cada,* can also take a consecutive sequel (but not *un,* for reasons I cannot explain):

(11) a. Juan es tan tonto (que se traga cualquier cosa).
    'John is so foolish (that he will swallow anything).'

---

  5. This example sharply contrasts with *¡Mirá! ¡El Nahuel Huapi es de bello!*, in which there are two independent clauses without embedding
  6. This constraint excludes so-called expletive negation (Espinal, 1992): *¡El tipo no (va y) dice cada barbaridad!* 'The guy doesn't (go and) say each nonsense!' Likewise, as has been noted, negative interrogative sentences can occasionally be used with an exclamative illocutionary force, so long as the relevant gradable expression is "plain": *¿No es hermoso este cuadro?* 'Isn't this picture beautiful!' Cf. *¿No es de bello este cuadro?* Far from being counterevidence, this fact supports my claim even further.

b. Hizo tal lío (que lo tuvieron que sacar a la fuerza).
'He made such trouble (that they had to bounce him out by force).'
c. El Nahuel Huapi es de lindo (que miles de turistas lo visitan año a año).
'The Nahuel Huapi is so nice (that thousands of tourists visit it year in, year out).'
d. El tipo dijo cada barbaridad (que el público lo silbó).
'The guy said each nonsense (that the audience jeered and catcalled at him).'
e. *Pedro es un vivo que siempre saca ventaja de uno.
'Peter is such a smart-aleck that he always takes advantage of one.'

As has been pointed out in the relevant literature, the close tie between exclamation and consecutive or resultative clauses cannot be overlooked. The unusual or undesired result in question (or "widening," in the sense of Zanuttini & Portner, 2001) follows naturally from the extreme (and therefore unexpected) degree feature of both exclamatives and intensifiers like *so* and *such*. For example, an extreme degree of weariness can prevent one from doing something as easy as sitting down (*John was so tired that he couldn't even sit down to dinner*; cf. *How tired John was! He couldn't even sit down to dinner*). In contrast, it would be very odd to say *Peter is so tired that he cannot even work 24 hours in a row*, since in the natural course of events no one is expected to work for a whole day (cf. *How tired Peter was! He couldn't even work 24 hours in a row*, which is equally odd). Besides, like exclamatives, sentences with consecutive clauses cannot be internally negated:

(12) *Juan no es tan alto que llega al techo.
'John is not so tall that he will reach the ceiling.'

However, once the resultative sequel is added, the sentence ceases to be exclamative in the true sense of the word, since the extreme degree variable is now "closed" or saturated by the sequel. In exclamatives proper (whether overt or covert), the extreme degree variable is bound by an operator. In other words, sentences with explicit consecutive clauses are not open. There is one more contrast between sentences with an implied result (or "suspended" resultatives, as they have been dubbed in the literature), which I am claiming are bona fide exclamatives, and sentences with explicit resultatives: while the first must necessarily be root, the latter can also be embedded (Ignacio Bosque, personal communication):

(13) a. Creo que el niño está tan grande que no cabe en la cuna.
'I think that the child is so big that he does not fit in the cot.'
b. *Creo que el niño está tan grande.
'I think that the child is so big.'

In conclusion, the above paradigms bear out the claim that the constructions under discussion are genuinely exclamative, since they show that they must meet the same requirements as overt wh-exclamatives and, moreover, are subject to the same restrictions. In the next section, I outline an analysis for covert exclamatives which allows us to account for the similarities pointed out above, while in section 5 I tentatively suggest that they behave in the same way with respect to island effects as well.

3. Analyzing Covert Exclamatives

There is general agreement that (partial) overt exclamatives contain a wh-element in Spec (CP)—or Spec of Focus Phrase—which binds an empty position *in situ* (whether we formalize this empty position in terms of traces or copies that later get deleted at PF is irrelevant here). Crucially, the wh-element is associated with both features required for exclamation: EXCLAMATIVE and EXTREME DEGREE (broadly understood to subsume extreme quantity as well). However, owing to PF-considerations, its displacement (or internal merge) entails pied-piping of the EXTREME DEGREE component along with its restrictor, just as in other cases of wh-movement, since they cannot be morphologically teased apart (Chomsky, 1995). In (14b) below, the fronted phrase *qué bello* realizes the exclamative operator per se, extreme degree (both conflated in *qué*), as well as its complement (or restrictor), that is, *bello*. I schematize my proposed analysis in (15), in which I adopt a Copy Theory of movement for concreteness:

(14) a. ¡Qué bello es el Nahuel Huapi!
'How beautiful the Nahuel Huapi is!'
b. ¡[Qué bello] $_{EXCL / EXTR DEG}$ es el Nahuel Huapi /[Qué bello] $_{EXCL / EXTR DEG}$!

On the basis of the parallel behavior of overt and covert exclamatives outlined in section 2 above, it naturally follows that covert exclamatives are also associated with the two required features, viz. EXTREME DEGREE and

EXCLAMATIVE. However, the EXCLAMATIVE feature is phonologically null and therefore "weak" (to use the well-known metaphor adopted in generative grammar). In traditional GB terms, we should propose LF movement to Spec (CP) of the covert exclamative expression, along the lines of Huang (1982) and others for interrogatives in Chinese, Japanese, Hindi, etc. On the other hand, if we were to follow Chomsky (1995), we should propose just feature movement at LF. However, since these two implementations have been abandoned, I propose instead a simpler solution: a base-generated OP with the feature EXCLAMATIVE binding the EXTREME DEGREE feature on the in situ phrase (for questions in Japanese, in which the OP generates in situ, cf. Watanabe, 2001). I schematize my analysis in (13):

(15) ¡OP $_{[\text{EXCL}]\,i}$ El Nahuel Huapi es [de bello]$_{[\text{EXTR DEG}]i}$!

Moreover, I claim that in the example we are considering (with partitive *de*) the extreme degree feature itself is phonologically null as well and that *de* is a marker of partitive case, as the diagram in (16) shows. This is not so, however, for covert exclamatives with the indefinite article and the quantifier *cada*. Instead, I assume that these two intrinsically contain an EXTREME DEGREE feature.

(16)
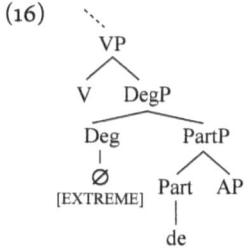

This is not different from other attested cases of the phonologically null expression of the extreme degree feature (with or without a partitive), as in (17):

(17) a. ¡Qué [e] de gente   que había   en la cola!
        What   of people that there-was in the line!
        'What an awful lot of people there were in the line!'
     b. Las cosas están [e] que explotan.
        The things are   that they-explode
        'Things have come to a pretty pass.'

The structure in (18) displays a complete analysis of a covert exclamative with partitive *de* (which can obviously be adapted for the other two covert exclamatives being considered in this chapter):

(18)

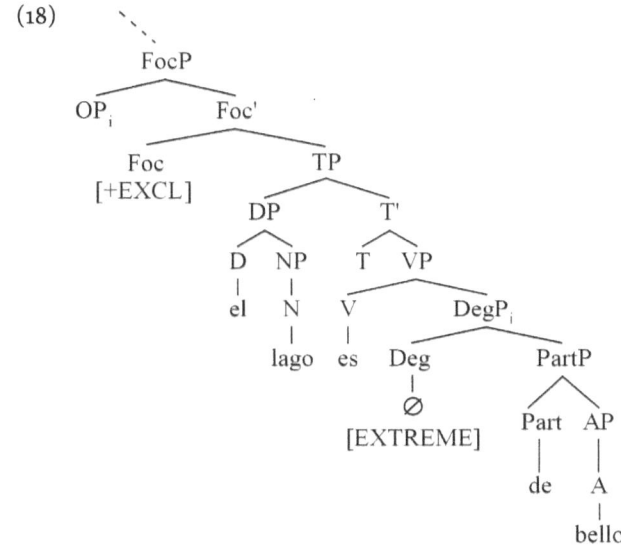

Having laid out our analysis, we can now proceed to account for the incompatibilities and restrictions pointed out in section 2. In the case of (5a) through (5c) the ungrammaticality follows from the fact that the overt interrogative operator leaves no room for the empty exclamative operator that must bind the *in situ* phrase with *de*, *un*, and *cada*. Likewise, Focus Phrase cannot host two different exclamative operators, nor can the same exclamative operator bind two different expressions bearing an extreme degree feature, which accounts for the ungrammaticality of (5d) through (5f). A similar clash obtains in (6), on the obvious assumption that these sentences contain a jussive, dubitative, and desiderative operator, respectively. As pointed out above, a sentence cannot be exclamative and declarative, interrogative, or jussive, etc., at the same time, as it would be uninterpretable at LF. If the expressions with *de*, *un*, and *cada* we are focusing on were not exclamative in nature, the observed incompatibilities would be hard to explain.

As Zanuttini & Portner (2003) claim, exclamatives are factive. Among other things, this property entails that they cannot be negated.[7] Sentences

---

7. D-linking and referentiality may override this restriction, as in *¡Cuántos libros interesantes no he leído en mi vida!* 'How many interesting books I have not read in my lifetime!' (see

(10a) through (10c) above show that this is true of covert exclamatives as well, as expected. Strictly speaking, factivity is intrinsically linked with extreme degree. As will be seen in section 4 below, plain elatives, i.e., expressions associated with extreme degree not necessarily occuring in exclamative sentences, are incompatible with negation, also owing to their factive nature. In turn, in Masullo (2012) this fact is further reduced to a violation of Relativized Minimality in the sense of Rizzi (1990), that is, negation acts as a barrier that prevents the operator in Focus Phrase from binding its target in situ, as is shown in (19):

(19) *¡OP $_{[EXCL]\,i}$ El Nahuel Huapi **no** es [**de** bello]$_{[EXTR\,DEG]\,i}$!

However, I will not pursue this difficult question any further here. For our purposes, the fact remains that both overt and covert exclamatives (and elatives in general) form a natural class in that they resist negation.

Given the word order possibilities of Spanish, which is quite permissive with regard to focusing (as well as topicalization), explicit movement of the non-wh-exclamative is generally also allowed as an option. In (20c) through (20e) the exclamative phrases *de lindo, un vivaracho,* and *cada barbaridad* have undergone "run-of-the-mill" fronting, much like the non-exclamative phrases *más dinero* and *hermosa* in (20a) and (20b):

(20) a. ¡Más dinero es lo que se necesita!
 'More money is what we need!'
 b. ¡Hermosa estuvo la obra de teatro!
 'How beautiful the play was!'
 c. ¡De lindo es el Nahuel Huapi!
 'How beautiful the Nahuel Huapi is!'
 d. ¡Un vivaracho es el chico!
 'How smart the child is!'
 e. ¡Cada barbaridad dijo el tipo!
 'What nonsense the guy talked!'

Not surprisingly, English, which shows more restrictions for focusing than Spanish, also allows fronting of *so* and *such*, which, as was pointed out above, are exclamative-like:

---

also Masullo, 2012).

(21) a. So severe had that winter been, that a lot of the crops were killed.
   b. Such a fuss did the customer make, that the manager had to be summoned.

Naturally, if (optional) focus-fronting of a covert exclamative takes place, the relevant features are locally checked. This would have been considered a case of "early altruism" in previous stages of Minimalism. I believe, however, that this fact shows optionality in a different light: far from being an exception, optionality is the norm. Only mandatory movement is special and must be accounted for. Whatever else is allowed may take place at any stage in the derivation, so long as all other independent principles and constrainsts are upheld—cf. Contreras (2009) for a smilar view regarding word order in general. This is undoubtedly a question of crucial theoretical import for Minimalism that must be further investigated.

4. Elatives and Exclamatives

4.1. INTRODUCTION

I now go on to discuss elative expressions in general (often also referred to as "ponderative," RAE-ASALE, 2009). As argued in Masullo (2012), elatives of all kinds, that is expressions that bear an EXTREME DEGREE feature, can also be used as exclamatives. Elative expressions abound in every natural language[8] and, moreover, seem to be subject to rich variation, dialectal, sociolectal, and diachronic. In current Argentinian Spanish new elatives keep coming into being. They are usually introduced by teenagers and, though most are short-lived and never make it to the standard, a few of them eventually do, as the often discussed prefix *re*,[9] now widely used to denote extreme degree in lieu of an adjective or adverb in *-ísimo*.

---

8. This fact can find a natural explanation at the C-I interface (Chomsky, 1995), particularly in the close relationship holding between certain aspects of language and emotion broadly understood (see Pinker, 2007).

9. Though I do not examine *re* in any detail here, I must however point out that while it was originally restricted to gradable adjectives, verbs, and adverbials (including prepositional phrases), it is now found as intensifiers of nouns as well, both count and mass: *Mis amigos tienen la re-casa/plata* 'My friends have a wonderful house/an awful lot of money.' In the case of mass nouns, the licensing of *re* is quite clear: quantity and degree belong to the same conceptual domain. In the case of count nouns, however, I assume that it is an understood gradable feature

Elatives that have entered colloquial Argentinian Spanish lately include expressions with an expletive accusative object, such as *romperla* (lit. 'break it') 'do something extraordinary,' 'excel,' 'outdo oneself,' etc., different kinds of quantifiers or quantitative nouns such as *todo* 'all' in conjunction with reflexive *se* and *banda* (lit. 'band'), adjectives such as *alto* 'tall' which have taken on a generic appreciative value, and, noticeably, the manner adverb *mal,* among several others. These are all illustrated below (example [22g] is also found in other varieties):

(22) a. Messi **la rompió** en el último partido.
 Messi it broke   in the last   game
 'Messi outdid himself in the last game.'
 b. Somos **una banda** en casa.
 We-are a   band   at home
 'There's an awful lot of us at home.'
 c. En este negocio facturan **banda**.
 In this store   they-bill band
 'They rake it in in this store.'
 d. Me costó **una bocha**   encontrar esa marca.
 Me it-cost a   bowling to-find   that brand
 'I had a very hard time finding that brand.'
 e. Nuestro profe   es **una masa**.
 Our   professor is a   mass
 'Our prof is {great/awesome}.'
 f. María **se**   bailó   **todo** anoche.
 Mary REFL danced all   last-night
 'Mary danced her feet off last night.'
 g. Maradona es **lo más** para muchos fanáticos del   fútbol.
 Maradona is the most for   many   fanatics of-the soccer
 'Maradona is God/a hero for many soccer fans.'
 h. ¡**Altas** zapatillas   te   compraste!
 Tall   tennis-shoes REFL you-bought
 'What gorgeous tennis shoes you've bought!'
 i. Juan estaba enojado **mal**   el   otro día.
 John was   angry   badly the other day.
 'John was hopping mad the other day.'

---

on one or more of the qualia of the noun (Pustejovsky, 1995) that licenses it. For example, *Mis amigos tienen la re-casa* may make reference to a very spacious, solid, well-built, or comfortable house, i.e., the extreme degree feature may be associated with the constitutive, formal, agentive, or telic qualia.

However, I must emphasize that these elatives should not be lumped together with the covert exclamatives dealt with in sections 2 and 3 above, even if associated with an EXTREME DEGREE feature, since, unlike them, they do not bear an intrinsic EXCLAMATIVE feature, so that they need not occur in exclamative sentences. As the following exchanges bear witness, the answers need not be exclamative. It is for this reason that they are being dubbed "plain elatives."[10]

(23) a. A: ¿Llovió   mucho anoche?
           'Did it rain a lot   last night?'
        B: Sí, (se) llovió todo
           Yes, REFL rained all
           'Yes, it rained an awful lot(!)'
     b. A: ¿Te gusta la casa?
           'Do you like the house?'
        B: Sí, es re-linda/¡Sí, es re-linda!
           'Yes, it's extremely nice(!)'

Nevertheless, expressing extreme degree, plain elatives are suitable targets for an exclamative operator, thus becoming covert exclamatives on a par with the ones with partitive *de, un,* and *cada.* Naturally the operator binding them must be empty. Overt wh-exclamatives could not possibly bind a plain elative for the simple reason that they already contain an inherent extreme degree feature, as seen in (24):

(24) ¡Qué tiene María una casa   re-linda!
     What has Mary a house RE-nice
     'What Mary has such a nice house!'
     (Cf. ¡Qué linda casa (que) tiene María! 'What a nice house Mary has!')

By the same token, plain elatives cannot co-occur with covert exclamatives, exactly for the same reason. Sentences (22c), (22d), and (22h) above become ungrammatical with the addition of *de, cada,* or the indefinite article:

(25) a. *¡Facturan de banda en este negocio!
        'They turn over a lot of money in this store!'

---

10. The distinction between covert exclamatives and elatives is somewhat blurred in Masullo (2012).

b. *¡Me costó {cada/una} bocha encontrar esa marca!
'I had a very hard time finding that brand!'
c. *¡De altas zapatillas te compraste!
'You bought such a gorgeous pair of tennis shoes!'

Although, as we have seen, plain elatives need not be bound by an empty exclamative operator, they are nonetheless akin to full-fledged exclamatives, whether overt or covert, in that they are factive, which explains why they always resist negation and why they cannot be used in jussive, desiderative, or dubitative sentences, as the ungrammaticality of the following sentences shows (for more details, see Masullo, 2012):

(26) a. *(¡)En este negocio no facturan banda(!) [OK as denial]
   In this store   no they-bill band
   'They don't rake it in in this store!'
b. *¡No te llores todo!
   Don't REFL cry all!
   'Don't cry your eyes out!'
c. *¡Sé re-bueno, por favor!¹¹
   Be re-good please!
   'Be extremely good, please!'
d. *¡(Ojalá) que el trabajo te cueste una bocha!
   (I wish) that the job you.DATcosts a bowling-ball
   'I hope you find the job extremely hard!'
e. *Tal vez se compró altas zapatillas.
   Perhaps REFL he-bought tall tennis shoes
   'Perhaps he bought gorgeous tennis shoes.'

Finally, I point out that when focus-fronted, plain elatives must necessarily receive an exclamative reading:

(27) a. ¡Una masa es nuestro profe! (cf. [22e])
   'My prof is {great/awesome}!'
b. ¡Todo se bailó María anoche! (cf. [22f])
   'Mary sure danced her feet off last night!'
c. ¡Lo más es Maradona para muchos fanáticos del fútbol! (cf. [22g])
   'Maradona sure is {God/a hero} for many soccer fans!'

---

11. See also Bosque (2002).

Plain elatives all deserve full treatment, possessing interesting formal and interpretable features of their own, apart from the general ones outlined above, which they all share. Dealing with each one of them in detail is beyond the scope of the present work, so I focus here on two of them only: the construction *se . . . todo*, as well as the new use of *mal* as an intensifier, illustrated in (22f) and (22i) above, respectively. I believe these two present the most interesting behavior from a syntactic standpoint. And, besides showing a high degree of productiviy, their diachornic development can be easily traced.

4.2. THE *SE . . . TODO* CONSTRUCTION

The *se . . . todo* construction has clearly come to stay in Argentinian Spanish. I characterize it as a construction because *todo* can take on an elative value only when used as the complement of a verb associated with the reflexive clitic *se* (to be further dealt with below). Though in all likelihood it started as an instance of hyperbole, the construction soon lost its literal meaning to become a true elative. However, it retains most of its formal properties, in particular, *todo* still behaves as an accusative object (to be precise, it is an argumental quantifier phrase in the sense of Bosque & Masullo, 1998). As the examples below show, it can be found with practically every transitive verb (though certain restrictions apply, as we shall see below):

(28) a. Ayer   me quedé en casa y   me   limpié   todo.
        Yesterday I-stayed at home and to-me I-cleaned all
        'I stayed home yesterday and cleaned like crazy.'
     b. ¡Marcos se   fuma   todo! ¡Como tres atados por día!
        Mark   REFL smokes all   About three packs a day
        'Mark {smokes like a chimney/is a chain smoker}!'
     c. María se   leyó todo en el verano.
        Mary REFL read all   in the summer
        'Mary read like crazy last summer.'

As one might expect, (28a) may also receive a literal interpretation. The high degree of fossilization and grammaticalization of this construction as an elative is borne out by the fact that its use has been extended to unergatives such as *hablar* 'speak,' *caminar* 'walk,' *llorar*, 'weep,' *dormir* 'sleep,' etc., which, as has been convincingly established, can assign accusative case to an object, cognate, or expletive (Burzio, 1986):

(29) a. ¡María se habla todo!
Mary REFL speaks all
'Mary {talks her head off/is a motor-mouth!}'
b. María se caminó todo cuando fue de vacaciones a la cordillera.[12]
Mary REFL walked all when she-went on vacation to the Cordillera
'Mary walked her feet off when she went on vacation to the Cordillera.'
c. ¡Se llovió todo anoche![13]
REFL rained all last night
'It rained cats and dogs last night!'
d. Se nevó todo en los cerros el fin de semana pasado.
REFL snowed all in the mountains the weekend last
'We had extremely heavy snowfalls in the mountains last week-end.'
e. Las chicas se lloraron todo con la película de Leonardo di Caprio.
The girls REFL cried all with the movie of Leonardo di Caprio
'The girls cried their hearts out watching the Leonardo di Caprio movie.'
f. ¡Juan se durmió todo anoche! Estaría exhausto.
John REFL slept all last night. He-would-be exhausted.
'John slept around the clock last night! He must have been exhausted.'

The above examples, apart from confirming the fact that unergatives are accusative case-assigners, also lend extra support to the hypothesis that they are hidden transitive predicates, as has been argued by Hale and Keyser (1993). And, though the status of atmospheric verbs is not always evident, the fact that they can occur in this construction goes to show that (at least

---

12. *Todo* may occasionally alternate with other expressions, for example, *la vida* 'the life,' as in *María se caminó la vida cuando fue de vacaciones a la cordillera* 'Mary walked her feet off when she went on vacation to the Cordillera.'

13. Examples will be randomly enclosed within exclamation marks. Remember that the *se . . . todo* construction can optionally be used exclamatively, like all other plain elatives.

in Spanish) they are also hidden transtives (and not unacusatives) associated with a Lexical Relational Structure along the lines of (30):

(30)
```
        VP
       /  \
      V    NP
      |    |
    [DO]   N
           |
         lluvia
         'rain'
```

Crucially, as predicted, unaccusative verbs are banned from appearing in this construction, since they could not possibly assign accusative case to *todo*:

(31) a. *María se llegó todo.
    Mary REFL arrived all
    'Mary arrived completely.'
  b. *La chica se desmayó todo.[14]
    The girl REFL fainted all
    'The girl passed out completely.'

The requirement that *todo* receive accusative case cannot be easily waived. Thus, prepositional verbs do not qualify, even if transitive, since they can't assign accusative case:

(32) a. El jefe prescinde de cualquier opinión en contrario.
    'The boss {dispenses with/ignores} any contrary opinion.'
  b. *El jefe se prescinde todo.
    'The boss ignores all contrary opinions.'

Schematically, and in a highly idealized manner, I summarize below the swift semantic shift this construction has undergone before becoming an elative:

Hyperbolic use → Elative use with accusative verbs → Extension to unergative verbs (probably, first to agentive unergatives and subsequently to weather verbs)

---

14. This sentence is doubly ungrammatical in fact: on the one hand, *todo* cannot receive its case and, on the other, *desmayar* already takes an anticausative *se* and so cannot take dative *se* as well.

With regard to the obligatorily required reflexive clitic *se* (or variants thereof), I believe it is formally the same *se* we find in the sentences below (despite their optionality):

(33) a. María (se) leyó diez novelas este verano.
'Mary read ten novels this summer.'
b. Pedro (se) comió tres porciones de pizza en la cena.
'Peter ate up three slices of pizza for dinner.'
c. Pedro (se) hizo un rico asado.
'Peter cooked himself a wonderful barbecue.'

The nature of *se* in the above sentences is a time-honored problem in both traditional and generative grammar, and, as expected, there is a vast literature on it, which I cannot even begin to review. However, for the purposes of this chapter I assume this *se* is a true reflexive in dative case, that is, it expresses the thematic role of auto-bene/malefactive. True enough, this use of the reflexive clitic has often been analyzed as perfective in the contemporary literature, but I believe the perfective interpretation associated with it is not primitive, but rather compositionally derived from the sense of completion entailed by the VP, whose *aktionsart,* as is self-evident, is that of an accomplishment. Moreover, being in dative case, it does not compete with *todo* for case, since the latter receives accusative. The *se . . . todo* construction is therefore incompatible with verbs such a *olvidarse* 'forget,' *quejarse* 'complain,' and a few others with "inherent" *se* (this *se* is analyzed as antipassive in accusative case in Masullo, 1992). It is well-known that Spanish does not allow two or more instances of *se* in the same VP, even if they belong to different categories. Thus the following sentences may only receive a literal interpretation:

(34) a. Pedro se olvidó todo.
Peter REFL forgot all
'Peter forgot everything.'
b. Pablo se acuerda todo.
Paul REFL remembers all
'Paul remembers everything.'

Strictly speaking, the EXTREME DEGREE feature in question does not pertain to the whole construction (which is elative only epiphenomenally), but rather to *todo,* which has semantically shifted from plain total quantification to extreme quantification. In any event, it is no accident that *todo* has become an elative in conjunction with *se*. Though formally a reflexive expressing an auto bene/malefactive, as I have assumed, it is often associated with the notion of overachievement or an unusual deed when used with certain verbs, thus reinforcing the elative character of the construction as a whole. In fact, it is not uncommon to find *se* with the colloquial light verb *mandar* 'make or do something extraordinary or unsual.' The verb *mandar* (literally 'send,' 'order,' 'command') in colloquial Argentinian Spanish deserves a study of its own. Apart from having been bleached to mean "make" or "do," it has been desemantized in other interesting ways which I cannot go into here. Suffice it to say, for the purposes of this study, that it is intrinsically elative itself, so that it selects only for objects somehow associated with an extreme degree feature, as the following examples show (notice, in particular, the unacceptability of [35d], with a non-elative object):

(35) a. Juan se mandó un asado espectacular.
 John REFL sent a barbecue spectacular
 'John cooked a spectacular barbecue.'
 b. Juan se mandó {un moco/una macana} terrible.
 John REFL sent {a snot/ a mistake} terrible
 'John fucked up big time.'
 c. Juan se mandó unos riquísimos mates.
 John REFL sent some very-good mates
 'John served some extraordinary mates.'
 d. *María se mandó una torta {común/sencilla}.
 Mary REFL sent a cake {common/simple}
 'Mary made a plain cake.'

It is no surprise then that *mandar* occurs quite naturally with the covert exclamatives dealt with in this chapter:

(36) ¡María se mandó {**un/cada**} error / un error **de** grave!
 Mary REFL sent {one/each error} /an error of grave!
 'Mary made such terrible/serious blunders!'

The restrictions observed above show that despite its fossilization and semantic shift, the formal properties of the construction are maintained, both with regard to *todo* and with regard to *se*. I now show that the basic *aktionsart* (or internal aspect) of the literal construction is also kept. It is obvious that sentences like *María se comió la manzana* 'Mary REFL ate the apple' is an accomplishment (an activity with an end-point that makes it telic).[15] It is therefore expected that stative transitive verbs should not occur in the *se . . . todo* construction, much in the same way as autobene/malefactive *se* with a perfective flavor cannot be used with stative verbs:[16]

(37) *María se   ama a todos sus hijos.
    Mary REFL love to all   her children
    'Mary loves all her children for herself.'

Examples in (38) fit within the same pattern.

(38) a. *Pedro se   admira a todos sus maestros.
       Peter REFL admire to all   his teachers
       'Peter admires all his teachers for himself.'
    b. *María se   ama todo.
       Mary REFL loves all
       'Mary loves (people) intensely.'
    c. *Pedro se   admira todo.
       Peter REFL admires all
       'Peter admires (everything) intensely.'

I conclude by pointing out that, as expected, the elative *se . . . todo* construction analyzed above cannot be (internally) negated and is in principle incompatible with dubitative, desiderative, interrogative, or exclamative operators in Focus Phrase:

(39) a. *¡No   te   llores todo!
        Don't REFL cry   all!
        'Don't cry your heart out!'

---

15. Compositionally, some of these sentences may be construed as states. Thus, *María se fuma todo* 'Mary smokes it all' can be construed as *María es una fumadora empedernida* 'Mary is an inveterate smoker,' but this is no counterexample, since *fumarse todo* is primarily an accomplishment at the lexical level, its stative interpretation being coerced by the habitual present; that is, the imperfective external aspect of the verb. Actually, there seems to be a more general restriction disallowing stative verbs with bene/malefactives altogether, reflexive or non-reflexive: *María le está contenta a la madre* 'Mary is happy for her mother's sake,' a question I will not develop any further here.

16. *Saber* and *conocer* 'know' seem to be exceptions, both in the literal and elative senses: *María se sabe muy bien la lección* 'Mary knows her lesson very well'; *¡María se sabe todo!* 'Mary knows so much!'

b. *Tal vez mañana   se   llueva todo.
       Perhaps tomorrow REFL rains all
       'Maybe it rains cats and dogs tomorrow'
   c. *¿Se   lloverá   todo mañana?
       REFL will-rain all   tomorrow?
       'Will it rain cats and dogs tomorrow?'
   d. ??¡Que se   llueva   todo mañana!
        That REFL rain.SUBJ all   tomorrow
       'May it rain cats and dogs tomorrow!'
   e. *¿Cuándo se   lloverá   todo?
       When   REFL will-rain all?
       'When will it rain cats and dogs?'
   f. *¡Cómo María se   fuma   todo!
       How   Mary REFL smokes all!
       'How Mary smokes like a chimney!'

4.3. *MAL* AS AN ELATIVE

The negative manner adverb *mal* 'ill,' 'badly' is being used more and more in colloquial Argentinian Spanish as an elative intensifier, both with positive and negative predicates:

(40) a. Mario {está enamorado/se enamoró}   mal.
        Mario is in-love/   has-fallen-in-love badly
        'Mario {is head over heels in love/has desperately fallen in love}.'
     b. Pedro es (un) conservador mal.
        Peter is (a)   conservative badly
        'Peter is {terribly conservative/a terribly conservative man}.'
     c. Se   trabaja mal   en temporada alta   en Bariloche.
        REFL works   badly in season   high in Bariloche.
        'We work like crazy during the high season in Bariloche.'
        (OK with a literal manner interpretation too)
     d. María es inteligente (pero) mal.
        Mary is intelligent (but) badly
        'Mary is extremely intelligent.'
     e. María es una adicta al   mate mal.
        Mary is an   addict to-the mate badly
        'Mary is terribly addicted to mate.'

f. María me gusta mal.
   Mary to-me likes badly
   'I like Mary an awful lot.'

This is not an entirely unexpected phenomenon. As we know, it is not uncommon in the world's languages for negative modifiers to gradually take on a (positive) elative meaning. For example, in English, *badly* can be used in a similar fashion, and adjectives and adverbs like *terrific(ally)*, *awful(ly)*, and *awesome* (all originally negative) are now used colloquially with a positive value, as the following examples illustrate:

(41) a. I {need/want/could do with} a cup of coffee/a rest badly.
     b. Kudos! The performance last night was {terrific/awesome}!
     c. I enjoyed the book an awful lot.
     d. These bagels are awfully good!

The same can be said of *bárbaro* 'barbarous,' *terriblemente* 'terribly' in many varieties of Spanish and *horrible* 'horrible' in Mexican Spanish (see Company, 2009), which can be used as positive elatives. In the opposite direction, originally positive items such as *bendito* 'blessed,' *santo* 'saintly,' *reverendo* 'reverend,' and a few others can be used as negative elatives (all instances of irony at its best):

(42) a. La fiesta de anoche estuvo {bárbara/ horrible}.
        The party of last- night was {barbarous/horrible}
        'The party last night was {terrific/awesome}.'
     b. María es terriblemente inteligente.
        'Mary is terribly intelligent.'
     c. Los chicos de hoy se la pasan en la computadora todo el santo día.
        The children of today REFL it.FEM pass in the computer all the saintly day
        'Nowadays, children spend all day long at their computer.'
     d. Juan es un reverendo idiota.
        John is a reverend idiot
        'John is a downright idiot.'

Going back to elative *mal*, the semantic shift involved is not difficult to reconstruct. Idealizing somewhat the (quite rapid) diachronic development, we may postulate the following stages:

Negative manner → extreme negative manner → extreme degree (negative properties) → extreme degree (all properties)

Like other run-of-the-mill elatives, *mal* can optionally be used in exclamative sentences, that is, it can optionally be bound by an empty exclamative operator in search of an expression expressing extreme degree:

(43) ¡Te emborrachaste mal anoche!
     You got-drunk badly last-night!
     'How drunk you got last night!'

The elative nature of this new use of *mal* is once again confirmed by the fact that, as predicted, it cannot occur in negative sentences, is incompatible with other elative expressions, and clashes with operators in Focus Phrase:[17]

(44) a. *Mario no está enamorado mal.
       Mario not is in-love badly
       'Mario is not badly in love'
       (Cf. *Mario no está muy enamorado* 'Mario is not very much in love.')
    b. *¿Quién se enamoró mal últimamente?
       'Who has fallen in love badly lately?'
    c. *¡No te enamores mal!
       'Don't fall in love badly!'
       (Cf. *¡No te enamores demasiado!* 'Don't fall too much in love!')

Apart from the fact that *mal* must be semantically licensed by a gradable element, just like other elatives (Cf. *Este es un tratado comercial mal* 'This is a commercial treaty badly,' in which the relational adjective *comercial* cannot license it), special attention must be paid to its syntactic behavior, since, unlike other elatives or intensifiers in general, it is to be analyzed as a VP-modifier or adjunct, not as a degree head selecting for a gradable predicate; that is, the semantic shift the adverb *mal* has undergone has left its categorial features intact. In this respect, it is comparable to degree adverbials such as *to a great extent, in a big way,* and *big time* in English, which are clearly modifiers within a VP, but do not take gradable expressions as complements,

---

17. Occasionally, we find elatives *re* and *mal* co-occuring. I don't think this poses a real problem for my analyis, if it is taken as a case of emphatic reinforcement: *El tipo es re-tonto mal* 'The guy is a downright fool.'

or else like *malamente* in Italian and some varieties of Spanish. The following contrasts fall naturally from this analysis:

(45) a. Mario es (un) {conservador mal/ *mal conservador}
    Mario is (a) {conservative badly/badly conservative}
    'Mario is terribly conservative.'
  b. Mario está {en peligro mal/*mal en peligro}.
    Mario is {in danger badly/badly in danger}
    'Mario is in terrible danger.'
  c. Esta planta es {invasiva mal/ *mal invasiva}.
    This weed is {invasive badly/badly invasive}
    'This weed is terribly invasive.'
  d. María corre {rápido mal/ *mal rápido}.
    Mary runs {rapid badly/badly rapid}
    'Mary runs incredibly fast.'

In (45a), *mal* is semantically licensed by the gradable predicate *conservador*, whether it is used as an adjective or a noun, but categorially licensed by V. As one might expect, the ungrammatical option in (45a) does not apply to the interpretation "J. is a bad convervative (person)."

The tree in (46a) shows the position of *mal* as an adjunct within the VP, like other manner adjuncts. In this respect it contrasts sharply with degree heads such as *re* (46b):

(46)
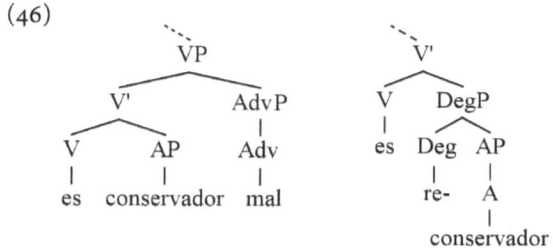

The ungrammaticality of the alternants with preposed *mal* observed in (45) can now be easily accounted for. Though they contain a gradable expression capable of licensing *mal*, this is a functional category acting as head of a degree phrase, rather than as a VP-adjunct.

I close this section by pointing out that, as far as can be ascertained, elative *mal* is always a bare adverb phrase, and like other elatives it can be preceded by *pero* 'but' in order to establish a contrast between "normal" or average degree and extreme degree, in which case *mal* tends to be the prosodic focus:

(47) a. A Pedro le   gusta el teatro {?? muy/tan} mal.
          To Peter DAT likes the theater {very/ so} badly
          'Peter likes drama {very/so} incredibly.'
     b. A Pedro le   gusta el teatro, pero MAL.
          To Peter DAT likes the theater, but BADLY
          'Peter likes drama, but very much indeed.'

5. Long-Distance Dependencies

It is an uncontested fact that wh-exclamatives, much like relative clauses and wh-questions, must meet locality constraints. The question of locality has traditionally been subsumed under Subjacency and the ECP (Empty Category Principle) in GB/PP, having been reformulated, in turn, in terms of the Minimal Link Condition in the Minimalist Program (Chomsky, 1995). However, ECP phenomena do not seem to have been completely recast in Minimalist terms yet, to the best of my knowledge. In fact, the whole question of locality and long-distance dependency is (or has been) in a constant state of flux in current generative theory and is awaiting a new unified solution. For my purposes, however, it suffices to point out that, like overt wh-exclamatives, covert exclamatives appear to meet the same locality conditions, however these are to be ultimately formulated and whatever axiomatic primitives they should be reduced to.

In the case of overt exclamatives (48), the bolded element forms a chain with the [e] in situ inside a nominal "island." In traditional GB/PP terms, locality has been violated by extracting out of a DP and out of a relative clause (see also Masullo, 2012):

(48) a. *¡**Qué interesante** leyó Juan ese libro [e]!
          How interesting read John that book!
          '*How interesting John read that book!'
          (Cf. *Juan leyó ese libro muy bueno* 'John read that very good book.')
     b. *¡**Cómo** vio Juan una película en la que llueve [e]!
          How saw John a movie   in the that rains!
          '*How much John saw a movie in which it rains!'
          (Cf. *Juan vio una película en la que llueve mucho* 'John saw a movie in which it rains very heavily.')

c. *¡**Cuánto**   **dinero** quiere María conocer un hombre que tenga [e]!
How-much money wants Mary to-know a man that has!
'*How much money Mary wants to know a man who has!'
(Cf. *María quiere conocer un hombre que tenga mucho dinero* 'Mary wants to meet a man with a lot of money.')

We find a similar situation in the case of the overt exclamatives with *de, un,* and *cada* dealt with in this chapter:

(49) a. *¡Juan leyó mi libro **de lindo**!
'*John read my book so nice!'
b. *¡No me gusta hablar con la gente que pone **una cara** cuando escucha!
'I don't like to talk to those people who put on such a face when they listen!'
(Cf. *No me gusta hablar con esa gente que pone cara de indiferente cuando escucha* 'I don't like to talk to people that put on an indifferent face when they listen.')
c. *¡No estoy de acuerdo con los que son **de tercos**!
'I don't agree with those that are so stubborn!'
(Cf. *No estoy de acuerdo con la gente muy terca* 'I don't agree with very stubborn people.')
d. *¡Ayer visité ese barrio que tiene **cada** casa!
'Yesterday I visited that neighborhood that has such houses!'
(Cf. *Ayer visité ese barrio que tiene casas imponentes* 'Yesterday I visited that neighborhood that has imposing houses.')

This fact can be explained in a natural manner by claiming that at LF the empty exclamative operator is blocked from binding the corresponding exclamative phrase inside the island in question. Thus the analysis that has been proposed here finds further support:

(50) *¡OP $_{[EXCL]\,i}$ Ayer visité ese barrio que tiene [**cada** casa]$_{[EXTR\ DEG]i}$!

I predict that the same constraints apply to plain elatives when used exclamatively since, as I have proposed, a chain must necessarily be formed between an empty exclamative operator and the elative in situ. This prediction is borne out:

(51) *¡Mirá a esa persona que se emborracha **mal** todas las noches!
'Look at that person who gets completely drunk every night!'

Plain elatives, however, should not be constrained in the same manner, since, as I have argued, they do not require an operator to bind their inherent extreme degree feature. In this respect, I depart from Masullo (2012), who lumps together *all* elatives and non-*wh* extreme degree expressions and therefore proposes "LF movement" in every case. This fact is confirmed by the grammaticality of the following sentences, in which such a movement would violate the complex NP-constraint (an NP with a relative or complement nominal clause):

(52) a. Me gustan esos días que se llueve todo.
'I like those days in which it rains cats and dogs.'
b. Me atraen las personas que son inteligentes mal.
'I am attracted to people that are extremely smart.'
c. La insinuación de que María canta malísimamente mal es absurda.
'The hint that Mary sings awfully badly is absurd.'

A similar situation seems to obtain when we extract out of adverbial clauses. As (53) shows, we cannot establish a long-distance dependency in the case of covert exclamatives:

(53) a. *Aunque Juan sea un loco, hay que admitir que trabaja muy bien [OK if *un* is not exclamative]
'Although John is such a crazy guy, we have to admit that he's a good worker.'
b. *Mientras (que) María es de loca, Pedro es mucho más razonable.
'While Mary is such a crazy woman, Peter is much more sensible.'
c. *Si Juan estuviera de loco, no podría tener un trabajo de tanta responsabilidad.
'If John was terribly crazy, he could not hold down such a responsible job.'

In contrast, and as expected, plain elatives seem to fare very well:

(54) a. Aunque Juan sea loquísimo, hay que admitir que trabaja muy bien.
'Though John is terribly mad, one has to admit he's a very good worker.'
b. Mientras (que) María es loca mal, Pedro es mucho más razonable.
'While Mary is so crazy, Peter is much more sensible.'

However, for independent reasons, plain elatives and conditionals are uneasy bed-fellows, given the non-factive nature of the latter:

(55) ??Si María es adicta a la cocaína mal, entonces no podrá conseguir empleo.
'If Mary is so addicted to cocaine, then she won't be able to get a job.'

This sentence strongly contrasts with *Si, como decís, María es adicta a la cocaína mal, entonces no podrá conseguir empleo* 'If, as you say, Mary is so addicted to cocaine, then she won't be able to get a job,' in which the elative *mal* is anaphorically licensed by *como decís* 'as you say.'

Given the colloquial nature of both covert exclamatives and plain elatives, which are not usually found in complex sentences, grammaticality judgements are not always accurate, but rather, slippery and fuzzy. In any case, the locality phenomena presented above prima facie confirm my analysis of covert exclamatives, as well as my account of plain elatives, whether these are used exclamatively or not. Matters are also blurred by different semantic factors that need to be carefully teased apart, as we saw in the case of (55) above, a question for future research.

6. Conclusions and Some Outstanding Questions

In this study I have attempted to establish a distinction between overt wh-exclamative sentences and covert exclamatives containing no overt operator in Spec (CP), but an expression *in situ* instead, which, I have argued, is associated with the features EXCLAMATIVE and EXTREME DEGREE at once. I have paid particular attention to three of these: those headed by the indefinite article, the partitive preposition *de,* and the quantifier *cada.* I have also claimed that we are to distinguish between *in situ* exclamatives proper, on the one hand, and plain elatives, on the other. The latter can only optionally be used as *in situ* exclamatives. Otherwise, they need not be bound by an operator, being intrinsically associated with extreme degree only. The chart below summarizes the analysis proposed:

Feature	Overt exclamatives	Covert exclamatives	Plain elatives
[EXCLAMATIVE]	On wh-element (strong)	On base-generated OP	On empty operator (optional)
[EXTREME DEGREE]	On wh-element	On *in situ* element	On *in situ* element

Apart from introducing recent elative expressions in colloquial Argentinian Spanish, I have examined carefully two in particular, the *se... todo* construction and the negative manner adverb *mal.* Nevertheless, insofar as covert and overt exclamatives as well as plain elatives are all factive, I have shown that they form a natural class at a higher level of abstraction. Thus, as I have shown, all three are incompatible with negation and cannot occur in interrogative, jussive, dubitative, or desiderative sentences.

My research has shown that what we call "exclamation" is not a homogeneous phenomemon, but a class of attitudinal meanings which may get encoded through various formal and structural means. Although I have followed along the lines of Masullo (2012), I have also demonstrated that finer-grained distinctions need to be made. However, it has not been my aim to cover all phenomena that may come under the umbrella of exclamation. For example, I have said nothing about "hidden" exclamatives (which somehow parallel hidden questions), introduced by the definite article or the neuter pronominal clitic *lo* (see Brucart, 1993; Contreras, 1999; RAE-ASALE, 2009; etc.). Neither have I dealt with "simple" exclamation as in the sentences below:

(56) a. ¡Salió el sol!
   'The sun's come out!'
 b. ¡Se prende fuego la casa!
   'The house is catching fire!'
 c. ¡Me robaron el celular!
   'They have stolen my cell phone!'

It can be argued that in this case the (empty) exclamative operator has scope over the entire propositional content and not just over an extreme degree expression (cf. RAE-ASALE, 2009, in which a distinction is suggested between total and partial exclamation). That is, although prototypically we show surprise or exclaim at the extreme degree of a property, we can also show surprise or exclaim at an unsual, unexpected, (un)desired, sudden, etc., situation. Thus, the "widening" effect requirement for exclamation (Zanuttini & Portner, 2003) is satisfied both in "total" and "partial" exclamatives.

In conclusion, complex and challenging though it may prove, the study of exclamative sentences and their "next of kin" provides us with insights into the rich interface between morphosyntax, semantics, pragmatics, and our conceptual-intentional systems. A thorough study of exclamation should also come to terms with the complex and nuanced prosodic aspects associated with exclamation, which once again places this phenomenon at the interfaces, this time with our articulatory and perceptual systems. These matters no doubt necessitate further collaborative research from different perspectives.

At-Issue Material in Spanish Degree Exclamatives
An Experimental Study

Xavier Villalba

1. Introduction: Levels of Meaning in Exclamatives

Since the initial studies in the seventies by Dale Elliott (1971, 1974), the exact categorization of the meanings conveyed by exclamatives has been a matter of debate, particularly concerning two main aspects: factivity and high degree. Hence, an exclamative sentence like (1) is commonly assumed (since Grimshaw, 1979) to involve the ascription of a property (2) and high degree meaning in (3).

(1) ¡Qué alta es María!
    What tall.F is Mary
    'How tall Mary is!'

(2) Mary is tall.

(3) Mary is tall beyond expectation.

I would like to thank Ignacio Bosque for his very useful comments and suggestions. Needless to say, all possible remaining errors are my own. This work was possible thanks to project FFI2104-52015 Compositionality of meaning. Theoretical and empirical perspectives awarded to UAB.

As for the ascription of a property, Elliott (1971, 1974) originally observed that exclamative clauses can only be selected by factive predicates, as the following pair shows:

(4) a. It's amazing how very expensive this wine is.
    b. *I asked how very expensive this wine was.

Grimshaw (1979, p. 320) took Elliott's observation a step further and argued that exclamatives were inherently factive:

> The claim that I want to make here is that in exclamations, what can be termed the "propositional content" is *inherently presupposed.* For an exclamation to be used appropriately, it must always be true that the corresponding proposition is presupposed to be true. The exclamation *How tall John is!* presupposes that John is tall, and an exclamation like *What big ears John has!* presupposes that John has big ears.

Consequently, Grimshaw (1979) could explain the fact that exclamatives made bad answers, for their content was presupposed (her ex. 150; the # mark is added), just as happened with the presuppositional constructions in (3) (for new arguments, see also Abels, 2010):

(5) Question: How tall is John?
    Answer: Very tall.
    Answer: #How tall John is!

(6) Question: Did John leave?
    Answer: #It's odd that he did.
    Answer: #I'd forgotten that he did.

Questioning whether a proposition p entails that p is not part of the common ground, hence p cannot be taken for granted in the answer. A similar contrast exists in the following pair of sentences:[1]

(7) a. She said that Peter quitted his job. Me, too.
       = "I said that, too."/"I will quit my job, too."
    b. She was surprised that Peter quitted her job. Me, too.
       = "I was surprised, too."/#"I will quit my job, too."

---

[1]. I am thankful to Ignacio Bosque for noting to me the relevance of these kind of examples.

The proposition selected by the factive predicate "be surprised" is clearly part of the background and cannot be reprised by the anaphoric element *too*.

Therefore, the received view is that the meaning in (2) is a presupposition—but see Castroviejo (2008a), Mayol (2008), and Beyssade (2009) for a different view and Abels (2010) for a positive reassessment of Grimshaw's analysis.

In contrast, the high degree meaning associated with exclamatives (3) has proved harder to classify. While some scholars argue it is a presupposition following from the presence of a higher order illocutionary operator (Gutierrez-Rexach, 1996, 2008), others defend the view that it is a conventional implicature generated by the semantic operation of domain extension ("widening") (Zanuttini & Portner, 2003). For example, Gutierrez-Rexach (1996) argues for a similar semantics for degree interrogatives and exclamatives based on a maximality operator (MAX) over degrees (d), which involves the presupposition of maximal degree. For instance, he proposes the following basic semantic representation for interrogative cases:

(8) How tall is John?

(9) $\iota p \, \exists d \, [p(w) \, \& \, p = \lambda w'[d = MAX(\lambda d'[tall(w')(j,d')])]]$

The formula in (9) reads as "What is the maximal degree d such that John is d-tall?" The exclamative sentence is obtained with the addition of an illocutionary intensional operator EXC on propositions, speakers (a), and worlds (w):[2]

(10) ¡{Qué/lo} alto que es Juan!
what/the-N tall that is Juan
'How tall Juan is!'

(11) $EXC(a)(w)(\iota p \, \exists d \, [p(w) \, \& \, p = \lambda w'[d = MAX(\lambda d'[tall(w')(j,d')])]])$

The formula in (10) reads as follows: "the speaker expresses an attitude (surprise, admiration, amazement) toward the fact that Juan is d-tall, where d is Juan's [maximal; XV] "degree of tallness (his height)" Gutierrez-Rexach (2008, p. 120).

Moreover, to capture the meaning of (9), one must encode the crucial fact that what really counts as a standard for height in an exclamative is

---

2. Gutiérrez-Rexach assigns this higher-order operator the type <i,<s,<<s,t>,t>>>, where *i* corresponds to the type of the speaker's variable and *s* to the type of the world variable.

not the normal standard or the standard salient in the current common ground, but rather the speaker's expectations (hence the surprise meaning typically associated with exclamatives). This semantic ingredient is assumed by Gutierrez-Rexach (1996, 2008) to be a presupposition:

> It would seem more adequate to treat this property not as an implicature but rather as a presupposition. A precondition that has to be met by the preceding discourse (or common ground) in order to be successfully updated with the content expressed by the exclamative. (Gutierrez-Rexach, 2008, p. 121)

Castroviejo (2008a, sec. 3.2) pursues a different track and argues that exclamatives lack any assertive content, but rather convey a background descriptive content (i.e., "Mary is tall to a high degree") and a derived "expressive presupposition" (i.e., "I am surprised [that Mary is tall to a high degree]"), following Schlenker's (2007) analysis of expressive constructions. The concept of "expressive presupposition" is important, for it departs from the basic tenets of the classical presupposition theory stemming from Karttunen (1973) and Stalnaker (1974), which is based on the assumption that a presupposition must be entailed by the speakers' common ground. Besides standard presuppositions in this sense, Stalnaker (1978) crucially includes in his discourse model the idea of accommodation (see also Lewis, 1979). Since these presuppositions modify the common ground rather than being entailed by it, one can technically label them "informative presuppositions." Yet, as Stalnaker remarks in latter work (Stalnaker, 2008, p. 542), even though informative, they are an inappropriate means to add new or controversial information to the common ground, for the accommodated presupposed content remains part of the common ground even if one rejects the asserted content they piggyback on. Castroviejo (2008a, p. 59) extends this idea to exclamatives in full:

> Moreover, expressing the speaker's emotional attitude does not modify the Common Ground like an assertion, but rather the same way as the goat does in Stalnaker's example above (see section 2.2); it is a nonlinguistic factor that models what mutual knowledge the participants in a conversation have. From the moment that a speaker utters an exclamative, the rest of the participants infer that s/he is emotional because of somebody's high degree of ADJ-ness, this becomes part of the Common Ground and influences the conversation.

In the Stalnakerian model, one must buy the presupposition, but can reject the asserted part. However, it is unclear then whether exclamatives involve any asserted content altogether.

Other scholars follow a different line of argumentation to account for this high/extreme degree. For example, Zanuttini and Portner (2003) analyze it as a conventional implicature (hence, pragmatic in nature) deriving from the semantic operation of "widening" involved in exclamatives, which places an individual in the extended interval built over the previous standard scale denoted by the predicate. The mechanism of widening is formally defined by Zanuttini and Portner (2003, p. 52) as follows:

Widening
For any clause S containing $R_{widening}$, widen the initial domain of quantification for $R_{widening}$, D_1, to a new domain, D_2, such that

(i) $[[S]]_{w,D_2,<} - [[S]]_{w,D_1,<} \neq \emptyset$ and;
(ii) $\forall x \forall y \, [(x \in D_1 \, \& \, y \in (D_2 - D_1)) \rightarrow x < y]$.

In prose, condition (i) requires that the extension of the domain include at least a new element, and condition (ii) states that any element of the widened domain not present in the initial domain must occupy a higher position in the scale than any element of the initial domain, i.e., the scale must be extended by its extreme. According to Zanuttini and Portner, this condition forces the generation of a conventional implicature of high/extreme degree. To support their analysis, they point out that the implicature cannot be conversational, for it is neither calculable, cancelable, or detachable (Grice, 1975, 1978, 1981), and offer the following examples:[3]

(12) a. #How very cute he is!—though he's not extremely cute.
     b. He's quite cute!—though not extremely cute.

In (12a) one can see that the high/extreme degree implicature cannot be canceled, and (12b) is intended to show that the implicature is attached to the exclamative form, not to the meaning of the sentence.[4]

---

3. The implicature cannot be calculated from the interaction of Grice's cooperative principle with any conversational maxim, unlike typical scalar conversational implicatures, which arise from apparent violations of the maxim of quantity.

4. Ignacio Bosque (personal communication) notes that wh-exclamatives are typically odd with concessive or adversative codas (his examples):

However, this characterization is controversial. On the one hand, as pointed out by Castroviejo (2006), continuations that do not cancel the implicature yield bad results as well (her exs. [79] and [81]):

(13) a. #How very cute he is!—but he lives a thousand miles away.
b. #How very cute he is!—because his mother is also extremely cute.

Note that the last example explicitly reasserts the high-degree implicature, which leads her to conclude that the problem has to do with the combination of two different speech acts, an exclamation and an assertion. I will turn back to cancellation in section 2.

On the other hand, it is far from being settled that the implicature is non-detachable. Villalba (2003) considers the case of Spanish hidden exclamatives (see Masullo, 1999), like the following:

(14) a. ¡Marta es de buena!
Marta is of good.F
'Marta is so good!'
b. ¡El chico es de travieso!
The boy is of naughty
'The boy is so naughty!'

Crucially, the application of the standard defeasibility test leads to the conclusion that this construction *does* carry the scalar implicature associated with overt exclamatives, which, consequently, cannot be attached to the exclamative form:

(15) a. ¡Marta es de buena! #Si es que lo es.
Marta is of good.F if is that it is
'Marta is so good! #If at all.'

(i) a. *¡Qué calor hace, aunque se está bien aquí!
'How hot it is, even though it is fine in here!'
b. *¡Cuánto dinero tiene Trump, pero no sabe emplearlo!
'How much money Trump has, but he doesn't know how to use it!'

Yet, some minor alterations ameliorate the sentences, which suggests that the problem is not a general incompatibility, but rather a pragmatic effect:

(ii) a. ¡Qué calor hace, a pesar de tener aire acondicionado!
'How hot it is, even though the air conditioning is on!'
b. ¡Cuánto dinero tiene Trump, pero qué mal que lo emplea!
'How much money Trump has, but how bad he uses it!'

b. ¡El chico es de travieso! #Aunque no demasiado.
   the boy is of naughty   although not too.much
   'The boy is so naughty! #Although not much.'

Hence, the conventional implicature defended by Zanuttini and Portner (2003) seems highly problematic and must be rethought on different grounds (see Villalba, 2008b). To sum up, our actual knowledge of the level of meanings involved in exclamative sentences is at best incomplete and points toward the somewhat disturbing fact that none of their meanings is asserted—indeed, Castroviejo's (2008a) position.

In this chapter I will attack the issue directly on the basis of our current understanding of the behavior of presuppositions and implicatures in order to determine the exact nature of the two meaning aspects associated with Spanish degree exclamatives (section 2). To help this task, in section 3, I will present the results of two experiments involving the interpretation and evaluation of these two meanings, which were aimed at offering psycholinguistic evidence for establishing which meanings are asserted ("at-issue") and which are backgrounded. The results will be discussed in section 4, where I will present some generalizations concerning the levels of meaning involved in Spanish degree exclamatives. Finally, section 5 will include the conclusions and pending issues.

2. An Experimental Approach to Exclamatives

While the debate described in the previous section has been lively and interesting on theoretical grounds, it has been alien to the current developments of experimental semantics and pragmatics (see, for instance, the papers in Noveck & Sperber, 2004; Sauerland & Yatsushiro, 2009; and Meibauer & Steinbach, 2011). In this chapter I offer a different point of view on the issue by taking into account a finer-grained typology of meanings stemming from Potts's (2005) approach to expressives, Roberts's (2011) extensive discussion of "only," and Tonhauser et al.'s (2013) study of projective content. My departing point will be the following typology of meanings, as presented in Mayol and Castroviejo (2013, p. 86):

- AT-ISSUE MEANING (Potts, 2005): the asserted content of an utterance, which can be described in terms of truth-conditions, and is open to discussion, acceptance or denial (it corresponds more or less to Grice's "what is said").

- CONVERSATIONAL IMPLICATURES: content inferred from the at-issue meaning with the help of general conversational principles (Grice, 1975, 1978, 1981), which can help to address the Question Under Discussion (QUD) making the at-issue meaning more informative.
- PROJECTIVE MEANING (Tonhauser et al., 2013): the content that may project over an entailment-canceling operator (i.e., presuppositions and conventional implicatures), which cannot address the current QUD. (Roberts, 1996)

As can be easily appreciated, the typology redefines the original Gricean picture including the insights of Potts's (2005) influential analysis of conventional implicatures as semantic contributions and Roberts's (1996) QUD as a guideline for helping us determine which content is at-issue.

By extending this idea to degree exclamatives, one can predict that, if presupposed, both meanings of exclamatives should be equally hard to be denied or corrected, for none of them would address the QUD.[5] That is, I could test the following patterns:

(16) a. ¡Qué alta es María!
    What tall.F is Mary
    'How tall Mary is!'
  b. No es cierto: no es alta.
    Not is true not is tall.F
    'That's not true: she is not tall.'
  b.' No es cierto: es alta, pero no tanto.
    Not is true is tall.F but not so-much
    'That's not true: she is tall, but not so tall.'

While the denial that Mary is tall (16a) seems perfectly natural to me, the one affecting just the degree part (16b) sounds less felicitous. If denials are fine for at-issue content only, one could thus conclude (1) that the "degree-beyond-expectation" meaning is not part of the at-issue meaning of exclamatives and (2) that the ascription to Mary of the property of being tall is at-issue content.

To sum up, the availability of felicitous denial seems a proper test to ascertain which part of the meaning of an exclamative sentence is at-issue, and I state the hypothesis that the property part is at-issue meaning, whereas the high

---

5. The complexities of the operations involved in denial are discussed at length in Geurts (1998). See also Mayol and Castroviejo (2013) for the cancellation of implicatures.

degree part is projective meaning. In order to test this hypothesis, I designed two experiments, which are described in detail in the following section.

3. Experimental Evidence for At-Issueness

In both cases, this experimental aspect of the research was intended to help us categorize the meanings involved in Spanish degree exclamatives, particularly its exact at-issue content. The departing idea was that the more a particular content was perceived as at-issue, the more it would be subject to denial. Hence, the experiments were designed to test this hypothesis both from an interpretation task (experiment 1) and from an evaluation task (experiment 2).

3.1. EXPERIMENT 1

The first experiment aimed at testing the preferred interpretation of a denial ("That's not true") of an exclamative sentence like ¡Qué alto es Juan! 'How tall John is!', namely whether it was intended to deny the ascription of the property ("It is not true that John is tall") or the high degree meaning involved ("It is not true that John is so tall"). The most favored option would be the best candidate for at-issueness.

3.1.1. Participants

The participants were 37 Spanish first course undergraduate students of the Faculty of Arts of the Universitat Autònoma de Barcelona (Catalonia, Spain). None had any training in linguistics.

3.1.2. Method and Procedure

Participants were explained the experiment procedure with a filler item that was not included in the test. Then they were asked to read a series of slides involving an interpretation task and a confidence evaluation. All the target items shared the following structure. First, a two-line dialogue between Pedro and Julia, where Pedro always uttered a degree exclamative (e.g., "How tall Mary is!") and Julia always replied denying such an utterance

Figure 5.1.
Reproduction of Target Item

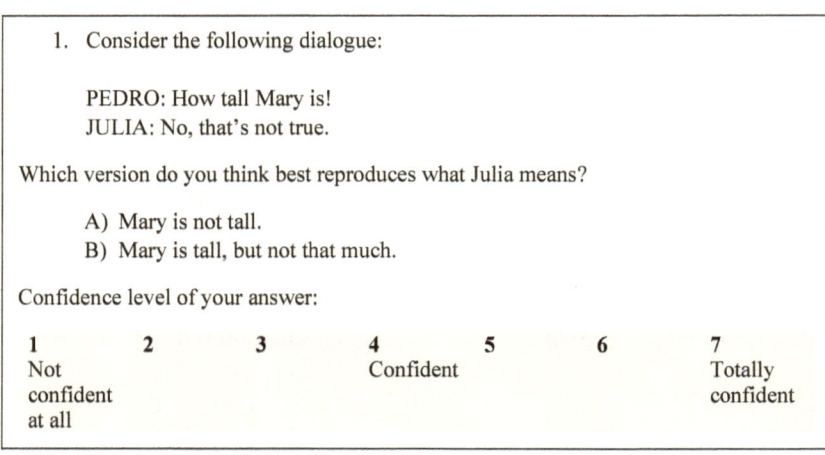

ambiguously ("No, that's not true"). Then participants were faced with two options for interpreting Julia's reply: a denial of the property (e.g., "Mary is not tall") or a denial of the high degree (e.g., "Mary is tall, but not that much"). The order of presentation of these two options was controlled: four targets had one order and the other four targets had the opposite order. Moreover, since the participants had a closed twofold option, a confidence evaluation was included by means of a seven-degree Likert-scale. A real target item is reproduced in figure 5.1 (all the materials were in Spanish). The degree-exclamative uttered by Pedro changed in each item to avoid adjective repetition, and the form of the options was consistent throughout the experiment (17a), with the exception of item 3 (17b), which served as a test of the influence of the form of the reply:

(17) a. x es ADJ, pero no tanto.
       x is ADJ but not so-much
       'x is ADJ but not that much.'
   b. x no es tan ADJ.
       x not is so ADJ
       'x is not so ADJ.'

Fillers shared the structure, but they involved no exclamative. Moreover, two fillers served as attention controllers. The test included eight target items and eight fillers, which were presented in alternation, beginning with a target. Each item was displayed on the screen for one minute and fifteen seconds.

Table 5.1.
Frequency of Answers to Experiment 1 and Confidence Level

	Denial of Property		Denial of High Degree		Confidence (1–7 scale)
	#	%	#	%	Average
1	29	78.37	8	21.62	5.51
3	8	21.62	29	78.37	4.86
5	32	86.48	5	13.51	5.37
7	23	62.16	14	37.83	4.45
9	34	91.89	3	8.10	5.56
11	21	56.75	16	43.24	5.13
13	24	64.86	13	35.13	4.64
15	33	89.19	4	10.81	5.43
totals	204	68.91	92	31.08	5.12

3.1.3. Results

The results showed that the denial of the property ascription ("Mary is not Adj") was perceived as more natural (68.91%) than the denial of the high degree ("Mary is Adj, but not that much") (31.08%), with an average confidence level of 5.12 out of 7; see Table 5.1 for details. Only one item (#3) broke this general pattern: the denial of the high degree was found more natural in 78.37% of the cases, against 21.62% who found the denial of the property more natural. If this case was discarded, the preference for property-denial boosted up to 75.67%. As for the confidence level, informants rated themselves over five out of seven on average (5.12; $s = 0.39$), without a sharp contrast between items. This value was not far from the average found for filler items: 5.70 ($s = 0.43$).

3.2. EXPERIMENT 2

The second experiment aimed at testing the naturalness of different denials of an exclamative sentence like ¡Qué alto es Juan! 'How tall John is!' Unlike experiment 1, informants were presented with three different replies that they had to evaluate using a Likert scale:

- assertion of the property plus denial of the high degree ("Yes, that's true, but John is not so tall");

Figure 5.2.
Example of Target Item of Experiment 2

1.

Consider the following dialogue:

    PEDRO: How fat Alberto is!

    JULIA: That's not true: he is not so fat.

How natural is Julia's reply?

utterly nonsense	very strange	strange	a bit strange	not very natural	quite natural	perfectly natural
1	2	3	4	5	6	7

- denial of the property ("No, that's not true: John is not tall");
- denial of the high degree ("No, that's not true: John is tall, but not so tall").

The option judged as most natural would be the best candidate for at-issueness.

3.2.1. Participants

The participants were 27 Spanish final course undergraduate students of the Faculty of Arts of the Universitat Autònoma de Barcelona (Catalonia, Spain). They had at least basic training in linguistics.

3.2.2. Method and Procedure

Participants were explained the experiment procedure with a filler item that was not included in the test. Then they were asked to read a written questionnaire involving an evaluation task. All the target items involved a two-line dialogue between Pedro and Julia, and participants were asked to evaluate the naturalness of Julia's reply using a seven-level Likert scale. Target items always involved a degree exclamative uttered by Pedro and a reply by Julia alternating the following three options:

    1) Yes, that's true, but X is not so Adj.

2) No, that's not true: X is not Adj.
3) No, that's not true: X is not so Adj.

Three lists of 18 items each (= nine targets + nine fillers) were created to avoid informants being confronted with different replies by Julia to the same utterance by Pedro. List 1 was answered by ten participants, list 2 by seven, and list 3 by ten. Informants had 18 minutes to answer the questionnaire. A real target item is reproduced in figure 5.2 (all the materials were in Spanish).

3.2.3. Results

The first option ("It is true, but X is not so Adj") was judged by informants as the least natural, with an average naturalness value of 3.23 out of 7. Direct denials were found far more natural: 5.72 for the denial of the property ("No, that's not true: X is not Adj") and 5.79 for the denial of the high degree ("No, that's not true: X is not so Adj"). Hence, there was no clear preference for any denial option, and standard deviation suggested no particular difference between them. The results for each item are displayed in Table 4. The sharp contrast between the first option, on the one hand, and the other two, on the other, can be easily grasped in figure 5.3.

4. Discussion

4.1. EXPERIMENT 1

Our initial expectation was that only the at-issue meaning of exclamatives would be cancellable. The results of experiment 1 (see 0) show that such an expectation was only fulfilled by the predication of the property (i.e., "Mary is tall"), but not for the high degree part ("Mary is tall to an unexpected degree"). The denial of the former was perceived as more natural (68.91%) than the denial of the latter (31.08%), which strongly suggests that hearers do not take the high degree involved in exclamatives as something at issue and hence subject to denial. This was so in 68.91% of the cases, with just one item (#3) falling outside the general pattern. In this case, when confronted with the dialogue in (18) 78.37% of the participants found the interpretation "It is not so slow" more natural, as opposed to 21.62% who found the reply "It is fast" more natural.

Table 5.2.
Results of Naturalness Test for Experiment 2

Item	"Yes, that's true, but X is not so Adj"	"No, that's not true: X is not Adj"	"No, that's not true: X is not so Adj"
2	3.5	6.0	6.4
4	3.1	4.9	6.5
6	3.5	6.9	6.0
8	3.1	4.5	5.6
10	3.4	5.7	5.3
12	3.2	6.8	6.0
14	3.2	5.1	5.6
16	2.7	6.3	5.0
18	3.4	5.3	5.7
Average	3.23	5.72	5.79
Standard Deviation	0.25	0.84	0.48

(18) PEDRO: How slow this computer is!
    JULIA: That's not true.

This was maybe due to the particular form of the reply, which did not include an explicit assertion of the predicate: "It is not so slow" vs. the general pattern, "It is slow, but not so slow," found in all other target items. Therefore, the different phrasing of the offered reading might be a potential disturbing factor to be taken into account carefully in future experiments.

Once this case is discounted, if Mayol and Castroviejo (2013) are correct in linking cancelation and QUD, this experiment half confirms and half corrects the received wisdom on the levels of meaning in exclamatives. On the one hand, it confirms that the high degree meaning is not part of the at-issue meaning of exclamatives, in accordance with the presupposition and the implicature analyses discussed in section 2. On the other hand, the fact that informants easily cancelled the property involved in the exclamative argues against Grimshaw's (1979, p. 320) claim—and Abels's (2010) revival—that "[t]he exclamation *How tall John is!* presupposes that John is tall, and an exclamation like *What big ears John has!* presupposes that John has big ears." Moreover, these data seem hard to conciliate with Castroviejo's (2008a) analysis of exclamatives as involving no asserted part at all (see section 1).

Figure 5.3.
Naturalness Evaluation Results of Experiment 2 on a 1–7 Likert Scale

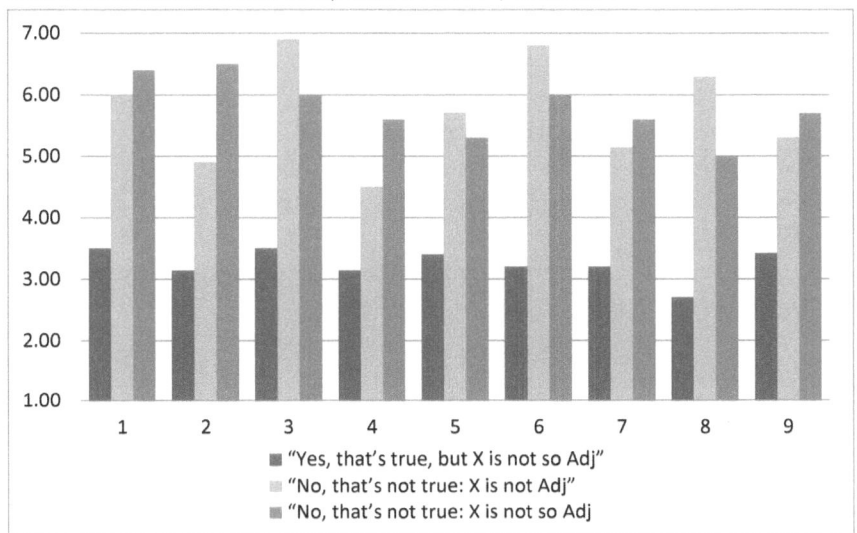

4.2. EXPERIMENT 2

Our second experiment aimed at testing the availability of denial from a naturalness evaluation task. The results did not perfectly match those of the first, for informants did not show a clear pattern concerning the material at-issue. On the one hand, denial of the property ("No, that's not true: X is not Adj") was judged quite natural (5.72 out of 7), in accordance with the results of experiment 1. On the other hand, denial of the high degree part was judged very differently regarding the form of the answer: whereas positive endorsement plus denial of the high degree ("Yes, that's true, but X is not so Adj") was perceived as the least natural (an average of 3.24 out of 7), negative denials of the high degree ("No, that's not true: X is not so Adj") were judged as the most natural option (a 5.78 average). These data are certainly difficult to interpret straightforwardly, but it seems clear that denial of high degree is not unnatural per se, as the latter case shows: it was rated even better than the denial of the property. This suggests that the poor rating of positive endorsement plus denial of the high degree should be interpreted as evidence that confirmations are perceived as endorsing all levels of meaning of exclamatives, namely both the property and the high degree, which yielded a contradictory feeling when denying the high degree part. In contrast, the strong denial ("No, that's not true: X is not Adj") wasn't restricted this way.

The overall picture arising from these experimental data is far from being crystal clear, but allows us to raise some generalizations. First, the ascription of the property in exclamatives is subject to denial, which clearly suggests it is (part of) the at-issue meaning of exclamatives, against Grimshaw's (1979) original claim and Abels's (2010) restatement. In contrast, the high degree meaning has proven more stubborn to classify: experiment 1 suggested that it is not part of the at-issue meaning, but this was only partially confirmed by experiment 2.

5. Conclusions

In this chapter I have offered empirical evidence concerning the nature of the levels of meaning involved in Spanish degree exclamatives. Particularly, by means of two denial experiments I have tested what speakers perceive as the at-issue meaning of an exclamative. The interpretation experiment showed that they more easily cancel the ascription of the property (i.e., "Mary is tall") than the high degree part (i.e., "Mary is taller than expected"), which was interpreted as evidence that only the former meaning was clearly at-issue.

The evaluation experiment yielded less clear results. It confirmed that denial of the ascription of the property was natural and hence part of the at-issue meaning. Yet in contrast with the former experiment, the denial of the high degree part showed a split behavior depending on the form: endorsement of the exclamative plus denial was clearly unnatural, in accordance with data in the interpretation experiment, but denial of the exclamative plus denial of the high degree was judged natural.

On the whole, our research contradicted the received wisdom, since Elliott (1974) that the core property ascription in exclamatives is presupposed. Rather, I have found in both experiments that this meaning is clearly at-issue and hence amenable to denial. In contrast, the high degree meaning has been found much harder to deny (but not impossible), in accordance with standard assumptions. However, to confirm this fact, and crucially to determine its exact nature as a presupposition or as a conventional implicature, further experimental research is needed on the projective behavior of this meaning.

Appendix: Items Included in Experiment 1

1.
PEDRO: ¡Qué alta que es María!
        'How tall María is!'
JULIA: No, no es verdad.
        'No, that's not true.'
A) María no es alta.
    'María is not tall.'
B) María es alta pero no tanto.
    'María is tall, but not that much.'

2. (filler)
PEDRO: La cerveza caliente es deliciosa.
        'Hot beer is delicious.'
JULIA: No, no es verdad.
        'No, that's not true.'
'Does Pedro like beer?'
A) Sí.
    'Yes.'
B) Sí, pero fría.
    'He does, but cold.'

3.
PEDRO: ¡Qué lento que es este ordenador!
        'How slow this computer is!'
JULIA: No, no es verdad.
        'No, that's not true.'
A) El ordenador no es tan lento.
    'The computer is not so slow.'
B) El ordenador es rápido.
    'The computer is quick.'

4. (Filler)
PEDRO: La cerveza caliente es deliciosa.
        'Hot beer is delicious.'
JULIA: No, no es verdad.
        'No, that's not true.'
'Do Pedro and Julia agree?'
A) Siempre.
    'Always.'
B) No.
    'No.'

5.
PEDRO: ¡Qué aburrida es María!
　　　　'How boring María is!'
JULIA: No, no es verdad.
　　　　'No, that's not true.'
A) María es divertida.
　　'María is funny.'
B) María es aburrida pero no demasiado.
　　'María is boring, but not so much.'

6.
PEDRO: La cerveza caliente es deliciosa.
　　　　'Hot beer is delicious.'
JULIA: No, no es verdad.
　　　　'No, that's not true.'
'Does Julia like beer?'
A) Sí, pero fría.
　　'She does, but cold.'
B) No.
　　'No.'

7.
PEDRO: ¡Qué burro es Juan!
　　　　'How silly Juan is!'
JULIA: No, no es verdad.
　　　　'No, that's not true.'
A) Juan es burro, pero no tanto.
　　'Juan is silly, but not so much.'
B) Juan es listo.
　　'Juan is smart.'

8.
PEDRO: Messi es argentino.
　　　　'Messi is an Argentinian.'
JULIA: No, no es verdad.
　　　　'No, that's not true.'
A) Messi no es argentino.
　　'Messi is not an Argentinian.'
B) Miguel es argentino.
　　'Miguel is an Argentinian.'

9.
PEDRO: ¡Qué fácil fue el examen!
　　　　'How easy the exam was!'
JULIA: No, no es verdad.
　　　　'No, that's not true.'

A) El examen no fue fácil.
'The exam was not easy.'
B) El examen fue fácil, pero no tanto.
'The exam was easy, but not so much.'

10. (filler)
PEDRO: María vendrá mañana.
'María will come tomorrow.'
JULIA: No, no es verdad.
'No, that's not true.'
A) María vendrá otro día.
'María will come some other day.'
B) María no vendrá.
'María will not come.'

11.
PEDRO: ¡Qué lejos aparcó el coche!
'How far away she parked the car!'
JULIA: No, no es verdad.
'No, that's not true.'
A) Aparcó el coche lejos, pero no demasiado.
'She parked the car far away, but not so much.'
B) No aparcó el coche lejos.
'She did not park the car far away.'

12.
PEDRO: En Italia no hay trabajo.
'There is no job in Italy.'
JULIA: No, no es verdad.
'No, that's not true.'
A) En Italia hay corrupción.
'There is corruption in Italy.'
B) En Italia hay mucho paro.
'There is much unemployment in Italy.'

13.
PEDRO: ¡Qué pesada que fue la charla!
'How dull the talk was!'
JULIA: No, no es verdad.
'No, that's not true.'
A) La charla fue divertida.
'The talk was funny.'
B) La charla fue pesada, pero no tanto.
'The talk was dull, but not so much.'

14.
PEDRO: La idiota de María llegó tarde.
　　　　'That idiot María arrived late.'
JULIA: No, no es verdad.
　　　　'No, that's not true.'
A) María no llegó tarde.
　　'María did not arrived late.'
B) María no es idiota.
　　'María is not an idiot.'

15.
PEDRO: ¡Qué borde se puso María!
　　　　'How naughty María behaved!'
JULIA: No, no es verdad.
　　　　'No, that's not true.'
A) María se puso borde, pero no demasiado.
　　'María behaved naughty, but not so much.'
B) María no se puso borde.
　　'María did not behave naughty.'

16.
PEDRO: La clase fue un aburrimiento.
　　　　'The class was an utter yawn.'
JULIA: No, no es verdad.
　　　　'No, that's not true.'
A) La clase no fue aburrida.
　　'The class wasn't boring.'
B) La clase fue divertidísima.
　　'The class was very funny.'

17. (filler: common to all three lists)
PEDRO: María juega a baloncesto.
　　　　'María plays basketball.'
JULIA: Sí, es cierto, pero no es alta.
　　　　'That's true, but she is not tall.'

18.
　　　　PEDRO: ¡Qué amables que son tus vecinos!
　　　　　　　　'How kind your neighbors are!'
list A: JULIA: No es cierto: no son tan amables.
　　　　　　　　'That's not true: they are not so kind.'
list B: JULIA: Sí, es cierto, pero no son tan amables.
　　　　　　　　'That's true, but they are not so kind.'
list C: JULIA: No es cierto: no son amables.
　　　　　　　　'That's not true: they are not kind.'

Exclamative Sentences and Extreme Degree Quantification

Raquel González Rodríguez

1. Introduction

It has been pointed out in the literature that exclamative sentences denote high or extreme degree (Postma, 1996; Masullo, 2005; among others). This means that an exclamative like (1a) expresses that the degree to which the property of intelligence holds is an extreme value. Thus, the sentence in (1a) could be paraphrased as in (1b), where we have a canonical extreme degree modifier (*extremadamente* 'extremely'):

(1) a. ¡Qué inteligente es Juan!
 'How intelligent John is!'
 b. Juan es extremadamente inteligente.
 'John is extremely intelligent.'

In spite of the parallelism that has been established between exclamative wh-phrases and extreme degree modifiers, little attention has been paid to determining whether the former behave exactly as the latter. The goal of this chapter is to compare exclamative wh-phrases with extreme degree

---

I would like to thank Ignacio Bosque for his very useful comments and suggestions. Needless to say, all possible remaining errors are my own.

modifiers such as *extremadamente* (henceforth "*extremadamente* modifiers" in Spanish). The paradigm of *extremadamente* modifiers includes the adverbs *extremadamente* and *sumamente*, as well as so-called morphological elatives (*inteligent-ísimo, super-inteligente*, etc.). Notice that adverbs such as *sorprendentemente* 'surprisingly,' *increíblemente* 'unbelievably,' *horriblemente* 'horribly,' etc., are not in that paradigm. As I will show in section 4, these modifiers behave in a rather different way. At this point, it is enough to mention that whereas *extremadamente* modifiers can appear in an exclamative wh-phrase, adverbs such as *sorprendentemente* cannot:

(2) a. ¡Qué extremadamente inteligente es Juan!
 'How extremely intelligent John is!'
 b. *¡Qué sorprendentemente inteligente es Juan!
 'How surprisingly intelligent John is!'

The comparison between exclamative wh-phrases and *extremadamente* modifiers will allow me to propose that exclamative wh-phrases do not denote extreme degree. They can convey an implicature of extreme degree, but this value is not a component of their meaning. Although one might argue that this idea is already present in the literature (Gutiérrez-Rexach, 1996, 2008; Castroviejo, 2006; Villalba, 2008b), I will deal with the issue from a different point of view, since I will focus on the (in)compatiblity of exclamative wh-phrases and *extremadamente* modifiers in negative environments. I will offer new data in favor of that proposal and develop two semantic analyses: one of exclamative wh-phrases and another one of *extremadamente* modifiers. I will study the behavior of these elements in negative contexts. Both types of modifiers are incompatible with negation (see [3]), which makes them positive polarity items:

(3) a. *¡Qué inteligente no es Juan!
 'How intelligent John is not!'
 b. *Juan no es extremadamente inteligente.[1]
 'John is not extremely intelligent.'

---

1. This example is ungrammatical if pronounced out of the blue, but it becomes grammatical if the negative operator has an external interpretation (Bosque, 1980a; Szabolcsi, 2004). In other words, the sentence in (3b) is grammatical when it refutes a previous statement or a

The ungrammaticality of (3) could be an argument in support of the idea that exclamative wh-phrases have the same denotation as *extremadamente* modifiers. The reason is that, according to semantic approaches of polarity, the sensitivity of positive polarity items is due to the fact that their semantics is incompatible with the context in which they are rejected (Israel, 1996; Giannakidou, 1998; Lahiri, 1998; Tovena, 1998; Chierchia, 2004, 2006; among others). Given that, the ungrammaticality of (3) could arise from certain incompatibility between negation and extreme degree denotation.[2] However, this argument makes incorrect predictions. I will show that, despite appearances, exclamative wh-phrases and *extremadamente* modifiers do not have the same distribution in negative environments. This provides evidence against the proposal that the denotation of exclamative wh-phrases equals that of *extremadamente* modifiers, that is, extreme degree.

This chapter is divided as follows: section 2 shows that exclamative wh-phrases and *extremadamente* modifiers are sensitive to different negative environments. It also proves that exclamative wh-phrases, unlike *extremadamente* modifiers, do not denote extreme degree. Section 3 offers two analyses: one of exclamative wh-phrases and another of *extremadamente* modifiers. The differences between them allow us to explain the asymmetries of these items regarding their distribution in negative environments. Section 4 gives further evidence for my hypothesis on modifiers such as *sorprendentemente* 'surprisingly.' Section 5 concludes the discussion.

2. Exclamative Wh-Phrases and *Extremadamente* Modifiers as Positive Polarity Items

In this section I will analyze the behavior of exclamative wh-phrases and *extremadamente* modifiers as positive polarity items. In section 2.1 I will establish a classification of both types of items that allows us to explain why some of them can co-occur with negation in spite of being positive polarity items. In section 2.2 I will argue against the idea that exclamative wh-phrases and *extremadamente* modifiers have the same denotation. I will show that these elements have a different distribution in negative contexts, which leads us to conclude that they do not have the same interpretation.

---

presupposed proposition. This interpretation, possible but irrelevant, must be excluded in all examples throughout this chapter.

2. See Masullo (2003, 2005) for a syntactic approach to this phenomenon.

2.1. DEGREE EXCLAMATIVES VS. AMOUNT EXCLAMATIVES

It has been pointed out in the literature that exclamative wh-phrases and *extremadamente* modifiers are positive polarity items, so that they cannot be in the scope of negation (Hernanz, 2001; González Rodríguez, 2008, 2010). The ungrammaticality of (4) illustrates the incompatibility between these elements and negation:

(4) a. *¡Qué alto no es Juan!
 'How tall John is!'
 b. *Juan no es extremadamente alto.
 'John is not extremely tall.'

I must hasten to point out that the grammaticality of the sentences in (5) does not constitute a counterexample to this conclusion:

(5) a. ¡Cuántos criterios no tuvo en cuenta!
 'How many criterions he did not take into account!'
 b. *No tuvo en cuenta muchísimos criterios.[3]
 'He did not take into account a lot of criterions.'

The difference between (4) and (5) lies in whether the quantitative DP expresses degree or amount (see Bosque, this volume). In (4), the quantifier modifies an adjective associated with a scale, measuring the degree to which the property holds, whereas in (5), it measures the amount of entities expressed by the restrictor.

This asymmetry affects the (im)possibility of having exclamative wh-phrases and *extremadamente* modifiers in negative sentences. As is shown in (4) and (5), whereas amount phrases may appear in a negative sentence (see [5]), degree phrases cannot (see [4]). Let me consider the behavior of these two types of phrases in detail and, specifically, the question of why the grammaticality of (5) does not contradict the claim that exclamative wh-phrases and *extremadamente* modifiers are positive polarity items.

---

3. The grammaticality judgment is restricted to the lower scope reading of the quantifier. *Muchísimos* 'many-ísimos' does not have an exact equivalent in English. The suffix *-ísimo* denotes extreme value.

Degree modifiers always have narrower scope than other operators in a sentence (Kennedy, 1997; Morón Pastor, 2004).[4] Thus, the only possible reading of (6) is the one in (6a), in which *muy* 'very' has narrow scope with respect to negation and is the constituent refuted.

(6) Carmen no es muy alta.
 'Carmen is not very tall.'
 a. There is a degree d, such that Carmen is tall to degree d, and d is not a high degree on the scale of tallness. [Neg > Very]
 b. #There is not a degree d, such that d is a high degree on the scale of tallness, and Carmen is tall to degree d. *[Neg > Very]
 c. #There is a degree d, such that d is a high degree on the scale of tallness, and Carmen is not tall to degree d. *[Very > Neg]

This means that in (6a) it is negated that Carmen has the property "tallness" to a high degree. The readings in (6b) and (6c) are not available. (6b), where negation takes wide scope, is not possible because it denies the existence of a high degree on the scale. The unavailability of the interpretation in (6c), in which the degree operator is not within the scope of negation, is due to the fact that this reading does not associate the individual with a degree on the scale.

Given that degree quantifiers always have narrow scope, the only expected interpretation in (4), repeated here as (7), is the one in (8a), where the wh-phrase has narrow scope and is refuted by negation. However, this reading is unavailable.[5] This proves that neither exclamative wh-phrases nor

---

4. This led Kennedy (1997) to propose that degree modifiers are not operators. In contrast, Morón Pastor (2004) argues that this fact does not necessarily mean that they are not operators.

5. Contrary to my judgments, as well as Kennedy's (1997) view, Gutiérrez-Rexach (2001, p. 175) and Villalba (2004, p. 15) defend that degree wh-phrases always have wide scope. To illustrate this, Villalba offers the example in (i) and points out that the only possible interpretation is the one in (a):

(i) How expensive all the books are!
 a. Only one degree d exists such that d is the maximal degree on the scale of expensiveness and such that for every y, y = book, y is expensive to degree d.
 b. *For every y, y = book, only one degree d exists such that d is the maximal degree on the scale of expensiveness and such that y is expensive to degree d.

I disagree. In my view the correct interpretation of this sentence is the one in (b), but removing "only." This naturally provides the reading according to which each book has a different price. Notice that if we assume that degrees are intervals on a scale (Kennedy, 1997, 2001; Schwarzschild & Wilkinson, 2002), the latter interpretation does not cancel the existence of

extremadamente modifiers can be in the scope of negation. As expected, the readings in (8b) and (8c) are not possible. The former denies the existence of a maximal degree on the scale. In the latter, the individual in question is not associated with a degree on the scale:

(7) a. *¡Qué alto no es Juan!
'How tall John is!'
b. *Juan no es extremadamente alto.
'John is not extremely tall.'

(8) a. #There is a degree d, such that Carmen is tall to degree d, and d is not the maximal degree on the scale of tallness. *[Neg > Quantifier]
b. #There is not a degree d, such that d is the maximal degree on the scale of tallness, and Carmen is tall to degree d. *[Neg > Quantifier]
c. #There is a degree d, such that d is the maximal degree on the scale of tallness, and Carmen is not tall to degree d. *[Quantifier > Neg]

Amount quantifiers are able to establish different scope relations with other operators. The sentence in (9) is ambiguous between the interpretations in (a) and (c):

(9) El violinista no tocó muchas sinfonías.
'The violinist did not play many symphonies.'
a. 'There are symphonies that the violinist played, and these are not many.' [Neg > Many]
b. #'There are not many symphonies that the violinist played.' *[Neg > Many]
c. 'There are many symphonies that the violinist did not play.' [Many > Neg]

In the former reading, the quantifier has narrow scope; in the latter, it takes scope over negation. Notice that the reading in which negation has wide scope is only possible if it affects the appraisal of the amount, as in (a),

---

a maximal degree on the scale. Any degree included in the highest interval is grammatically codified as an extreme degree.

but not if the resulting interpretation implies the non-existence of a certain number of symphonies, as in (9b).

Since amount modifiers may establish different scope relations with other operators, the quantifiers in (5), repeated here as (10), may have wide scope over negation.

(10) a. ¡Cuántos criterios no tuvo en cuenta!
'How many criterions he did not take into account!'
b. No tuvo en cuenta muchísimos criterios.
'He did not take into account a lot of criterions.'

This is illustrated in (11c). The reading resulting from the negation having wide scope (as in [11a]) is expected (see [9a]), but is not available:

(11) a. #There were criterions that he took into account, and these were not many.   *[Neg > Quantifier]
b. #There were not many criterions that he took into account.
*[Neg > Quantifier]
c. There were many criterions that he did not take into account.
[Quantifier > Neg]

This shows that, when exclamative wh-phrases and *extremadamente* modifiers express amounts, they behave in the same way as they do when they denote degrees: they are rejected in the scope of negation. On the other hand, the reading in (11b) is not expected because it denies the existence of a certain number of criterions that someone did not take into account.

Notice that the grammaticality of (10a) does not imply that amount exclamatives are always compatible with negation. Their compatibility depends on whether or not the wh-phrase is able to display a wide scope reading. If this scope relation cannot be established, the sentence is ungrammatical, as in (12), where *cuánto* is followed by a mass noun:

(12) *¡Cuánto coraje no tuvo!
'How much courage he did not have!'

This sentence, unlike (10a), does not allow for the reading in which negation has narrow scope ("There were much courage that he did not have"). According to González Rodríguez (2008), exclamative wh-phrases may take scope over negation if the latter is able to affect the wh-phrase's denotation.

This happens when the wh-phrase allows the individualization of the wh's domain, as in (10), where it is easy to imagine a situation in which *cuántos criterios* refers to a specific set of individuals. In (7) and (12), the individualization of the wh-phrase's domain is not possible, and, as a consequence, the quantifier cannot have wide scope either.[6] In section 3 I will deal with the impossibility that exclamative wh-phrases and *extremadamente* modifiers take narrow scope with respect to negation.

Summarizing, neither exclamative wh-phrases nor *extremadamente* modifiers can have narrow scope with respect to negation, regardless of whether they express amount or degree. When they denote amount, they have wide scope and, therefore, are not incompatible with negation. However, the only reading available is the one resulting from that scope relation. Since I am only interested in the reading in which quantifiers display narrow scope with respect to negation, I will avoid the use of amount modifiers, which are able to outscope negation causing the grammaticality of the sentence.

2.2. AGAINST A UNIFIED ANALYSIS

In the previous section I have shown that exclamative wh-phrases and *extremadamente* modifiers behave as positive polarity items. According to semantic theories of polarity, the sensitivity of positive polarity items is due to the fact that their denotation is incompatible with the semantics of the contexts in which they are rejected. As a consequence, if two expressions have the same denotation, both of them must be incompatible with the same contexts. This situation is apparently found with exclamative wh-phrases and *extremadamente* modifiers: both denote extreme degree and cannot co-occur with negation. However, facts are more complex. As shown below, both types of modifiers have a different behavior if we take into account other negative environments.

In order to describe the behavior of exclamative wh-phrases and *extremadamente* modifiers as positive polarity items, one must pay attention to their (in)compatibility with several negative contexts. Since Ladusaw's (1980) work, negative contexts, which license negative polarity items, have been characterized as downward-entailing environments (Hoeksema, 1983; van der Wouden, 1997; Zwarts, 1998; among others). Following this theory, there are three types of polarity triggers: downward-entailing functions,

---

6. For a detailed explanation of this restriction see González Rodríguez (2008).

anti-additive functions and anti-morphic functions.[7] Van der Wouden (1997) shows that these contexts are also relevant for positive polarity items, which are incompatible with certain environments. Depending on whether positive polarity items cannot co-occur with downward-entailing, anti-additive or anti-morphic operators, van der Wouden distinguishes between strong, medium and weak positive polarity items, respectively.

Consider first the behavior of exclamative wh-phrases and *extremadamente* modifiers in anti-morphic contexts. Sentential negation is anti-morphic. As shown in (7), exclamative wh-phrases and extreme degree quantifiers cannot be within the scope of negation, and, therefore, they are at least sensitive to anti-morphic environments.[8] The preposition *sin* 'without' is an anti-additive function and allows us to check whether exclamative wh-phrases and *extremadamente* quantifiers are sensitive to anti-additive contexts. As the contrast between (13a) and (13b) shows, *extremadamente* modifiers are compatible with *sin* (see [13a]), whereas exclamative wh-phrases are not (see [13b]):

(13) a. Les sedujo sin ser extremadamente simpático.
      'He seduced them without being extremely nice.'
   b. *¡Sin qué labia les sedujo!
      'Without such a loquacity he seduced them!'

The behavior of exclamative wh-phrases and *extremadamente* modifiers in downward-entailing environments is also different. For example, *raramente* 'rarely' is a downward-entailing operator, and exclamative wh-phrases cannot have narrow scope with respect to it (see [14a]). In contrast, *extremadamente* modifiers can co-occur with that operator without causing ungrammaticality (see [14b]):

---

7. A function is downward-entailing iff $X \subseteq Y \rightarrow f(Y) \subseteq f(X)$; that is, downward-entailing functions support inferences from sets to subsets ("His children rarely eat vegetables" → "His children rarely eat spinach"). A function is anti-additive iff $(X \cup Y) = f(X) \cap f(Y)$. That is, a disjunction in the scope of an anti-additive function is equivalent to a wide scope conjunction. "Without," for example, is anti-additive because "John went to work without eat or sleep" is equivalent to "John went to work without eat and without sleep." A function is anti-morphic if (a) $f(X \cup Y) = f(X) \cap f(Y)$ and (b) $f(X \cap Y) = f(X) \cup f(Y)$. Thus, an anti-morphic function is characterized by the following properties: (a) a disjunction in its scope is equivalent to a wide scope conjunction, and (b) a conjunction in its scope is equivalent to a wide scope disjunction. Sentential negation is an anti-morphic function because "It wasn't John who ran or swam" is equivalent to "It wasn't John who ran and it wasn't John who swam," and "It wasn't John who ran and swam" is equivalent to "It wasn't John who ran or it wasn't John who swam."

8. See González Rodríguez (2010) for a more detailed description of the sensitivity of *extremadamente* modifiers to anti-morphic contexts.

(14) a. *¡Qué motivados están raramente sus empleados!
'How rarely motivated his employees are!'
b. Sus empleados raramente están extremadamente motivados.
'His employees are rarely extremely motivated.'

The data above show that exclamative wh-phrases and *extremadamente* modifiers are positive polarity items. However, whereas the former are sensitive to downward-entailing contexts, the second are only incompatible with anti-morphic environments. In other words, exclamative wh-phrases are strong positive polarity items, whereas *extremadamente* modifiers are weak positive polarity items. Assuming that the sensitivity of positive polarity items is due to their denotation, the asymmetries illustrated above demonstrate that exclamative wh-phrases and *extremadamente* modifiers do not have the same meaning, contrary to what it might appear.

3. Widening a Domain of Quantification vs. Closing an Open Scale

After demonstrating that exclamative wh-phrases and *extremadamente* modifiers have a different distribution and, as a consequence, a different denotation, I will introduce a semantic analysis of each of these quantifiers. In section 3.1. I will focus on *extremadamente* modifiers. I will defend the claim that they denote extreme degree because they close an open scale and associate some individual with the maximal value on that scale. In section 3.2 I will argue that exclamative wh-phrases widen a domain of quantification, in line with Zanuttini and Portner (2003). This proposal allows us to explain that, whereas exclamative wh-phrases are rejected in downward-entailing contexts, *extremadamente* modifiers are incompatible with anti-morphic environments.

3.1. CLOSING AN OPEN SCALE

The semantic analysis of *extremadamente* modifiers that I want to propose is based on the structure of scales developed by Kennedy and McNally (2005a). These authors address the set of degrees that adjectival scales may express and distinguish four types:

a) (Totally) open scales lack a minimal and a maximal element, that is, they do not contain a degree whose value is greater or less than the others in the set. The adjectives *tall* and *short* are associated with open scales, since it is possible to imagine a higher degree with respect to any degree of tallness.[9]
b) (Totally) closed scales have a minimal and a maximal element. This means that they contain a degree whose value is lower than the others in the set, together with another that is the highest on the scale. *Full* and *empty* are closed scale adjectives because their scale has a limit with respect to the degree in which the property may hold. In the case of *full* this limit determines that the scale has a maximal value; in the case of *empty*, the limit causes the existence of a minimal value.
c) Lower closed scales lack a maximal element but have a minimal one; in other words, they include a degree whose value is the lowest on the scale, but not a degree whose value is greater than that of all the others. This is what happens with *loud* and *quiet*. Whereas there is not a maximal degree associated to the positive adjective *loud*, there is a minimal value with respect to the negative adjective *quiet*.
d) Upper closed scales have a maximal value and lack a minimal one. The adjectives *safe* and *dangerous* are associated with a scale of this type. The reason is that the scale of safety contains some highest degree. However, it does not include a degree whose value is less than the others on the scale.

In order to represent these scales, Kennedy and McNally (2005a, pp. 353–354) assume that "degrees are values that are isomorphic to the real numbers between 0 and 1" and offer the representation of scales illustrated in (15), where R refers to the ordering relations and Δ is the dimension for the scale:

(15) A typology of scale structures
    a. <D(0,1), R, Δ > (totally) open scale.

---

[9]. The minimal value of a scale corresponds to the highest degree that the property denoted by the negative adjective is able to express. Assuming this, one may refer to that extreme by just mentioning the minimal value of the scale or the maximal degree of the negative adjective. This asymmetry does not arise in the other extreme of the scale, the highest one. This extreme corresponds to the maximal value of the scale and to the highest degree of the positive adjective.

b. <D[0,1), R, Δ > lower closed scale.
c. <D(0,1], R, Δ > upper closed scale.
d. <D[0,1], R, Δ > (totally) closed scale.
(Kennedy and McNally 2005a: 354)

Bearing in mind this classification, let me go back to the denotation of *extremadamente* modifiers. Whereas these modifiers are compatible with open scale adjectives (see [16a]), they cannot co-occur with closed scale adjectives (see [16b]):

(16) a. Su madre es extremadamente guapa.
'His mother is extremely beautiful.'
b. *El vaso está extremadamente lleno.
'The glass is extremely full.'

This fact seems to come into conflict with the extreme degree denotation of a modifier such as *extremadamente*. Moreover, it is not possible to dissolve the paradox by arguing that *extremadamente* does not express extreme degree, but just a high degree on the scale. Evidence for the extreme degree denotation of *extremadamente* comes from the impossibility of continuing (16a) with expressions such as *pero menos que* 'but less than,' as in (17).

(17) Su madre es extremadamente guapa, #pero menos que María.
'His mother is extremely beautiful, but she is less beautiful than Mary.'

Since *extremadamente* associates the individual with the maximal value on the scale, it is not possible to add adversative tags implying the existence of a higher degree.[10] One should then conclude that *extremadamente* modifiers denote extreme degree and, at the same time, modify open scale adjectives (that is, scalar adjectives without a maximal value). Any analysis of these modifiers must offer a satisfactory answer to this paradox. My proposal is

---

10. Castroviejo (2006, p. 27) points out that the ungrammaticality of *How very cute he is!—though he's not extremely cute* is due to the incompatibility between exclamative and declarative modalities. I agree with her that denoting extreme degree does not constitute an explanation of the ungrammaticality of that sentence, since I have proposed that exclamative quantifiers do not have that denotation. However, notice that the situation is not the same in (17), where there is no combination of modalities.

that *extremadamente* modifiers close an open scale and associate the subject of predication with the maximal value on the scale that has been closed. The meaning of modifiers such as *extremadamente* is illustrated in (18):[11]

(18) $[[\text{extremadamente}]] = \{<G_{(0, 1)}, G_{[0, 1]}>\} \wedge \lambda G \lambda x. \exists d \, [d = \max(S_G) \wedge G(d)(x)]$

This proposal allows us to solve the paradox of denoting extreme degree with respect to an open scale. Moreover, this analysis accounts for the incompatibility between *extremadamente* modifiers and the particle *no*. Remember that in a sentence like (19), the only expected reading is the one in (19a), where *extremadamente agradable* has narrow scope with respect to negation and is the refuted constituent. The readings in (19b) and (19c) are not expected. The former expresses that the individual has a property to the maximal value, but under this reading, that specific degree does not exist. The latter is not expected because degree phrases always have narrow scope:

(19) *Roberto no es extremadamente agradable.
 'Roberto is not extremely nice.'
 a. #There is a degree d, such that Roberto is nice to degree d, and d is not the maximal degree on the scale of niceness.
 *[Neg > Quantifier]
 b. #There is not a degree d, such that d is the maximal degree on the scale of niceness, and Roberto is nice to degree d.
 *[Neg > Quantifier]
 c. #There is a degree d, such that d is the maximal degree on the scale of niceness, and Roberto is not nice to degree d.
 *[Quantifier > Neg]

The relevant question is why the reading in (19a), although expected, is not available; in other words, why (19) cannot have the same interpretation as the sentence "Roberto is not very nice" ("There is a degree d, such that Roberto is tall to degree d, and d is not a high degree on the scale of niceness"). The answer to this question is related to the meaning of

---

11. I use Kennedy and McNally's (2005a) notation here: *G* refers to arguments that have the semantic type of adjectives associated with scales; *d*, to arguments of type "degree"; *x*, to arguments of type "entity"; S_G to the scale associated with a gradable adjective; and *max*, to the maximal element of the scale.

extremadamente modifiers. Assuming my semantic analysis of these quantifiers, the unavailability of the interpretation in (19a) can be easily explained. When *extremadamente* is refuted, the relevant meaning of the modifier is the one that associates the individual with the maximal degree on the scale. The problem is that if the scale has not been closed before, that denotation is not available because the existence of a maximal degree has not been established. It is not possible to deny the degree in which an individual has a property if that degree does not exist.

3.2. WIDENING A DOMAIN OF QUANTIFICATION

As I have shown, exclamative wh-phrases are not sensitive to the same contexts as *extremadamente* modifiers, and, therefore, their denotation has to be different. In this section, I will address the semantics of exclamative wh-phrases and I will derive their polar sensitivity (Israel, 1996; Giannakidou, 1998; Lahiri, 1998; Tovena, 1998; Chierchia, 2004, 2006; among others). As noted by Zanuttini and Portner (2003), exclamative quantifiers are operators that bind a variable, inducing a scalar implicature. These elements express that the scale in question has been extended far beyond the speaker's expectations. Based on Kadmon and Landman (1993), Zanuttini and Portner (2003) name this property "widening" because the bound variable is out of the domain of quantification expected by the speaker. For instance, in (20), the expected domain with regards to prices of a plane ticket would be that in (21a). The exclamative operator would then widen the domain as in (21b):

(20) ¡Qué caro ha sido el billete!
'How expensive the ticket was!'

(21) a. D1: {400 euros, 500 euros, 600 euros}.
b. D2: {400 euros, 500 euros, 600euros, 700 euros, 800 euros, 900 euros}.

This proposal allows us to explain the polar sensitivity of exclamative wh-phrases. Zanuttini and Portner (2003, p. 50, footnote 15) suggest that there is a certain relation between the widening that exclamative sentences convey and the one involved in the meaning of the negative polarity item *any* (Kadmon & Landman, 1993), but they do not explore the nature of that relation. I would like to propose that this relation exists and also that it is essential to understand the sensitivity of exclamative wh-phrases, in a manner parallel to Kadmon and Landman's (1993) and Chierchia's (2004) account of the polar sensitivity of *any*. As Kadmon and Landman (1993) point out, *any* widens a domain of quantification because, in an NP of the form *any NP,* the quantifier *any* extends the interpretation of the common noun. Thus, in (22), for example, *any* widens the domain of quantification in D_1 to the one illustrated in D_2:

(22) a. I don't have any potatoes.
 b. D1: {cooking potatoes}.
 c. D2: {cooking potatoes, non-cooking potatoes}.
 (adapted from Kadmon & Landman, 1993, p. 359)

According to Chierchia (2004), the domain-widening function must be universally closed. This closure is subject to a strengthening condition, that is, the result must be a stronger statement, giving rise to a gain of information.[12] In the case of *any,* the closure "must lead to something stronger than the corresponding meaning with a plain indefinite" (Chierchia, 2004, p. 76).

The combination between the widening effect and the strengthening principle allows Kadmon and Landman (1993) and Chierchia (2004) to derive the sensitivity of *any,* which implies that this item can only occur in downward-entailing contexts.[13] When it appears in these environments, the strengthening condition is satisfied, the reason being that downward-entailing operators create entailments from sets to subsets. As shown in (23), the statement in which the domain has been extended (see [23a]) entails the one in which the domain has not been widened (see [23b]):

(23) a. WIDE: We don't have potatoes, cooking or others.
 b. → NARROW: We don't have cooking potatoes.
 (Kadmon & Landman, 1993, p. 370)

In contrast, the strengthening condition is not satisfied when *any* occurs in affirmative contexts, since the direction of the entailments is the opposite. As shown in (24), the result of the widening in affirmative environments does not lead to a stronger statement, violating the strengthening principle:

---

12. Kadmon and Landman (1993) argue that this requirement is a lexical property of *any.*
13. See Krifka (1995) and Lahiri (1998) for a similar proposal.

(24) a. WIDE: We have potatoes of SOME kind (cooking or other).
b. - ↛ NARROW: We have cooking potatoes.
(Kadmon & Landman, 1993, p. 370)

The use of *any* in these contexts leads to a loss of information, causing the ungrammaticality of the sentence:

(25) *I have any potatoes.

Assuming this approach to negative polarity, and accepting that exclamative wh-phrases widen a domain of quantification, the incompatibility between these modifiers and downward-entailing contexts can be naturally explained. Exclamative wh-phrases are positive polarity items because they induce a domain-extension that creates a stronger statement, not in downward-entailing contexts, but in affirmative environments. Thus, when exclamative quantifiers occur within the scope of a downward-entailing operator, the strengthening condition is not satisfied, causing the ungrammaticality of the sentence. As I have pointed out, exclamative quantifiers extend the interval of the scale that is relevant to localize the subject of predication. The widening involved in exclamative quantifiers is illustrated in (26), where D_1 constitutes the initial domain and D_2 exemplifies the widened domain:

(26) a. ¡Qué alto es Juan!
'How tall John is!'
b. D1: {1.70m(eters), 1.80m.}. [narrow domain]
c. D2: {1.70m., 1.80m., 1.90m., 2m., 2.10m.}. [widened domain]

Exclamative quantifiers widen the domain of quantification toward the top of the scale, expressing that the degree to which the property holds is higher than the one expected by the speaker. As a consequence of the direction in which the quantifier extends the domain, the resulting statement is stronger than it would be without the widening process in affirmative contexts. In other words, the widening associated with exclamative quantifiers leads to a gain of information. Given a degree x and a degree y, such that x is higher on the scale than y, the sentence "John is x" entails "John is y." In other words, the direction of entailments is the one indicated by the arrow in (27):

(27)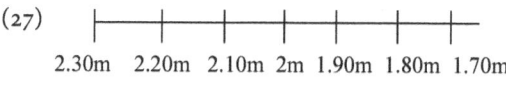
2.30m   2.20m   2.10m   2m   1.90m   1.80m   1.70m

Therefore, as shown in (28), if it is the case that an individual is two meters tall, it must also be the case that he is 1.90 meters tall, 1.80 meters tall, etc.:[14]

(28) John is 2 meters tall → John is 1.80 meters tall.

This shows that the widening of the quantification induced by exclamative quantifiers satisfies the strengthening constraint in affirmative contexts.[15] In contrast, this principle is not satisfied in downward-entailment environments, in which the widening induced by exclamative quantifiers leads to a loss of information. Let us consider a negative context in particular. The result of the widening induced by the exclamative wh-phrase in the negative sentence illustrated in (29a) is the same as the one in the affirmative construction. That is, the interval of the relevant scale is extended toward the top (see [29b–29c]):

(29) a. *¡Qué alto no es Juan!
  'How tall John is not!'
  b. D1: {1.70m., 1.80m.}. [narrow domain]
  c. D2: {1.70m., 1.80m., 1.90m., 2m., 2.10m.}. [widened domain]

Crucially, the result of the domain expansion in (29) does not lead to a stronger statement, but to a weaker one, the opposite of what we attest in affirmative sentences (see [28]). The reason is that (30a) does not imply (30b). In fact, (30a) entails that John is not 2.5 meters tall, three meters tall, and so on (see [30c]):[16]

---

14. Notice that this reading arises when the sentence is interpreted as in (ia), but not when it is paraphrased as in (ib):

(i) a. John reaches two meters tall.
    b. John is exactly two meters tall.

Since exclamative sentences express the former reading, the second interpretation must be excluded.

15. I will not address the question whether this requirement is a lexical property of exclamative quantifiers (Kadmon & Landman, 1993) or a condition that the universal closure associated with the domain expansion must satisfy (Chierchia, 2004).

16. Remember that I am not dealing with the interpretation of (30a), which can be paraphrased as "John is not exactly two meters tall" (see footnote 14). According to this reading, (30a) does not entail (30b). In contrast, this relation holds under the other reading ("John does not reach two meters"), as shown by the anomaly of "John does not reach two meters, although he reaches 2.25 meters."

(30) a. John is not two meters tall.
    b. - ↛ John is not 1.80 meters tall.
    c. → John is not 2.10 meters tall.

The negative operator reverses entailments, so that the direction of the entailments is the one indicated by the arrow in (31):

(31) Downward-entailment contexts

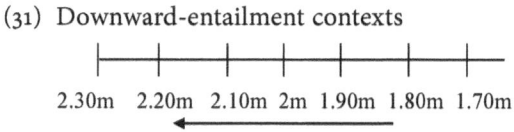

2.30m 2.20m 2.10m 2m 1.90m 1.80m 1.70m

Since the negative operator, just like the rest of downward-entailing functions, reverses scalar entailments, the widening associated with exclamative wh-phrases does not satisfy the strengthening condition. The violation of this principle causes the ungrammaticality of the sentence in (29), as well as the ungrammaticality of the exclamatives in which the wh-phrase must be interpreted within the scope of a downward-entailing function.

To summarize, the fact that exclamative wh-phrases and *extremadamente* modifiers are sensitive to different contexts provides evidence strong enough as to argue that they have a different denotation. The latter close an open scale and express that the degree to which a property holds is the maximal value on the scale. In contrast, the former do not denote extreme degree, but they widen a domain of quantification; in other words, they express that the bound variable is out of the domain of quantification expected by the speaker. As Zanuttini and Portner (2003) point out, this could give rise to an implicature of extreme degree. However, as I have argued, exclamative wh-phrases widen a domain of quantification, but, unlike *extremadamente* modifiers, they do not express extreme degree. This explains the different distribution of these modifiers in negative environments.

4. Further Evidence

More empirical evidence for my proposal comes from a certain type of quantifiers that extend a domain of quantification without being exclamatives, such as *sorprendentemente* 'surprisingly', *increíblemente* 'amazingly', etc.

Morzycki (2008) argues that when these operators modify an adjective, they widen a domain of quantification toward the top of some scale.[17] This author considers that the semantic contribution of these adverbs is related to one of the corresponding adjectives. By doing so, he deals with the relationship between sentences such as the ones in (32):

(32) a. Carmen es sorprendentemente alta.
 'Carmen is surprisingly tall.'
b. Es sorprendente cómo de alta es Carmen.
 'It is amazing how tall Carmen is.'

According to Morzycki, both sentences express that Carmen is tall, so that the surprising information is the degree in which Carmen owns this property. This author claims that the meaning of adverbs such as *sorprendentemente* is similar to the one of embedded exclamatives. Given this, Morzycki extends Zanuttini and Portner's analysis of exclamatives to adverbs such as *sorprendentemente*. Following these linguists, Morzycki assumes that exclamative sentences denote a set of propositions; for example, the exclamative sentence *What surprising things he eats!* has the denotation in (33):

(33) [[What surprising things he eats!]] = {*p*: *p* is true and there is a surprising thing x such that p is the proposition that he eats x}
(Morzycki, 2008, p. 110)

In consequence, when *sorprendente* 'surprising' embeds an exclamative clause, its semantics is the one in (34), where the adjective selects a set of propositions. This set contains a proposition that is surprising:

(34) $[[amazing]] = \lambda E_{<<s, t>, t>}, \exists\, p[E(p) \wedge amazing(p)]$
(Morzycki, 2008, p. 111)

Consequently, the denotation of a sentence like that in (35a), is the one illustrated schematically in (35b):

(35) a. It is amazing how tall Clyde is.

---

17. See Morzycki (2008) on the extension of his proposal to the meaning of these modifiers in other structural positions, as in *Surprisingly, John attended the meeting*.

b. ∃p[p∈{'Clyde is 6 feet 1 inch tall,' ... 'Clyde is 6 feet 2 inches tall,' ... 'Clyde is 6 feet 3 inches tall,' ... 'Clyde is 6 feet 4 inches tall.'} ∧ amazing(p)]
(Morzycki, 2008, p. 111)

The relevant property of this set of propositions is the degree of tallness; therefore, Morzycki replaces that set with a set of degrees, as illustrated in (36):

(36) amazing (^∃p[p∈ {'Clyde is 6 feet 2 inches tall,' ... 'Clyde is 6 feet 3 inches tall,' ... 'Clyde is 6 feet 4 inches tall.'} ∧ amazing(p)])
(Morzycki, 2008, p. 112)

As said above, Morzycki proposes that the denotation of adverbs such as *sorprendentemente* is parallel to the one of exclamatives (see [32]). According to Morzycki, (37b) illustrates the interpretation of (37a):

(37) a. Clyde is remarkably tall.
  b. remarkable (^ ∃d [d∈{6 feet 1 inch, ... 6 feet 2 inches, ... 6 feet 3 inches, ... 6 feet 4 inches} ∧ Clyde is d-tall]).
(Morzycki, 2008, p. 111)

However, this analysis does not capture one of the two properties that, following Zanuttini and Portner (2003), characterize exclamative sentences and, by extension, adverbs such as *sorprendentemente*; namely, the widening of a domain of quantification.[18] As recalled above, a domain of quantification is widened when the bound variable is out of the domain expected by the speaker. Thus, if the speaker expected that the tallness of Carmen is within the domain in (38a), the exclamative sentence widens the domain into (38b):

(38) a. D1: {1'60, 1'70, 1'80}.
  b. D2: {1'60, 1'70, 1'80, 1'90, 2}.

This implies that exclamatives (and, therefore, adverbs such as *sorprendentemente*), do not only convey that the degree in which the property holds is surprising, but they entail as well that this degree must be out of the

---

18. The other property of exclamatives is that they are factive (Zanuttini & Portner, 2003). I will not discuss whether adverbs such as *sorprendentemente* have this property.

domain of quantification expected by the speaker. In order to account for this property, Morzycki assumes that contextual domain restrictions (von Fintel, 1994; Westerstal, 1995; Martí, 2003) are included in the extended projection of adjectival phrases. Assuming this postulation, the denotation of a sentence like *Clyde is tall* contains a variable C, which restricts an existential quantifier over degrees on the scale of tallness:

(39) $[[\text{Clyde is tall}C]] = \exists d\ [d\ \epsilon C \wedge \text{tall (Clyde) } (d) \wedge d \geq \text{Stall}_n]$
(Morzycki, 2008, p. 113)

Bearing in mind this assumption, Morzycki reformulates his semantic analysis of modifiers such as *sorprendentemente* in order to capture their effect of domain widening. This author introduces two variables that restrict the domain of quantification: *C*, which refers to the expected domain, and *C*,' which refers to the widened domain and excludes the expected one:[19]

(40) $[[\text{Clyde is remarkably tall}_C]] = \text{remarkable } (\wedge\ \exists d \exists C'\ [C' \supset C \wedge d\ \epsilon C'\text{-}C \wedge \text{tall (Clyde)}(d) \wedge d \geq S_{\text{tall}}])$ (Morzycki, 2008, p. 114)

Morzycki's proposal basically reduces the semantics of adverbs such as *sorprendentemente* to that of exclamative sentences. These adverbs express that the subject of predication has a property to a degree out of the domain of quantification expected by the speaker. Modifiers such as *soprendentemente*, like exclamative wh-phrases, widen a domain of quantification. Given these assumptions, it is expected that modifiers such as *sorprendentemente* and exclamative wh-phrases are rejected in the same negative environments. The expectation is met. As shown in (41), *sorprendentemente* is incompatible with anti-morphic (see [41a]), anti-additive (see [41b]) and downward-entailing contexts (see [41c]):

(41) a. *Sus hijos no son sorprendentemente valientes.
 'His/Her children are not surprisingly courageous.'
 b. */??Conquistó a María sin ser sorprendentemente guapo.
 'He won Mary without being surprisingly handsome.'
 c. */??Los asesinos raramente están sorprendentemente locos.
 'Killers are rarely surprisingly crazy.'

---

19. Although this linguist does not reformulate the analysis of embedded exclamatives in the same way, these two variables should be also introduced in embedded exclamatives.

5. Conclusions

This chapter has compared exclamative wh-phrases to extreme degree modifiers such as *extremadamente* in negative environments. I have shown that, although both types of quantifiers are positive polarity items, they are sensitive to different contexts: whereas exclamative wh-phrases are incompatible with downward-entailing operators, modifiers such as *extremadamente* cannot co-occur with anti-morphic operators. Since the sensitivity of a positive polarity item depends on its denotation, that asymmetry provides new evidence that exclamative wh-phrases, unlike modifiers such as *extremadamente*, do not denote extreme degree. My proposal regarding the semantics of these elements is that *extremadamente* modifiers close an open scale and express the degree to which a property holds is the maximal value on the scale. As Zanuttini and Portner (2003) point out, exclamative wh-phrases widen a domain of quantification because they express that the scale in question has been extended far beyond the speaker's expectations. I have explained how this analysis is able to account for the sensitivity of exclamative wh-phrases and extreme degree modifiers.

Embedded Exclamatives and the Ingredients of Grounded Belief

Javier Gutiérrez-Rexach and Patricia Andueza

1. Exclamatives and Embedding

A great deal of recent research has focused on the structure and interpretation of Spanish exclamatives (for a relatively recent compilation, cf. Villalba, 2008a). Nevertheless, there has been less emphasis on analyzing the occurrence of exclamatives as embedded expressions and the restrictions associated with embedding such constructions. Theories about embedded exclamatives can be divided into two groups. For some scholars—most prominently Grimshaw (1979), Elliot (1974), Zanuttini and Portner (2003), and Gutiérrez-Rexach (2008)—only emotive predicates have the capability of embedding exclamative constructions. For example, the wh-expression *cuánto bebe* 'How much he drinks' is interpreted with exclamatory content when embedded by an emotive verb or as a question when embedded by a question-selecting verb such as *preguntarse* 'wonder.' Such an expression cannot be embedded by declarative-embedding verbs such as *creer* 'believe,' as shown in (1):

We would like to thank the audiences at the "41st Linguistic Symposium on Romance Languages" (University of Ottawa, May 2011), the "21st Colloquium on Generative Grammar" (Universitat Autònoma de Barcelona, March 2012), and the "AMPRA/Pragmatics of the Americas Conference" (University of North Carolina, Charlotte, October 2012) for observations and comments related to partial aspects of the content. We would also like to thank Ignacio Bosque for his very detailed comments on the final version of this chapter.

(1) a. Es increíble cuánto bebe.
'It is unbelievable how much he drinks.'
b. Me pregunto cuánto bebe.
'I wonder how much he drinks.'
c. *Creo cuánto bebe.
*'I believe how much he drinks.'

Advocates of the second theory—Lahiri (1991, 2002), D'Avis (2002), and Abels (2004)—claim that wh-clauses embedded by emotive predicates have to be treated as wh-interrogatives. The issue thus remains as to which elements are critical in order to determine or condition the possibility of embedding and how they relate to the basic properties of exclamative constructions. In this chapter, it will be argued that exclamative sentences not only express a specific type of speech act (with exclamatory force), but also involve *de re* reference in a process that we will be calling "grounding." Embedding is possible when properties related to this process, mostly related to semantic and pragmatic conditions, are satisfied. Thus, it is shown that several classes of verbs can actually embed exclamatives, most prominently factive emotive predicates. The embedding process can take place only if certain conditions are met. Some of these conditions are also satisfied by other verb classes, such as certain directive predicates, explaining the exclamatory flavor of a variety of related expressive constructions. Thus, from a grammatical point of view, it seems that what is required is the compatibility between certain features of the embedding verb and the embedded exclamative complement.

2. Exclamatives and the Grounding Process

Both traditional grammar approaches and formal analyses—from those emanating from the philosophical tradition developed after speech-act theory to current formal semantic/pragmatic approaches—have concluded that different sentence types can be established according to what has been labeled as *actitud del hablante* 'speaker's attitude' in traditional grammar, a criterion that is currently known as "sentential force" in philosophical and pragmatic terms. Sentence types can thus be classified not only according to standard grammatical or syntactic parameters, but also with respect to semantic and pragmatic criteria. For example, declarative sentences are semantically assumed to denote truth values and be used by speakers to express assertions about facts, beliefs, etc. Interrogative sentences denote questions—modeled, for example as sets of proposition, as in Karttunen (1977)—and are used to express requests; imperatives denote commands and are used to express orders or instructions. Finally, exclamatives denote "exclamations" and are used by conversation participants to express speaker-based attitudes, mostly with an emotive content, the one that brings about the relevant "exclamation." More specifically, when uttering an exclamative, a speaker expresses a contextually dependent motive attitude toward the content of his utterance. By uttering (2), the speaker is expressing an emotive attitude (e.g., surprise, amazement, elation) toward the fact that the gift is wonderful (to a point that exceeded his expectations if he had them regarding the object at issue):

(2) ¡Qué regalo tan maravilloso me dio por mi cumpleaños!
'What a wonderful present he gave me for my birthday!'

There are normally one or more linguistic clues that allow the addressee to figure out the relevant emotive content. With respect to (2), the presence of the adjective *maravilloso* indicates that there is an element of surprise and/or counterexpectation in the underlying speaker's attitude, something that is not necessarily the case with other examples, as pointed out by Bosque (chapter 1; cf. *¡Qué bonita mañana!* 'What a beautiful morning!'). Gutiérrez-Rexach (1996) claims that the logical representation of exclamative constructions has as its essential attribute the presence of a force operator, EXC—cf. also Grosz (2011) for an application of this idea to a wider variety of constructions. Semantically, the exclamative operator EXC introduces an emotive property P that holds (is true of) an agent (the speaker) and the proposition p expressed by the exclamative expression at the utterance world w if the speaker holds such an emotive property towards p at w. In formal terms, the following holds:

(3) EXC (a) (w) (p) iff $\exists P_{emot}[P(w)(a)(p)]$

Exclamative utterances satisfy all the prerequisites and conditions to be considered genuine speech acts. When uttering an exclamative expression a speaker expresses a very specific illocutionary attitude of an emotive nature and also makes certain commitments, which may be encoded as presuppositions. Consider (4):

(4) ¡Qué alto es Juan!
'How tall Juan is!'

A speaker would utter (4) felicitously in a situation s if and only if he has received new information or assessed all information leading him to an update of his beliefs. This update could thus be new information, if he did not know how tall Juan was, or a revision of his beliefs, if for instance he expected Juan to be shorter. It is the accommodation of this information in the common ground, and the associated updated belief state, that would serve as the proper context for uttering (4). More specifically, a speaker may utter (4) when he realizes that Juan is tall to a degree that exceeds a standard or his expectations about him. For instance, in a situation where the speaker's expectation is that Juan is 5'8" tall but he learns that in the actual world Juan is much taller than that, then he can felicitously utter (4) to express his surprise at this fact.

The belief state associated with the utterance of an exclamative sentence is a very specific type of belief: grounded belief. A belief is grounded when it is connected in a direct fashion to a fact about an individual in the common ground. For someone to believe that a fact is true he needs to have a *de re* belief about it. In order for this *de re* belief to be possible, a causal connection between the believer and the *de re* element is required as well: S knows p if and only if S believes p *de re* of some fact exemplifying p (cf. Kratzer, 1990). In a situation s where Juan is as tall as expected or less tall than expected, an exclamative such as (4) would express either: (1) a misleading, false proposition, (2) a rhetorical proposition,[1] or (3) a non-informative proposition. For scenarios (1) and (2) to hold, the speaker has to know the grounding fact, namely that Juan's height does not exceed standard expectations. He would then deliberately utter (4) to mislead the addressee, possibly with an ulterior purpose, or utter it rhetorically, with the goal of ironically conveying that Juan is short. Scenario (3) would hold if the speaker does not know the grounding fact. In such a case, uttering an exclamatory expression would be at least partially inconsistent with the necessary conditions for such an utterance, so performing such an utterance would be unwarranted. Consider an utterance of (4) in a situation in which Juan is not tall or even actually quite short but the speaker believes him to be tall. Such an utterance would be communicating false information to other participants, although not with a deliberate ulterior purpose necessarily. The speaker would be expressing an

---

1. Andueza and Gutiérrez-Rexach (2011) claim that rhetorical exclamatives differ from standard exclamatives in the fact that the speaker assumes not the truth of the utterance but of its negation. When a speaker utters (4) rhetorically, he knows that Juan's height has not exceeded his assumptions but pretends that it has. Therefore, the implied meaning of (4) is "How no-tall Juan is!"

emotive attitude toward a proposition that is actually not factual (not true in the world of utterance).

In all the scenarios described in the preceding paragraph, the exclamative utterance would be pragmatically infelicitous (or used rhetorically). In other words, an actual grounded belief is the trigger of the exclamative, but the speaker needs to have certain previous expectations, assumptions, or beliefs about the propositional content of the exclamative or other propositional content related to it, as well as some evidence about the actual grounding fact(s) for an exclamative utterance to be successful.

3. Subordination and Exclamative Content

Reference to degrees has been recently claimed to be essential to determine the content of certain exclamatives, especially those involving the use of wh-expressions (Castroviejo, 2006, 2008a; Rett, 2011). In such cases there are two degrees involved: (1) a reference degree obtained by applying a gradable property to an individual and (2) a standard degree taken from context. There is a scalar implicature associated with the exclamative sentence (Gutiérrez-Rexach, 2001; Zanuttini & Portner, 2000, 2003; Villalba, 2003). The implicature marks a high point in a contextually determined scale, triggering the high-degree reading that is so characteristic of sentences of this type.

(5) ¡Qué alumno tan inteligente es!
    'What a smart student he is!'

The standard level of intelligence (standard degree) is established in (5) by the speaker's expectations, and the relevant student's intelligence (reference degree) is located at a point higher than the standard one in the relevant scale of intelligence.

A speaker's commitments (presuppositions) when uttering an exclamative include having a grounded belief about the fact at issue, involving a degree property in many cases, and also having evidence that this fact is remarkable or unexpected with respect to his assumptions; such evidence would be the basis for the relevant emotive attitude. As was discussed above, if the belief is not properly grounded, the resulting utterance leads to a false, misleading, or non-informative utterance.

The speaker is the only individual who is able to assess *de re* the propositional content associated with the exclamative. In other words, if the exclamative is uttered in a conversational exchange context (a dialogue), the fact that the addressee might know the grounding fact would not constitute proper grounding for the utterance. The addressee would always assume that the speaker is expressing an emotive attitude about a fact, not that the speaker is anticipating the addressee's knowledge (or lack thereof) about it.

In this respect, exclamatives have been claimed to be factive constructions.[2] Kiparsky and Kiparsky (1970) characterize factivity as follows: "[a factive operator] presupposes that the embedded clause expresses a true proposition, and makes some assertion about the proposition." Elliot (1974) and Grimshaw (1979) isolate a class of predicates selecting exclamatives: emotives. These predicates express a subjective assessment about a proposition rather than mere knowledge about it or its truth value. Factive emotive predicates are emotive predicates presupposing the truth of their complements. For example, the following predicates are factive emotives: *es importante* 'it is important,' *es una locura* 'it is crazy,' *es raro* 'it is odd,' *es relevante* 'it is relevant,' *lamento* 'I regret,' *Me da rabia* 'I resent,' etc. There is wide agreement on the fact that exclamatives are factive (Elliot, 1974; Grimshaw, 1979; Zanuttini & Portner, 2003; Gutiérrez-Rexach, 1996). The essential ingredient of factivity is that the propositional content in the scope of the factive operator is presupposed. When uttering (6), the speaker presupposes that the relevant group has been assigned a (long) book:

(6) ¡Qué libro tan largo nos ha puesto como tarea!
'What a long book we have been assigned!'

Proposition-selecting factive emotive predicates presuppose their complement. For instance, both (7a) and (7b) entail sentence (7c):

(7) a. Es extraño que esté lloviendo.
'It is odd that it is raining.'
b. No es extraño que esté lloviendo.
'It is not odd that it is raining.'

---

2. Kiparsky and Kiparsky (1970) distinguish between factive and non-factive predicates. Factive predicates include "*significant, odd, tragic, exciting, relevant, matter, count, make sense, suffice, amuse, bother . . . regret, be aware (of), grasp, comprehend, take into consideration, take into account, bear in mind, ignore, make clear, mind, forget (about), deplore, resent, care (about),*" etc. Non-factive predicates include expressions such as "*likely, sure, possible, true, false, seems, appear, happen, chance, turn out . . . suppose, assert, allege, assume, claim, charge, maintain, believe, conclude, conjecture, intimate, deem, fancy, figure . . .*"

c. Está lloviendo.
'It is raining.'

Other predicates can be characterized as non-factive emotives: *temer* 'fear,' *desear* 'desire,' *querer* 'want,' *ser vital* 'it is vital,'etc. (Mindt, 2011). These cannot embed exclamatives. For example, *Temo que {estaba/estará} enfadado* 'I fear that he was/will be angry' does not presuppose *{Estaba/estará} enfadado* 'He was/will be angry.' Elliot (1974) and Grimshaw (1979) claim that complements of a particular semantic type are selected by predicates of the same type, a requirement that Grimshaw dubs "semantic selection" (s-selection), to contrast it with standard categorial or syntactic selection, also called subcategorization. Without entering here on the difficult issue of how to characterize semantic selection or whether such one-to-one correspondence is tenable in all cases, a proposal of this sort would explain why exclamatives are embedded only by factive emotive predicates and not by non-factive predicates such as *ignorar* 'not know,' *temer* 'fear,' *preguntar* 'ask,' or *preguntarse* 'wonder,' as the contrast between (8) and (9) illustrates.

(8) a. Es increíble lo alto que es Pepe.
'It is amazing how tall Pepe is.'
b. Me sorprende lo rápido que corre Pepe.
'I'm surprised at how fast Pepe can run.'

(9) a. *Temo qué loco está.
*'I fear what a fool he is.'
b. Paco se pregunta cómo de alto es Pepe.
'Fred is wondering how tall Pepe is.'

The embedded complement in (8a) is a genuine exclamative when in root contexts, namely when it occurs unembedded (*¡Lo alto que es Pepe!* 'How tall Pepe is!'). As such, it can be embedded by an emotive verb stating the relevant emotive attitude that the grounding fact actually triggers (amazement). The embedded complement in (9a) is also a genuine exclamative, an expression that can only be interpreted as having exclamatory force (*¡Qué loco está!* 'What a fool he is!') and not as any other type of wh-expression (interrogative). A non-factive predicate such as *temer* 'fear' cannot embed this sentential complement because doing so would conflict with the factivity presupposition of the embedded exclamative. Finally, the propositional complement in sentence (9b) only has the non-exclamatory meaning.

Zanuttini and Portner (2003) claim that exclamatives can be embedded by factive emotive predicates because they contain a covert factive morpheme (FACT) hosted in the specifier of the complementizer phrase (CP). This factive morpheme generates a pragmatic effect of "widening." They propose that exclamatives such as (10) have two domains of quantification:

(10) ¡Qué cosas tan extrañas come Luisa!
'What strange things Luisa eats!'

(11) D_1 = {eats (she, poblanos), eats (she, serranos),eats (she, jalapeños)}.
D_2 = {eats (she, poblanos), eats (she, serranos), eats (she, jalapeños), eats (she, gueros), eats (she, habaneros)}.

The first domain (D_1) would be the set of individuals denoted by the wh-clause in a standard situation; for example, mild hot peppers in the intended utterance situation corresponding to (10). The second domain (D_2) would be a larger domain containing not only the expected individuals, but also unusual ones; very hot peppers in (10). The presence of a factive operator makes the non-standard alternatives in this latter quantificational domain presupposed. In sum, the analyses proposed by Elliot (1974), Grimshaw (1979), and Zanuttini and Portner (2003) agree in considering factivity a property of both the predicate and the exclamative clause. Nevertheless, it still not clear how we can restrict the class of exclamative-selecting predicates to just emotive factives.

Gutiérrez-Rexach (1996, 2008) claims that factivity is one of the ingredients of the intensional exclamative operator on propositions (EXC) associated with exclamative sentences. Additionally, a contextually dependent emotive property is predicated on the relevant presupposed proposition. Emotive factives embed exclamatives because they encode the exclamative operator. Root exclamatives can be considered factive because of the presence of a null emotive predicate, associated with the presence of the exclamative operator at the sentential level in the level of representation of logical form (LF), as assumed in generative approaches to natural language syntax. Grosz (2011) proposes a variant of this operator-based theory.

Lahiri (1991, 2002) makes the interesting observation that wh-clauses embedded under predicates of surprise are not interpreted as exclamatives obligatorily. However, he only mentions those wh-clauses that cannot be matrix exclamatives, such as *quién vino a la fiesta* 'who came to the party' in (12):

(12) Es sorprendente quién vino a la fiesta.
'It is surprising who came to the party.'

D'Avis (2002) and Abels (2004) claim that the exclamative reading is the result of embedding a wh-interrogative clause under an exclamative/ surprise predicate. Different predicates relate to different aspects of the wh-complement. Consider (13):

(13) Me sorprende lo alto que es Pablo.
'It amazes me how tall Pablo is.'

The denotation of this sentence involves two answers ($answer_1$ and $answer_2$), as proposed in Heim (1994): (1) $answer_1$ is the set of worlds making the proposition *Pablo is d-tall* true, and (2) $answer_2$ is the set of worlds where the proposition corresponding to $answer_1$ relative to the wh-clause is the same as in the actual world. The agent of an utterance of (13) would know $answer_2$ (Pablo is *d*-tall) and most likely did not expect $answer_1$ (Pablo is *d*-tall).

To summarize the predictions of the different theories on the embedding issue, the picture is not uniform or clear cut and does not seem to make room for cross-linguistic variation. Grimshaw (1979) and Elliot (1974)'s proposals entail that embedding would be possible as long as semantic selection requirements are satisfied (the complement denotes/presupposes a fact). For Zanuttini and Portner (2003), embedding is associated with widening without any further qualifications. Finally, for Lahiri (1991, 2000, 2002), D'Avis (2002), and Abels (2004), embedding is related to the nature of the wh-complement, namely embedding is allowed as long as the wh-complement has $answer_1$ and $answer_2$ and the matrix predicate relates these two answers.

4. Types of Spanish Exclamatives

In the remainder of the chapter, a semantic analysis of the conditions allowing embedded exclamatives will be proposed. The literature on exclamatives has mostly focused on wh-exclamatives. Nevertheless, exclamatives are not uniform. There are several types of exclamatives in Spanish with important differences in their syntactic and semantic characteristics. We will briefly characterize these types in what follows: [3]

---

3. See Alonso-Cortés (1999b) and Bosque (this volume) for a more detailed description.

4.1. WH-EXCLAMATIVES

Exclamatives of this sort are introduced by certain wh-words, such as *qué* 'what', *cuánto* 'how many/much', and *cómo* 'how', but not *por qué* 'why', *para qué* 'what for', *dónde* 'where', or *cuándo* 'when'. The wh-phrase, which occurs in a displaced position in the left periphery of the sentence, can be headed by a noun phrase (14a), an adjectival phrase (14b), or an adverbial phrase (14c):

(14) a. ¡Qué cosas dice Juan!
    'The things that Juan says!'
 b. ¡Qué divertido es Juan!
    'How funny Juan is!'
 c. ¡Qué bien habla Juan!
    'What a good speaker Juan is!'

As was mentioned above, there are two degrees involved in wh-exclamatives: (1) a reference degree obtained by applying a gradable property to an individual and (2) a standard degree taken from context. The availability of such degrees is direct or argumental in adjectives, such as *divertido* 'funny' in (14b), where *divertido* denotes a relation between individuals and degrees (x is funny to degree d). On the other hand, degree availability is indirect with nouns, such as *qué cosas* in (14a). Only certain nouns allow the availability of a related degree property. In (14a) such degree might be related to the property of being outlandish or inappropriate (statements are outlandish/inappropriate to degree d).

The scalar implicature associated with the exclamative sentence indicates a high point in a contextually determined scale, triggering the high-degree reading. Consider (15):

(15) ¡Qué inteligente es Juan!
    'How intelligent Juan is!'

In (15) the standard level of intelligence (standard degree) is established by the speaker's assumptions/beliefs (Gutiérrez-Rexach, 1996), and Juan's intelligence (reference degree) is located in a point higher than the standard one in the relevant height scale. The standard level of intelligence (standard degree) is established by the speaker's expectations, and Juan's intelligence (reference degree) is located in a point higher than the standard one in the relevant scale of intelligence.

4.2. DEFINITE AND FREE-RELATIVE EXCLAMATIVES

Free-relative exclamatives or relatives introduced by definite determiners may have exclamatory force with a degree reading when occurring as root elements:

(16) a. ¡Lo alto que es tu hermano!
'How tall your brother is!'
b. ¡Las cervezas que bebe!
'The number of beers s/he drinks!'

In the case of (16a), the adjective displaced to the left periphery of the sentence is in a focus position pied-piped by the neuter determiner. In (16b) noun displacement is triggered by the definite determiner (Gutiérrez-Rexach, 2001).

4.3. EVIDENTIAL EXCLAMATIVES

There are exclamatives introduced by evidential adjectives whose reading is clearly propositional. In (17a) and (17b) the relevant alternatives are not based on degrees or kinds, but on propositions (cf. Andueza & Gutiérrez-Rexach, 2011):

(17) a. ¡Claro que te lo voy a dar!
'Of course, I will give it to you!'
b. ¡Evidentemente que te voy a devolver el libro!
'Evidently, I will give the book back to you!'

When uttering (17b), a speaker asserts that it is evident that he is going to give the relevant object to the addressee, and he also expresses a contextually determined emotive attitude toward that assertion. For instance, this sentence can be uttered in a situation in which the addressee has expressed his doubts about getting a book back and, by uttering this exclamative, the speaker expresses his surprise or resentment toward the fact that the addressee does not trust him.

4.4. DECLARATIVE SENTENCES

Gutiérrez-Rexach (1996) claims that the following declarative sentences can be considered genuine exclamative expressions from a prosodic and illocutionary point of view:

(18) a. ¡Juan se lo ha comido todo!
'Juan ate everything!'
b. ¡Juan es muy divertido!
'Juan is so funny!'

They exhibit the characteristic intonational contour of these types of sentences and, when uttering them, a speaker expresses an emotive attitude toward the content of his utterance. In the case of (18a) the relevant attitude is directed toward the fact that Juan has eaten everything; (18b) is interpreted as "Juan is an instance of the kind of funny man I am referring to."

The content of exclamatives is thus not only about degrees, but also about propositions. We claim that these four structural types of exclamatives can be merged into two different semantic groups (Andueza & Gutiérrez-Rexach, 2011): (1) exclamatives whose content is a degree property, such as wh-exclamatives or free-relative exclamatives, and (2) exclamatives whose content is propositional, such as exclamatives with a declarative structure and exclamatives introduced by an evidential expression. Following Rett (2009), it can be assumed that these two groups of exclamatives have different requirements. The exclamatives in the first group are expressively correct when their content is about a degree that exceeds the speaker's assumptions/beliefs. The content of the exclamatives in the second group must be about a fact that contradicts the speaker's assumptions/beliefs.

5. *De Re* Ascription and Spanish Exclamatives: A Survey

A problem for contemporary theories of embedding is that predicates do not seem to embed exclamatives uniformly. In other words, not all emotives can do it and, furthermore, not all emotive predicates are able to embed exclamative expressions. Andueza and Gutiérrez-Rexach (2012a, 2012b), analyzing Spanish exclamative constructions, report that there are significant embedding asymmetries with wh-complements in Spanish, as illustrated in the following examples.

(19) a. {Es increíble/Me sorprende} cómo se viste Pepe.
'{It is incredible/It amazes me} how well Pepe dresses.'
b. Es {increíble/sorprendente} cuánto habla Pepe.
'It is {incredible/amazing} how much Pepe talks.'

    c. *{Me sorprende/Es increíble} qué historias cuenta Juan.
    '{It surprises me/It is incredible} what stories Juan tells.'
    d. *Es increíble quiénes vinieron.
    'It is incredible who came.'
    e. *Es {sorprendente/increíble} qué listo es Juan.
    *'{It surprises me/It is incredible} how smart Juan is.'
    f. *Es increíble qué bien cuenta las historias Juan.
    *'It is incredible who well Juan tells his stories.'

The problem seems to be that factive emotive predicates are able to embed wh-exclamatives but not uniformly. The claim that will be defended in this chapter is that exclamatives can be embedded by emotive predicates only if they can be grounded to a fact about a specific entity (degree). Two semantic conditions have to be satisfied: (1) the complement of the predicate involves reference to a specific degree, and (2) the relationship between the predicate and its complement has to be an expression of *de re knowledge*.

A test survey was conducted among a population of native Spanish speakers from Spain (Andueza & Gutiérrez-Rexach, 2012a). A group of thirty individuals from northern Spain was selected, all belonging to the same age cohort (35–38 years old) and with similar educational backgrounds (all having a university degree). The survey was conducted during three days using standard testing measures to minimize data bias and errors (order randomization, insertion of fillers, etc.).[4] The most accepted embedded wh-exclamatives in the survey are those headed by *cómo* 'how'(20/30) and *cuánto* 'how many' (27/30):

(20) Es increíble{cómo/cuánto} habla Pepe.
    'It is incredible how much Pepe talks.'

---

    4. The group consisted of 20 males and 10 females. The main goal of the study was to investigate a native speaker's acceptability of the embeddability of different types of exclamatives (wh-constructions, free relatives, etc.) by emotive predicates. Since one of the main proposals of the embedding problem is that interrogatives and exclamatives behave alike in this respect, it seemed desirable to test whether native speakers would accept any type of wh-constructions as complements of emotive predicates even if such constructions do not constitute proper root exclamatives. The participants were presented with a total of 30 short contexts, each one of which was followed by three possible sentences that could be deemed grammatical (or not) in the context provided. Participants were instructed to read carefully the contexts and choose sentences according to grammaticality criteria (perform a grammaticality judgment task). In addition to the experimental items, 10 filler items were included to avoid certain participant bias. Five of the filler items were embedded interrogatives, and five were embedded declaratives.

In the case of *cómo* 'how' and *cuánto* 'how much,' the specific-degree property clearly comes from the wh-word, since these are both degree words. Wh-forms of this sort behave as degree words not only in exclamatives, but also in interrogative sentences:

(21) ¿Cómo es de alto Juan?/¿Cuánto mide Pepe?
'How tall is Juan?' ('What is the degree *d* . . . ?')

Notice that *cómo* is not interpreted as a manner adverbial under this construction:

(22) a. Es increíble cómo {habla/come} este tío.
'It is incredible how much this guy {talks/eats}.' (Not the manner in which he does it.)
b. Me sorprende cómo se viste.
'It is incredible how {bad/well} he dresses.' (Not the manner in which he does it.)

As the above paraphrases show, the proper interpretation of the above sentences is not one in which *cómo* is associated with a manner reading. When uttering (22a), a speaker is not surprised at how the individual under consideration eats. Rather, he is surprised at a degree property: the amount he eats (which exceeds a standard or threshold). The degree interpretation is preferred because it immediately makes a degree available, whereas such is not the case for the manner reading, except for certain contexts. For example, uttering (22b) in a situation in which a boy is trying to put his pants on over his head would be associated with a degree based on a manner interpretation (the oddness of dressing oneself in such a fashion). Evidence for *de re* knowledge ascription comes from the fact that exclamatives such as (23) would be infelicitous in a situation in which the speaker lacks knowledge about the degree under consideration:

(23) ¡{Cómo/cuánto} habla Pepe!
'How much Pepe talks!'

Much lower grammaticality rates are attested in our survey for the following wh-expressions: *qué* 'what' + adv, *qué* 'what' + noun, *qué* 'what' + adj, and "what for." These are judged as ungrammatical by most speakers (90%):

(24) a. *Es increíble qué páginas tiene este libro.
'It is incredible what pages this book has.'
b. *Es increíble qué agua sale del grifo.
'It is incredible what water comes out of the faucet.'

Some instances improve when there is an obvious degree reading potentially derived from a contextually dependent degree variable in the wh-phrase:

(25) a. ??Es increíble qué listo es Pepe.
'It is incredible how smart Pepe is.'
b. ??Es increíble qué bien dibuja Pepe.
'It is incredible how well Pepe draws.'
c. ??Es increíble qué libros lee Pepe.
'It is incredible which books Pepe reads.'

Certain speakers find complements introduced by *para qué, dónde, por qué*, or *cuándo* to be fine when embedded by emotive predicates, although they do not constitute root exclamatives:

(26) a. *¡{Para qué/dónde/por qué/cuándo} trabaja Pepe!
'For {what/where/why/when} Pepe works!'
b. Es increíble {dónde/cuándo} trabaja Pepe. [Ok for many speakers.]
'It is incredible {where/when} Pepe works.'
c. ??Es increíble {por qué/para qué} te pones ese gorro.
'It is incredible why you wear that hat.'
d. Es inaudito con qué desparpajo le robó el bolso.
'It is amazing how bold he was when he stole her purse.'

The wh-words *dónde* 'where' and *cuándo* 'when' introduce measure-based denotations (time, location) facilitating the association with an (extreme) degree: "It is incredible how remote the place where Pepe works is," "It is incredible how late Pepe works." Such accommodation is more difficult with rationale/goal clauses, although not impossible: "It is incredible that you wear that hat for such outlandish reasons." Ignacio Bosque (personal communication) points out that wh-words introduced by a preposition occur quite naturally in certain embedded exclamatives, as in (26d). In these cases, the preposition brings about the required association with a measure (degrees of boldness in the example), something that would not be available if the wh-word occurred as a non-prepositional argument.[5]

These deviant results would be the result of an inappropriate embedding not meeting the two necessary semantic requirements for embedding that we have postulated so far. In other words, the reason why many *qué*-exclamatives cannot be embedded is that the two conditions for embedding described above are not met in general: (1) *qué* is not intrinsically a degree word, i.e., the quantificational domain of *qué*-words is a universe of individuals, and (2) *qué*-words do not presuppose *de re* attitude attribution. Matrix *qué*-exclamatives receive their degree reading from the exclamative illocutionary operator. When an exclamative is embedded, this operator is not available. Only when such an operator is contextually available, through an accommodation or similar inferential process, does embedding become possible.

Castroviejo (2006, 2008a) claims that wh-exclamatives in Catalan cannot be embedded by emotive factive predicates in general, with some minor exceptions (27c):

(27) a. ?Es increíble que alt que ets.
'It's amazing how tall you are.'
b. *No em puc creure quina feina tan meravellosa que heu fet a Nepal.
'I can't believe what a wonderful job you did in Nepal.'
c. Es increíble como ets d'alt.
'It is incredible how tall you are.'

From this evidence, we can conclude that exclamative expression in Catalan is a root phenomenon. Emotive factives do not embed wh-elements, and the ability to embed exclamatives or to embed expressions of one type or other is not a universal phenomenon, as the contrasting behavior in Spanish clearly shows.

---

5. Here are two examples in which *qué* is the term of a preposition and the resulting construction is grammatical when embedded by an emotive factive verb:

(i) a. Es inaudito con qué chulería campan a sus anchas esos facinerosos.
'It is incredible the cocky fashion in which those criminals walk around.'
b. Es una vergüenza con qué facilidad la administración hace uso del dinero de los contribuyentes.
'It is a shame how the government uses the taxpayers' money.'

6. Non-Sentential Exclamatives in Embedded Contexts

Exclamative constructions belonging to other structural types, fundamentally of a non-sentential nature, can be argued to be subject to similar restrictions as sentential ones if they undergo embedding. Nominal exclamatives will be considered first in this section. Nominal exclamatives are expressions of a nominal nature with the ability to occur as root exclamatives (Portner & Zanuttini, 2005). For example, the nominal exclamatives in (28a) can be embedded, as shown in (28b, 28c):

(28) a. ¡La de libros que lee Juan!/¡Los libros que lee Juan!
   'Juan reads so many books!'
   b. Es increíble la de libros que lee Juan.
   'It is incredible the amount of books Juan reads.'
   c. ?Es increíble los libros que lee Juan.
   'It's incredible the books Juan reads.'

There is proper degree reference in (28b), given that the non-embedded correlate only has a degree or amount-based reading. An emotive attitude is expressed toward the amount (number) of books read by Juan. On the other hand, in (28c) and in its matrix correlate, there would only be accommodated degree reference. When such a reference is necessary, it is accommodated to prevent a conflict or clash of presuppositions. This is so because free relatives have individual-based denotations, namely, they can be viewed as definite descriptions in disguise (Jacobson, 1995). Consider the following contrast:

(29) a. ?Es increíble   lo   que dices.
      It's incredible lo-NEUTER that you-say
      'It's incredible the things you say.'
   b. Me   sorprende lo   que cuentas.
      Me-CL surprises lo-NEUTER that you-tell
      'It surprises me the things you say.'
   c. Averiguó   lo   que cuentas de   él.
      He-found-out lo-NEUTER that you-tell about him
      'He found out what you say about him.'

Sentence (29a) is slightly marginal because reference to a degree has to be accommodated from reference to individual propositions (the set of statements under consideration). What is stated to be incredible is not what the addressee is talking about (statements are not gradable entities), but the outrageous or transgressive nature of its content. This aspect would trigger the contextually appropriate emotive attitude of incredulity. When such emotive attitude characterizes the belief state of a speaker, the required degree ascription becomes rooted to the speaker's assessment of a grounding fact. On the other hand, embedding under a standard question/statement subordinating verb, such as *averiguar* 'find out' in (29c), requires no accommodation because such verbs do not impose a degree requirement. The embedded complement is not an exclamative.

Embedded complements of factive emotives are normally degree relatives, instantiating the structure "*lo* + ADJ + sentential expression," such as the one in (30a), with embedded counterparts as in the ones in (30b, 30c):

(30) a. ¡Lo   listo que es Juan!
         lo-NEUTER clever that is Juan
         'How clever Juan is!'
     b. Es increible lo   listo   que es Juan.
         it's incredible lo-NEUTER clever that is Juan
         'It is incredible how clever Juan is.'
     c. Es increíble lo   bien que trabaja Juan.
         It's incredible lo-NEUTER well that works Juan
         'It is incredible how well Juan works.'

The neuter *lo* is a neuter degree pronoun in (30a). In general, neuter degree relatives refer to a (maximal) degree (Gutiérrez-Rexach, 1999). This degree would be the maximal degree of cleverness/intelligence that Juan is capable of in example (30a). Thus, proper grounded reference can be established in these constructions and embedding by emotive predicates is allowed, as further illustrated by (30b, 30c).

Concealed exclamatives are DPs without intrinsic exclamative interpretation. They only have it when embedded (Baker, 1968; Elliott, 1974; Grimshaw, 1979; Castroviejo, 2006), as the following examples show. The DP in (31a) lacks an intrinsic exclamatory structure, but can be embedded by an emotive predicate and then have an exclamatory reading (31b).

(31) a. la altura de ese edificio.
         'the height of the building.'

b. Es alucinante la altura del edificio.
'It is incredible the height of the building.'

What makes the embedded DP a concealed exclamative is that the emotive predicate relates the emotive attitude to a high degree proposition associated with the content of the relevant DP. In (31b) what is incredible is the (extreme) degree of height of the building under consideration. The relevant degree is associated to the head noun *altura* in (31b), but it can also be a high degree associated with a contextually accommodated property associated with the noun. Such a property would be associated with the individual's behavior in in (32b):

(32) a. su conducta.
   'his behavior.'
   b. Es increíble su conducta.
   'It is incredible her behavior.'

Concealed exclamatives satisfy the definiteness restriction, i.e., only weak or indefinite-like determiners can occur in the construction:[6]

(33) Es increíble {*una/esa} ventana del edificio.
   'It is incredible {*a/that} window of the building.'

They all associate with extreme degree and require restrictive modification, indicating the proper contextual environment for the degree assertion. The following examples would be ungrammatical if the restrictive elements between parentheses were omitted:

(34) a. Es increíble los propósitos (tan extraños) (por los que trabaja Juan).
   'It is incredible the (strange) purposes Juan works for.'
   b. Es increíble los sitios (tan extravagantes) (en los que trabaja Juan).
   'It is incredible the (extravagant) places where Juan works.'

---

6. As pointed out by I. Bosque (personal communication), this property extends to a wide variety of matrix wh-exclamatives:

(i) ¡Qué alto es {el/*un} niño!
   'How tall {the/*a} boy is!'

The use of the indefinite would go against *de re* reference to a fact/degree.

Portner and Zanuttini (2005) claim that concealed exclamatives have clause-like meaning, following Kayne's (1994) analysis of relative clauses. According to this account, the definite article indicates factivity. There are potential connections with propositional theories of concealed questions (Nathan, 2006; Frana, 2010), namely, a concealed exclamative can be argued to denote a proposition, making it equivalent to a full-fledged exclamative. Their "exclamative flavor" has also been claimed to be derived from the meaning of the embedding predicate (Castroviejo, 2006). All of these factors would explain their embedding by emotive predicates.

Summarizing, the interplay of structural and contextual factors would explain variability in the possibility of embedding an exclamative construction or in achieving an exclamative interpretation under a verb that normally embeds such a construction (i.e., standard factive emotive predicates). First, the embedded exclamative has to directly express or accommodate a reference to a specific degree. Additionally, a process of ascription of *de re* belief to such a degree via the embedding predicate has to take place. The extension to other measure-based denotations (time, location, etc.) is possible, as long as there is accommodation of a degree-based grounding fact. Finally, other non-standard or non-propositional exclamative constructions, such as free relatives/nominal/concealed exclamatives, are fine for an embedding process as long as thesegeneral conditions are satisfied.

7. Operator Interaction

Embedding by emotive factives is facilitated by the occurrence of certain sentential operators, but the exclamatory interpretation is canceled. For example, the addition of genericity triggers blocks such interpretation. In (35), the adverb of quantification *siempre* 'always' or the verb *soler* 'use to' cancel the exclamatory meaning:

(35) a. ?Es increíble quién tiene que ocuparse siempre de todo en esta casa.
'It is incredible who has to take care of everything in this household.'
b. Le suele parecer {lamentable/increíble/sorprendente} qué alto ponen el volumen en la discoteca.
'He usually finds {appalling/incredible/surprising} how loud the music is at the disco.'

Generic statements express generalizations over worlds or individuals and have been analyzed as involving reference to kinds (Carlson, 1977). Generic quantification is incompatible with *de re* reference to actual individuals in the utterance world. If the line of reasoning we are advocating here is correct, this would entail that beliefs about kinds (i.e., generic beliefs) would not necessarily be factually grounded beliefs about the utterance situation/world and would not support exclamatory interpretations. This correctly predicts the readings available for the examples in (35).

Such sentences are reports of expressive attitudes toward a given (generic) proposition, but they do not report exclamatory content (an emotive attitude by a given *de re* fact in the utterance situation). It is worth noticing that although imperfective tenses are inductors of genericity, tense specification is not sufficient to turn the examples in (19) above and similar ones into grammatical sentences. There seems to be a requirement for an explicit adverbial (*siempre*) or verbal (*soler*) inductor.

Several other sentential operators are also able to block an exclamative interpretation. In general, it is not possible to embed exclamatives in questions or under negation. In the following examples it can clearly be seen that the wh-proposition lacks an exclamative interpretation:

(36) a. ¿No te sorprende qué cosas suele hacer?
    'Aren't you surprised by the things he does?'
  b. No me sorprende lo que puede hacer.
    'It does not surprise me what he does.'

The embedding predicate relates to the question-answer meaning, i.e., to the set of individuals under consideration, not to a salient degree property of such individuals. Sentence (36a) expresses the speaker's usual surprise at the content of the addressee's assertions. Questions and negation also block attribution of *de re* knowledge and facilitate answer-like interpretations. When embedding occurs in the scope of an interrogative or negative operator, exhaustive (mention all) readings and non-exhaustive readings (mention some) are allowed. For example, (36b) may be asking for an exhaustive list of the things the individual under discussion does (mention all) or for one or more instances illustrative of a pattern (mention some). These are typical readings associated with interrogative sentences (Groenedijk & Stokhof, 1989), and thus indicate clear departure from an exclamative interpretation. If one is asking about a particular individual or proposition, he cannot have factual knowledge about the same information, which would be incompatible with this type of speech act. Thus, the content of the embedded sentences in (36) is closer to a question than to an exclamative: it relates to the individuals satisfying the relevant set expression and does not involve an emotive attitude about a *de re* entity.

Finally, as pointed out by Bosque (personal communication), degree adverbs with lower reference points or thresholds seem to cancel or interfere with the high degree requirement associated with the emotive predicate, as in *Me sorprende (*muy poco) a qué extremos hemos llegado* 'It is (*very little) surprising to me the extent to which we have taken things.' Facts of this sort, as well as the ones considered in this section, highlight the need for considering the embedding problem as a compositional one, not just as a mere lexical-selection issue.

8. Beyond Emotives

The evidence presented so far indicates that exclamative expressions are only embedded by emotive factive predicates. This is not completely correct from an empirical perspective. Several non-emotive and non-factive predicates are able to embed genuine exclamative expressions. One of the most common predicates used for this purpose is *mira* 'look':

(37) a. ¡Miren ustedes qué cosas dice!
'Look at the things he says!'
b. ¡Mirad quiénes se presentaron!
'Look who showed up!'

This construction is actually very common, especially in colloquial discourses, as attested by the following corpus examples:

(38) a. ¡Mira qué guapísimo es! (*El corpus del español*)
'Look at how handsome he is!'
b. ¡Mira qué bien viene la pregunta! (*CREA*)
'Look at how appropriate the question is!'
c. ¡Mira qué perrillo! (*CREA*)
'Look at that (nice) doggie!'
d. ¡Mira cuántas chinitas hay! (*CREA*)
'Look at how many pebbles there are!'
e. ¡Mira cuánto has hablado! (*El corpus del español*)
'Look at how much you talked!'

 f. Pero, ¡mira cómo beben! (*El corpus del español*)
  'Look at how they are drinking!'
 g. ¡Y mira dónde estoy ahora! (*El corpus del español*)
  'Look at where I am now!'
 h. ¡Mira dónde estás y con quién hablas! (*El corpus . . .*)
  'Look where you are and who you talk to!'

Mira 'look' is a directive perception verb. It instructs the addressee to pay attention to a fact. There are other directive perception verbs allowing exclamative embedding, such as *fíjate/fijaos* (also *fijaros*) 'pay attention':

(39) a. ¡Fíjate qué locuras dice!
   'Watch out for her nonsense!'
  b. ¡Fija(r)os cuántos han venido!
   'Look at how many came!'
  c. ¡Fija(r)os qué alto está!
   'Look at how tall he is!'
  d. ¡Fíjate dónde ha puesto la ropa!
   'Look at where he put his clothes!'

Nevertheless, other directive perception verbs (*oír* 'hear,' *escuchar* 'listen,' and *atender* 'pay attention') cannot embed exclamative expressions. In some cases, they are not able to embed wh-complements in general. The intended construction would be ungrammatical even in a non-exclamatory interpretation, as the following examples illustrate:

(40) a. *¡Oye qué locuras dice!
   'Hear her nonsensical statements!'
  b. *¡Escucha qué alto está!
   'Listen at how tall he is!'
  c. *¡Atended dónde lo he visto!
   'Pay attention to where I have seen him!'

There are several restrictions on the availability of exclamative readings under directive perception verbs. First, only true imperative forms are accepted.[7] Suppletive imperative forms, such as the first-person plural pres-

---

  7. The distinction between true and suppletive surrogative imperatives is well established in the literature (Joseph & Philippaki Warburton, 1987; Rivero & Terzi, 1995). Morphologically

ent or matrix sentences headed by the complementizer *que*, do not allow embedded exclamatives, even if they would convey a meaning that would be very close to a genuine exclamative. This point is illustrated by the examples below:

(41) a. *¡Miremos qué guapísimo está!
    'Let us look at how very handsome he is!'
   b. *¡Vamos a mirar qué alto está!
    'We are going to look at how tall he is!'
   c. *¡Que miren qué cosas dice!
    'You look at the things he says!'

Second, changes in tense specification or the addition of sentential operators such as negation make embedding possible, but only with an interrogative interpretation, not with an exclamative one, as (42) shows.

(42) a. Miraré cómo beben.
    'I will look at how they drink.'
   b. (No) Me fijé *(en) cuántos han venido.
    'I did not pay attention to how many came.'

The data in Andueza and Gutiérrez-Rexach (2012a) corroborate this point. The verbs *mira* 'look' or *fíjate* 'watch out' are found to embed exclamatives more frequently (84%) than standard embedders (such as *es increíble* 'it is incredible'). These verbs were also judged by speakers in the survey to be more appropriate than emotives to express unambiguous exclamatory content (76%). It is significant to notice that *qué*-exclamatives are allowed as complements of these directive predicates, whereas they were only marginal when embedded under emotive factives. Wh-complements headed by *qué* are even more frequent (55.4%) than those headed by *cómo* (19.6%) and *cuánto* (11.3%), also in contrast to the data resulting from embedding by emotive factives. Other wh-exclamatives are also possible, although less common.

We will be calling the subclass of perception verbs with the ability to embed wh-exclamatives directive mirative factives (DMFs), with *mira/fíjate*

---

true imperatives belong to a distinct verbal paradigm and have imperative force exclusively. On the other hand, suppletive imperatives belong to a morphological paradigm (subjunctives, indicatives, infinitives) and have a variety of additional pragmatic uses.

as the canonical members of this class. Let us explain why. First, they have the property of factivity, as illustrated in (43):

(43) a. *¡Mira qué cosas dirá!
    *'Look at the things he will say!'
 b. *¡Mira qué me parece que dijo!
    *'Look what seems that he said!'

The ungrammaticality of the sentences above can be attributed to the fact that statements about future events are intrinsically not factive, since such events have not occurred yet. Another property of DMFs is that they are lexically mirative. Mirativity conveys information that is new or unexpected to the speaker (De Lancey, 2001; Rigau, 2003), as illustrated in (44):

(44) a. Me dio el libro y mira qué tapas tiene.
    'He gave me the book and look at its cover!'
 b. #Me dio el libro y mira qué ejemplar es.
    'He gave me the book and look what copy it is!'

The second conjunct in (44a) adds new or unexpected information triggering the speaker's attitude of surprise (the book's cover looks unusual or surprising). On the other hand, the information in the second conjunct in (44b) is analytic or redundant, so it cannot be embedded under *mira*. Additionally, exclamative constructions with DMFs instantiate actual directivity, i.e., an instruction to perform a cognitive action, such as paying attention, in the utterance situation. The addressee is instructed to consider something in the actual world/time (utterance time or world of evaluation). It is not possible to use expressions of this type to ask the addressee to consider facts or propositions in a near or distant future, for example.

Let us now characterize DMFs in a formal fashion. We say that a proposition *p* can be embedded by a DMF predicate if and only if the speaker has *de re* knowledge about the fact supporting *p* in the actual world and is instructing the speaker to consider *p*. When exclamatives are embedded by these predicates, the speaker calls the addressee's attention to a specific *de re* proposition. The speaker asks the addressee to ascertain a fact about the specific *de re* element triggering the exclamative. Interestingly, there is no degree requirement on the entity referred to. Such an entity (*de re*) may be an individual. Consider (45):

(45) ¡Mira quién habla!
'Look who is talking!'

This sentence does not express an emotive attitude toward the degree to which a property holds. Rather, the speaker is instructing the addressee to consider a contextually relevant proposition about a salient individual. The individual referred to (*de re*) is not the one that the speaker expected to be talking, and this triggers the utterance. If this reasoning is correct, it points out the need to consider *mira* as a genuine and fully operational DMF operator, not as a mere interjection (RAE-ASALE, 2009; Rodríguez Ramalle, 2008c).

9. Embedding Non-Wh-CPs and Mixed Exclamatives

In the preceding sections, we have considered emotives and their ability to embed wh-expressions denoting exclamatives. Nevertheless, emotive predicates also embed non-wh-propositional complements, as (46) shows:

(46) ¡Es increíble que tenga esa pinta!
'It is incredible that he looks that bad!'

The expressive content of (46) is also exclamatory in nature and the embedding predicate plays a critical role in triggering it. The speaker expresses an emotive attitude (incredulity) toward the embedded proposition. It is thus completely natural for emotive predicates to embed declarative propositional complements. DMFs also embed non-wh-propositions. The expressive content is not necessarily exclamative, i.e., expressing surprise, amazement, etc. In the following examples, it can be seen that DMFs are associated with expressive contents of a somewhat diverse nature, indicated between parentheses in the following examples:

(47) a. ¡Mira que tiene gracia la cosa! [exclamative: anger/regret]
   'Look, that's not amusing at all!'
   b. ¡Mira que te tengo dicho que comas más! [exhortative/optative]
   'Look, I've repeatedly told you that you should eat more!'
   c. ¡Mira que me voy! [warning]
   'Look, I'm leaving!'

d. ¡Mira que te pego! [threat]
'Look, I'm about to hit you!'

Other defective verbal forms that have traditionally been considered interjections (*vaya, anda, venga*) embed propositional complements too. They also have a mixed or more flexible expressive content. In other words, they are used to express exclamatory content plus other content of an expressive nature, or just this separate expressive content. Consider the following examples in which exclamative content related to "surprise" is associated with other expressive elements, such as defiance, refutation, etc.:

(48) a. ¡Vaya {que/sí} se ha comido la sopa! [excl. + incredulity]
'He ate the soup!'
b. ¡Vaya {que/sí} me voy a ir! [excl.+ defiance/threat]
'Of course, I am leaving!'

(49) ¡Anda que no tienesdinero! [excl. + refutative]
'So you didn't have any money!'

(50) ¡Venga con que no quieres salir! [excl. + emphatic]
'Come on, so you don't want to leave?'

A sentence such as (48a) would normally be uttered to convey incredulity: the speaker expected the relevant individual to not like the soup or not eat it, when in fact he has eaten it. Similarly, sentence (48b) could be uttered to express defiance or a threat: the speaker would be asserting that he is leaving no matter what. By uttering (49), a speaker would normally refute a previous claim by the addressee stating his rather impoverished financial situation or a similar claim. Sentence (50) would be felicitous, for example, as a reply to a statement by the addressee indicating that he does not want to go out. Mixed exclamatives of this sort have several properties of interest for our purposes. There is no factivity requirement and no *de re* knowledge requirement with respect to an entity (degree/individual). In other words, it is possible to have an exclamative interpretation without the satisfaction of these requirements. For example, (48b) expresses a plan defying some previous restriction, norm, or order. The added emotive exclamatory content may be triggered by contextual factors; for instance, if someone has just expressed opposition to such a plan, etc. The exclamative content is introduced by the embedding verb, encoding the exclamative operator. The speaker expresses a mixed expressive attitude toward a proposition at the utterance time, introducing what we might call an actuality requirement.

Other mixed exclamative expressions include embedders not of a verbal nature. They are adverbial embedders from a categorical perspective (Gutiérrez-Rexach, 2001), such as *bien* and *por supuesto* in (51):

(51) a. ¡Bien que te fastidia esto!
   'You are really bothered by this!'
 b. ¡Por supuesto que te lo daré!
   'Of course I will give it to you!'

It is interesting to compare this occurrence of exclamative embedding *bien* with emphatic *bien* (Hernanz, 1999, 2011). The latter is illustrated in (52):

(52) ¡Bien habló el decano ayer!
   'Yesterday's speech by the Dean was great!'

In this sentence the emphatic element *bien* is not just related to exclamative content but also to the event characterized in the proposition. It would be uttered felicitously when the speaker is conveying that the Dean talked a lot or more than expected. In this respect, this instance of *bien* is not an "embedder." It is just an occurrence of an exclamative marker displaced to the left periphery (Gutiérrez-Rexach, 2001).

Optional adverbials also work as indicators of differential mixed expressive content, mostly exclamatory plus optative, desiderative or exhortative as respectively illustrated in (53a), (53b), and (53c). There are also non-adverbial evidentiality markers, such as *¡Cuidado/ojo/claro que* ... *!*

(53) a. ¡(Por favor) que no vuelva!
   'Please, I wish he didn't come back!'
 b. ¡(Dios mío) que me quede como estoy!
   'God, I wish I could stay as I am!'
 c. ¡(Ojalá) que llegue pronto!
   'I hope he is here soon!'

These ideas, although still tentative, provide us with a good roadmap for tackling the difficult issue of how to characterize the content of what can be called mixed expressives. These expressive elements can be claimed to introduce expressive operators, in the same fashion as genuine or non-mixed exclamatives do. This would require us to propose and develop an expansion of what 'expressivity' is and how to make an inventory of its ingredients. Formally, a set EXP can be defined as a family of operators: $EXP = \{EX_1 \ldots Ex_n\}$. The EXP family of operators would generalize the EXC operator (Gutiérrez-Rexach, 1996; Grosz, 2011) and include expressive content in general—cf. also Potts and Roeper (2006), Potts (2005), and Kaplan (1989). For $1 \leq i \leq n$, an utterance of $EX_i(\phi)$, where the proposition ϕ is in the scope of the EX_i operator, conveys the following: the speaker at the point of utterance has an emotion ε (or at least an evaluative attitude ε) toward ϕ, and ϕ is univocally associated with EX_i. The speaker intends to express ε, rather than describe ε (Grosz, 2011). This condition relates to the need for the utterance to be a genuine expressive/mixed-exclamative speech act, not a description of one. Additionally, on the pragmatic side, several felicity conditions have to be satisfied so that the expressive attitude is genuine and appropriate in the utterance situation. Finally, ε involves a scale S on which ϕ exceeds a salient threshold. EX_i only combines with scales that are anchored to the speaker and are evaluative/emotive. An approach of this sort would have the advantage of providing the needed flexibility for charting the territory of "exclamativity" in all of its forms and associated meanings.

10. Conclusions

Using data from Spanish as a starting point, it has been argued that the distribution of embedded exclamatives is a byproduct of several factors: the nature of exclamatives as speech acts, the presuppositional requirements of exclamatives, and the semantics of the embedding predicates. Exclamatives as speech acts express an emotional attitude toward a given fact, which normally is unexpected. Propositionally, they ascribe a *de re* belief to a degree (cf. Katz, 2005). An embedded exclamative expression has to preserve or be consistent with these requirements in order to preserve its exclamatory nature. Thus, embedded exclamatives are *de re* ascriptions and degree-referring. The semantics and pragmatic requirements of emotive-factive predicates allow for the embedding of exclamative constructions headed by certain degree wh-words (*cómo* and *cuánto*) or degree relative propositions (NEUT ART + *que*, ART + *que*).Certain directive predicates embed exclamatives in general and impose differential conditions. Other elements embed "mixed" exclamatives, each with its own requirements. To summarize, embedding exclamatory content in the broad sense of this term is not a transparent process. Rather, there is an intricate interaction between the pragmatic and semantics requirements of the embedding element and the embedded content.

Abels, K. (2004). Why surprise-predicates do not embed polar interrogatives. *Linguistische Arbeitsberichte, 81*, 203–222.

Abels, K. (2005). Remarks on Grimshaw's clausal typology. In E. Maier, C. Bary, & J. Huitink (Eds.), *Proceedings of SuB9. A collection of papers presented at the 9th Sinn und Bedeutung*, pp. 1–15. Nijmegen, Netherlands: Radboud University.

Abels, K. (2007). Deriving selectional properties of "exclamative" predicates. In A. Späth (Ed.), *Interfaces and interface conditions*, pp. 115–140. Berlin, Germany: De Gruyter.

Abels, K. (2010). Factivity in exclamatives is a presupposition. *Studia Linguistica, 64*, 141–157.

Abney, S. P. (1987). *The English noun phrase in its sentential aspect* (Unpublished doctoral dissertation). MIT, Cambridge, MA.

Abrusán, M. (2014). *Weak islands semantics*. Oxford, United Kingdom: Oxford University Press.

Aikhenvald, A. (2004). *Evidentiality*. Oxford, United Kingdom: Oxford University Press.

Aikhenvald, A. (2012). The essence of mirativity. *Linguistic Typology, 16*, 435–485.

Allan, K. (2006). Clause-type, primary illocution, and mood-like operators in English. *Language Sciences, 28*, 1–50.

Almela Pérez, R. (1982). *Apuntes gramaticales sobre la interjección*. Murcia, Spain: Universidad de Murcia.

Alonso-Cortés, Á. (1999a). *La exclamación en español*. Madrid, Spain: Minerva Ediciones.

Alonso-Cortés, Á. (1999b). Las construcciones exclamativas. La interjección y las expresiones vocativas. In I. Bosque & V. Demonte (Eds.), *Gramática descriptiva de la lengua española* (vol. 3, pp. 3993–4050). Madrid, Spain: Espasa.

Alonso-Cortés, Á. (2011). *Ojalá que llueva café*: Una construcción optativa del español. In V. Escandell, M. Leonettin & C. Sánchez (Eds.), *60 problemas de gramática dedicados a Ignacio Bosque* (pp. 24–30). Madrid, Spain: Akal.

Androutsopoulou, A., & Español-Echevarría, M. (2006). Unpronounced *much* and the distribution of Degree Expressions in Spanish. In D. Torck & W. L. Wetzels (Eds.) *Romance languages and linguistic theory 2006: Selected papers from "Going Romance"* (pp. 1–16). Amsterdam, Netherlands: John Benjamins.

Andueza, P. (2011). *Rhetorical exclamatives in Spanish* (Unpublished doctoral dissertation). The Ohio State University, Columbus, OH.

Andueza, P., & Gutiérrez-Rexach, J. (2010). Negation and the interpretation of Spanish rhetorical exclamatives. In C. Borgonovo & M. Español-Echevarría (Eds.), *Selected proceedings of the 12th Hispanic Linguistics Symposium* (pp. 17–25). Sommerville, MA: Cascadilla Press.

Andueza, P., & Gutiérrez-Rexach, J. (2011). Degree restrictions in Spanish exclamatives. In L. Ortiz López (Ed.), *Selected proceedings of the 13th Hispanic Linguistics Symposium* (pp. 286–295). Sommerville, MA: Cascadilla Press.

Andueza, P., & Gutiérrez-Rexach, J. (2012). Embedding Spanish exclamatives. Paper presented at the 41st Linguistic Symposium on Romance Languages, University of Ottawa, Ottawa, Canada.

Anscombre, J.-C. (2013). Les exclamatives: Intensification ou haut-degré. *Langue française, 177*, 23–36.

Arce Castillo, Á. (1999). Intensificadores en español coloquial. *Anuario de Estudios Filológicos, 22*, 37–48.

Bacha, J. (2000). *L'exclamation*. Paris, France: L'Harmattan.

Baker, C. L. (1968). *Indirect questions in English* (Unpublished doctoral dissertation). MIT, Cambridge, MA.

Bastos-Gee, A. C. (2011). *Information structure within the traditional nominal phrase: The case of Brazilian Portuguese* (Unpublished doctoral dissertation). University of Connecticut, Storrs, CT.

Batllori, M., & Hernanz, M. L. (2009). En torno a la polaridad enfática en español y en catalán: Un estudio diacrónico y comparativo. In J. Rafel (Ed.), *Diachronic linguistics* (pp. 319–352). Girona, Spain: Documenta Universitaria.

Batllori, M., & Hernanz, M. L. (2013). Emphatic polarity particles in Spanish and Catalan. *Lingua, 128*, 9–30.

Bello, A. (1964). *Gramática de la lengua castellana*. Buenos Aires, Argentina: Sopena. (Original work published 1847)

Benincà, P. (1995). Il tipo esclamativo. In L. Renzi, G. Salvi, & A. Cardinaletti (Eds.), *Grande grammatica italiana di consultazione* (vol. 3, pp. 127–152). Bologna, Italy: Il Mulino.

Benincà, P. (1996). La struttura della frase exclamativa alla luce del dialetto padovano. In P. Benincà, G. Cinque, T. de Mauro, & N. Vincent (Eds.), *Saggi di grammatica per Giulio C. Lepsky* (pp. 23–43). Rome, Italy: Bulzoni.

Benincà, P., & Munaro, N. (2010). Frasi esclamative. In G. Salvi and L. Renzi (Eds.), *Grammatica dell'italiano antico* (pp. 1187–1198). Bologna, Italy: Il Mulino.

Beyssade, C. (2009). Exclamation and presupposition. In P. Egré & G. Magri (Eds.), *Presuppositions and implicatures: Proceedings of the MIT-Paris Workshop* (pp. 19–35). Cambridge, MA: MIT.

Beyssade, C., & Marandin, J-M. (2006). The speech act assignment problem revisited: Disentangling speaker's commitment from speaker's call on addressee. In O. Bonami & P. Cabredo Hofherr (Eds.), *Questions empiriques et formalisation en syntaxe et sémantique 6* (pp. 37–68). Paris, France: Sciences de L'Homme et de la Societé.

Biezma, M. (2007). An expressive analysis of exclamatives in Spanish. Paper presented at Going Romance 21, Lisbon, Portugal.

Biezma, M. (2008). On the consequences of being small: Imperatives in Spanish. In A. Schardl, M. Walkow, & M. Abdurrahman (Eds.), *Proceedings of NELS 38* (vol. 1, pp. 89–101). Amherst, MA: University of Massachusetts Amherst.

Biezma, M. (2010). Inverted antecedents in hidden conditionals. In S. Kan, C. Moore-Cantwell, & R. Staubs (Eds.), *Proceedings of NELS 40* (vol. 1, pp. 59–70). Amherst, MA: University of Massachusetts Amherst.

Biezma, M. (2011a). Optatives: Deriving desirability from scalar alternatives. In I. Reich et al. (Eds.), *Proceedings of Sinn und Bedeutung (SuB) 15* (pp. 117–132). Saarbrücken, Germany: Saarland University Press.

Biezma, M. (2011b). *Anchoring pragmatics in syntax and semantics* (Unpublished doctoral dissertation). University of Massachusetts Amherst, Amherst, MA.

Boisvert, D., & Ludwig, K. (2006). Semantics for nondeclaratives. In B. Smith & E. Lepore (Eds.), *The Oxford handbook of the philosophy of language* (pp. 864–892). Oxford, United Kingdom: Oxford University Press.

Bosque, I. (1980a). *Sobre la negación*. Madrid, Spain: Cátedra.

Bosque, I. (1980b). Retrospective imperatives. *Linguistic Inquiry, 11*, 415–419.

Bosque, I. (1984a). Sobre la sintaxis de las oraciones exclamativas. *Hispanic Linguistics, 1*, 283–304.

Bosque, I. (1984b). La selección de las palabras interrogativas. *Verba, 11*, 245–273.

Bosque, I. (2001). Adjective position and the interpretation of indefinites. In J. Gutiérrez-Rexach & L. Silva (Eds.), *Current issues in Spanish syntax and semantics* (pp. 17–38). Berlin, Germany: Mouton-De Gruyter.

Bosque, I. (2002). Degree quantification and modal operators in Spanish. In J. Gutiérrez-Rexach (Ed.), *From words to discourse* (pp. 263–288). Amsterdam, Netherlands: North-Holland.

Bosque, I. (2012). Mood. Indicative vs. Subjunctive. In J. I. Hualde, A. Olarrea, & E. O'Rourke (Eds.), *Handbook of Hispanic Linguistics* (pp. 373–394). Oxford: Blackwell.

Bosque, I., & Demonte, V. (Eds.). (1999). *Gramática descriptiva de la lengua española* (Vols. 1–3). Madrid, Spain: Espasa.

Bosque, I., & Masullo, P. (1998). On verbal quantification in Spanish. In O. Fullana & F. Roca (Eds.), *Studies on the syntax of Central Romance languages* (pp. 9–64). Girona, Spain: Universitat de Girona.

Bresnan, J. (1973). Syntax of the comparative clause construction in English. *Linguistic Inquiry, 4*, 275–343.

Brown, L. A. (2008). The semantics of exclamatives: Refining the domain of quantification. Paper presented at the annual conference of the Canadian Linguistic Association, Vancouver, Canada.

Brucart, J. M. (1993). Sobre la estructura de SCOMP en español. In A. Viana (Ed.), *Sintaxi: Teoria i perspectives* (pp. 59–102). Lleida, Spain: Publicacions de la Universitat de Lleida.

Brucart, J. M. (1994). Syntactic variation and grammatical primitives in generative grammar. In A. Briz & M. Pérez-Saldanya (Eds.), *Lynx. Categories and functions. A monographic series in linguistics and world perception* (pp. 145–176). Minneapolis, MN/Valencia, Spain: University of Minnesota/Publicacions de la Universitat de València.

Burnett, H. (2009). Pitch accent, focus, and the interpretation of non-wh exclamatives. In S. Colina, A. Olarrea, & A. M. Carvalho (Eds.), *Romance linguistics 2009. Selected papers from the 39th Linguistic Symposium on Romance Languages (LSRL)* (pp. 369–386). Amsterdam, Netherlands: John Benjamins.

Burzio, L. (1986). *Italian syntax*. Dordrecht, Netherlands: Kluwer.

Bustos Kleiman, A. (1974). *A syntactic correlate of semantic and pragmatic relations: The subjunctive mood in Spanish* (Unpublished doctoral dissertation). University of Illinois Urbana-Champaign, Champaign, IL.

Carbonero Cano, P. (1990). Configuración sintáctica de los enunciados exclamativos. *Philologia Hispalensis, 5*, 111–137.

Carlson, G. (1977). *Reference to kinds in English* (Unpublished doctoral dissertation). University of Masachussetts Amherst, Amherst, MA.

Casas, A. (2004). Exclamativas y expletividad. El *que* enfático. *Revista de Filología Española, 64*, 265–284.

Casas, A. (2005). *Gramática del enunciado exclamativo* (Unpublished doctoral dissertation). Universidad de Oviedo, Oviedo, Spain.

Casas, A. (2006). Truncamiento y remate de las construcciones comparativas. *Verba, 33*, 281–311.

Castroviejo, E. (2006). *Wh exclamatives in Catalan* (Unpublished doctoral dissertation). Universitat de Barcelona, Barcelona, Spain.

Castroviejo, E. (2007). A degree-based account of wh- exclamatives in Catalan. In E. Puig-Waldmüller (Ed.), *Proceedings of Sinn und Bedeutung 11* (pp. 134–149). Barcelona, Spain: Universitat Pompeu Fabra.

Castroviejo, E. (2008a). Deconstructing exclamations. *Catalan Journal of Linguistics, 7*, 41–90.

Castroviejo, E. (2008b). An expressive answer. Some considerations on the semantics and pragmatics of wh-exclamatives. In M. Bane (Ed.), *Proceedings of CLS 44* (vol. 2, pp. 3–17). Chicago, IL: Chicago Linguistic Society.

Chernilovskaya, A. (2010). Wh-exclamatives and other non-interrogative questions. In *Proceedings of the 26th annual meeting of The Israel Association for Theoretical Linguistics*. Ramat Gan, Israel. Retrieved from http://linguistics.huji.ac.il/IATL/26/TOC.html

Chernilovskaya, A. (2011). Embedding high degrees. Paper presented at Grammar of Attitudes, the 33rd Meeting of the German Linguistic Society, Utrecht, Netherlands.

Chernilovskaya, A., & Nouwen, R. (2012). On wh-exclamatives and noteworthiness. In M. Aloni, V. Kimmelman, F. Roelofsen, G. W. Sassoon, K. Schulz, & M. Westera (Eds.), *Logic, language and meaning* (pp. 271–280). Berlin, Germany: Springer.

Chierchia, G. (2004). Scalar implicatures, polarity phenomena, and the syntax/pragmatics interface. In A. Belleti (Ed.), *Structures and beyond. The cartography of syntactic structures* (pp. 39–103). Oxford, United Kingdom: Oxford University Press.

Chierchia, G. (2006). Broaden your views: Implicatures of domain widening and the "logicality" of language. *Linguistic Inquiry, 37*, 535–590.

Chomsky, N. (1981). *Lectures on government and binding*. Dordrecht, Netherlands: Foris.

Chomsky, N. (1995). *The minimalist program*. Cambridge, MA: MIT Press.

Cinque, G. (1994). On the evidence for partial n-movement in the Romance DP. In G. Cinque (Ed.), *Paths towards universal grammar. Essays in honor of Richard S. Kayne* (pp. 85–110). Washington, DC.: Georgetown University Press.

Company, C. (2009). Entre el bien y el mal. Una pauta de lexicalización en la lengua española. *Revista de Historia de la Lengua Española, 4*, 29–45.

Contreras, H. (1999). Relaciones entre las construcciones interrogativas, exclamativas y relativas. In I. Bosque & V. Demonte (Eds.), *Gramática descriptiva de la lengua española* (vol. 2, pp. 1931–1963). Madrid, Spain: Espasa.

Contreras, H. (2009). Word order and minimalism. In P. J. Masullo (Ed.), *Romance linguistics 2007* (pp. 69–87). Amsterdam, Netherlands: John Benjamins.

Contreras, L. (1960). Oraciones independientes introducidas por *si*. *Boletín de Filología, 12*, 273–290.

Corpus diacrónico del español. (CORDE). (n.d.). Retrieved from http://corpus.rae.es/cordenet.html

Corver, N. (1991). The internal syntax and movement behavior of Dutch "wat voor" construction. *Linguistische Berichte, 133*, 190–228.

Corver, N. (1997). *Much*-support as a last resort. *Linguistic Inquiry, 28*, 119–164.

Corpus de referencia del español. (CREA). (n.d.). Retrieved from http://corpus.rae.es/creanet.html

D'Avis, F. J. (2002). On the interpretation of wh-clauses in exclamative environments. *Theoretical Linguistics, 28*, 5–31.

De Cuba, C. F. (2007). *(Non) factivity* (Unpublished doctoral dissertation). Stony Brook University, Stony Brook, NY.

De Lancey, S. (2001). The mirative and evidentiality. *Journal of Pragmatics, 33*, 371–384.

Dehé, N., & Kavalova, Y. (Eds.). (2007). *Parentheticals*. Amsterdam, Netherlands: John Benjamins.

Demonte, V., & Fernández Soriano, O. (2009). Force and finiteness in the Spanish complementizer system. *Probus, 21*, 23–49.

Demonte, V., & Fernández Soriano, O. (2013). El *que* citativo, otros que de la periferia izquierda oracional y la recomplementación. In D. Jakob & K. Plooj (Eds.), *Autour de que* (pp. 47–67). Frankfurt, Germany: Peter Lang.

Demonte, V., & Fernández Soriano, O. (2014). Spanish matrix *que* at the syntax-pragmatics interface. In A. Dufter & A. Octavio de Toledo (Eds.), *Left sentence peripheries in Spanish: Diachronic, variationist, and typological perspectives* (pp. 217–252). Amsterdam, Netherlands: John Benjamins.

Di Tullio, Á. (2004). El argentinismo *es de lindo*... y la gramática de la exclamación. *RASAL, 1*, 101–120.

Di Tullio, Á. (2008). La gramática de la réplica en el español rioplatense. In *Jornadas académicas hispanorrioplatenses sobre la lengua española* (pp. 213–221). Buenos Aires, Argentina: Academia Argentina de Letras.

Di Tullio, Á., & Kailuweit, R. (2012). Las oraciones copulativas enfáticas del español y sus varias realizaciones. In F. Lebsanft, W. Mihatsch, & C. Polzin-Haumann (Eds.), *El español, ¿desde las variedades a la lengua pluricéntrica?* (pp. 141–160). Madrid, Spain: Iberoamericana.

Dufter, A., & Octavio de Toledo, Á. (Eds.). (2014). *Left sentence peripheries in Spanish: Diachronic, variationist, and typological perspectives*. Amsterdam, Netherlands: John Benjamins.

Dumitrescu, D. (1998). Subordinación y recursividad en la conversación: Las secuencias integradas por intercambios ecoicos. *Diálogos Hispánicos, 22*, 277–314.

Edeso, V. (2009). *Contribución al estudio de la interjección en español*. Bern, Germany: Peter Lang.

El corpus del español. Created by Mark Davies, Brigham Young University. Available at: http://www.corpusdelespanol.org/

Elliot, D. (1971). *The grammar of emotive and exclamatory sentences in English* (Unpublished doctoral dissertation). The Ohio State University, Columbus, OH.

Elliot, D. (1974). Toward a grammar of exclamatives. *Foundations of Language, 11*, 231–246.

Embick, D. (2007). Blocking effects and analytic/synthetic alternations. *Natural Language and Linguistic Theory, 25*, 1–37.

Embick, D., & Noyer, R. (2001). Movement operations after syntax. *Linguistic Inquiry*, 32, 555–598.

Escandell Vidal, M. V. (1984). La interrogación retórica. *Dicenda*, 3, 9–38.

Escandell Vidal, M. V. (1999). Los enunciados interrogativos. Aspectos semánticos y pragmáticos. In I. Bosque and V. Demonte (Eds.), *Gramática descriptiva de la lengua española* (vol. 3, pp. 3929–3991.). Madrid, Spain: Espasa.

Escandell Vidal, M. V., & Leonetti, M. (2014). Fronting and irony in Spanish. In A. Dufter and Á. Octavio de Toledo (Eds.), *Left sentence peripheries in Spanish: Diachronic, variationist, and typological perspectives* (pp. 309–342). Amsterdam, Netherlands: John Benjamins.

Espinal, M. T. (1992). Expletive negation and logical absorption. *The Linguistic Review*, 9(4), 333–358.

Espinal, M. T. (1997). Non-negative negation and *wh*- exclamatives. In D. Forget, P. Hirschbühler, F. Martineau, & M. L. Rivero (Eds.), *Negation and polarity. Syntax and semantics* (pp. 75–93). Amsterdam, Netherlands: John Benjamins.

Espinal, M. T. (2000). Expletive negation, negative concord and feature checking. *Catalan Working Papers in Linguistics*, 8, 47–69.

Etxepare, R. (2007). Aspects of quotative constructions in Iberian Spanish. *ASJU*, 16(2), 25–58.

Etxepare, R. (2008). On quotative constructions in Iberian Spanish. In R. Laury (Ed.), *Crosslinguistic studies of clause combining. The multifunctionality of conjunctions* (pp. 35–78). Amsterdam, Netherlands: John Benjamins.

Etxepare, R. (2010). From hearsay evidentiality to samesaying relations. *Lingua*, 120(3), 604–627.

Evans, N. (2007). Insubordination and its uses. In I. Nikolaeva (Ed.), *Finiteness. Theoretical and empirical foundations* (pp. 366–431). Oxford, United Kingdom: Oxford University Press.

Frana, I. (2010). *Concealed questions: In search of answers* (Unpublished doctoral dissertation). University of Massachusetts Amherst, Amherst, MA.

Gallego, Á. (2007). *Phase theory and parametric variation* (Unpublished doctoral dissertation). Universitat Autònoma de Barcelona, Barcelona, Spain.

Gandon, F. (1988). Les "noms de qualité." Syntaxe ou semantique? Le débat entre J.-C. Milner et N. Ruwet. *Lingvisticæ Investigationes*, 12, 157–179.

Garrido Medina, J. (1999). Los actos de habla. Las oraciones imperativas. In I. Bosque and V. Demonte (Eds.), *Gramática descriptiva de la lengua española* (vol. 3, pp. 3879–3928). Madrid, Spain: Espasa.

Gérard, J. (1980). *L'exclamation en français*. Tübingen, Germany: Niemeyer.

Geurts, B. (1998). The mechanisms of denial. *Language*, 74(2), 274–307.

Giannakidou, A. (1995). Subjunctive, habituality and negative polarity items. In M. Simons & T. Galloway (Eds.), *Proceedings of SALT V* (pp. 94–111). Ithaca, NY: Cornell University.

Giannakidou, A. (1997). *The landscape of polarity items* (Unpublished doctoral dissertation). University of Groningen, Groningen, Netherlands.

Giannakidou, A. (1998). *Polarity sensitivity as (non)veridical dependency*. Amsterdam, Netherlands: John Benjamins.

Giannakidou, A. (2006). *Only*, emotive factive verbs, and the dual nature of polarity dependency. *Language*, 82(3), 575–603.

Gili Gaya, S. (1961). *Curso superior de sintaxis española*. Barcelona, Spain: Bibliograf.

Girón, J L. (2014). Del léxico a la gramática. Sobre si hay o no exclamativas indirectas totales en español. In J. L. Girón & D. M. Sáez (Eds.), *Procesos de gramaticalización en la historia del español* (pp. 45–57). Madrid, Spain: Iberoamericana.

González Calvo, J. M. (1984). Sobre la expresión de lo "superlativo" en español I. *Anuario de Estudios Filológicos, 7,* 172–205.

González Calvo, J. M. (1985). Sobre la expresión de lo "superlativo" en español II. *Anuario de Estudios Filológicos, 8,* 113–146.

González Calvo, J. M. (1986). Sobre la expresión de lo "superlativo" en español III. *Anuario de Estudios Filológicos, 9,* 129–153.

González Calvo, J. M. (1987). Sobre la expresión de lo "superlativo" en español IV. *Anuario de Estudios Filológicos, 10,* 101–132.

González Calvo, J. M. (1988). Sobre la expresión de lo "superlativo" en español V. *Anuario de Estudios Filológicos, 11,* 159–174.

González Calvo, J. M. (1998). *Variaciones en torno a la gramática española*. Cáceres, Spain: Universidad de Extremadura.

González Calvo, J. M. (2001). Revisión de la clasificación de la oración según el "modus." *Anuario de estudios filológicos, 24,* 207–221.

González-Rivera, M. (2011). *On the internal structure of Spanish verbless clauses* (Unpublished doctoral dissertation). The Ohio State University, Columbus, OH.

González Rodríguez, R. (2006). Negación y cuantificación de grado. In M. Villayandre Llamazares (Ed.), *Actas del XXXV Simposio Internacional de la Sociedad Española de Lingüística* (pp. 853–871). León, Spain: Universidad de León.

González Rodríguez, R. (2007a). Reconstruction and scope in exclamative sentences. In L. Eguren & O. Fernández-Soriano (Eds.), *Coreference, modality, and focus* (pp. 89–112). Amsterdam, Netherlands: John Benjamins.

González Rodríguez, R. (2007b). Sintaxis y semántica de la partícula de polaridad *sí*. *Revista Española de Lingüística, 37,* 311–336.

González Rodríguez, R. (2008). Exclamative wh-phrases as positive polarity items. *Catalan Journal of Linguistics, 7,* 91–116.

González Rodríguez, R. (2009). *La gramática de los términos de polaridad positiva* (Unpublished doctoral dissertation). Universidad Complutense de Madrid, Madrid, Spain.

González Rodríguez, R. (2010). Consecuencias gramaticales de la estructura de las escalas adjetivales. *Verba, 37,* 123–148.

Grande Rodríguez, V., & Grande Alija, F. J. (2004). Entre la interrogación y la exclamación: La construcción *¡Qué bien lo haría, que hasta le dieron un premio!* In M. Villayandre (Ed.), *Actas del V Congreso de Lingüística General* (pp. 1429–1440). Madrid, Spain: Arco Libros.

Gras, P. (2013). Entre la gramática y el discurso: Valores conectivos de *que* inicial átono en español. In D. Jacob & K. Ploog (Eds.), *Autour de que. El entorno de que. Studia romanica et linguistica* (pp. 89–112). Frankfurt am Main, Germany: Peter Lang.

Gras, P. (2016). Revisiting the functional typology of insubordination: *Que*-initial sentences in Spanish. In N. Evans & H. Watanabe (Eds.), *Dynamics of insubordination* (pp. 113–144). Amsterdam, Netherlands: John Benjamins.

Grice, H. P. (1975). Logic and conversation. In P. Cole & J. Morgan (Eds.), *Syntax and semantics 3: Speech acts* (pp. 64–75). New York: Academic Press.

Grice, H. P. (1978). Further notes on logic and conversation. In P. Cole (Ed.), *Syntax and semantics 9: Pragmatics* (pp. 113–127). New York: Academic Press.

Grice, H. P. (1981). Presupposition and Conversational Implicature. In P. Cole (Ed.), *Radical pragmatics* (pp. 183–198). New York: Academic Press.

Grimshaw, J. (1979). Complement selection and the lexicon. *Linguistic Inquiry, 10,* 279–326.

Groenedijk, J., & Stokhof, M. (1982). Semantic analysis of wh complements. *Linguistics and Philosophy, 5*, 175–233.

Groenedijk, J., & Stokhof, M. (1989). *Studies in the semantics of questions and the pragmatics of answers* (Unpublished doctoral dissertation). University of Amsterdam, Amsterdam, Netherlands.

Grohmann, K., & Etxeparre, R. (2003). Root infinitives: A comparative view. *Probus, 15*, 201–236.

Grosu, A., & Landman, F. (1998). Strange relatives of the third kind. *Natural Language Semantics, 6*(2): 125–170.

Grosz, P. G. (2011). *On the grammar of optative constructions* (Unpublished doctoral dissertation). MIT, Cambridge, MA.

Gutiérrez-Rexach, J. (1996). The semantics of exclamatives. In E. Garret & F. Lee (Eds.), *Syntax at sunset. UCLA working papers in linguistics* (pp. 146–162). Los Angeles, CA: UCLA.

Gutiérrez-Rexach, J. (1997). The semantic basis of NPI licensing in questions. *MIT Working Papers in Linguistics, 31*, 359–376.

Gutiérrez-Rexach, J. (1998). Rhetorical questions, relevance and scales. *Revista Alicantina de Estudios Ingleses, 11*, 139–156.

Gutiérrez-Rexach, J. (1999). The structure and interpretation of Spanish degree neuter constructions. *Lingua, 109*, 35–63.

Gutiérrez-Rexach, J. (2001). Spanish exclamatives and the interpretation of the left periphery. In J. Rooryck, Y. de Hulst, & J. Schroten (Eds.), *Selected papers from Going Romance 1999* (pp. 167–194). Amsterdam, Netherlands: John Benjamins.

Gutiérrez-Rexach, J. (Ed.). (2002). *From words to discourse.* Amsterdam, Netherlands: North-Holland.

Gutiérrez-Rexach, J. (2008). Spanish root exclamatives at the syntax/semantics interface. *Catalan Journal of Linguistics, 7*, 117–133.

Gutiérrez-Rexach, J., & Andueza, P. (2016). The pragmatics of embedded exclamatives. In A. Capone & J. L. Mey (Eds.), *Interdisciplinary studies in pragmatics* (pp. 767–790). Berlin, Germany: Springer.

Gutiérrez-Rexach, J., & González-Rivera, M. (2013). Spanish PredNPs and the left periphery. In J. Cabrelli Amaro, G. Lord, A. de Prada Pérez, & J. E. Aaron (Eds.), *Selected proceedings of the 16th Hispanic Linguistics Symposium* (pp. 1–14). Somerville, MA: Cascadilla Proceedings Project.

Gutiérrez-Rexach, J., & González-Rivera, M. (2014). Spanish predicative verbless clauses and the left periphery. In A. Dufter & Octavio de Toledo (Eds.), *Left sentence peripheries in Spanish: Diachronic, variationist, and typological perspectives* (pp. 101–124). Amsterdam: John Benjamins.

Hale, K., & Keyser, S. (1993). On argument structure and the lexical expression of syntactic relations. In K. Hale & S. Keyser (Eds.), *The view from building 20* (pp. 59–109). Cambridge, MA: MIT Press.

Halle, M., & Marantz, A. (1993). Distributed morphology and the pieces of inflection. In K. Hale & S. Keyser (Eds.), *The view from building 20* (pp. 111–176). Cambridge, MA: MIT Press.

Hamblin, C. L. (1973). Questions in Montague English. *Foundations of Language, 10*, 41–53.

Heim, I. (1982). *The semantics of definite and indefinite noun phrases* (Unpublished doctoral dissertation). University of Massachusetts Amherst, Amherst, MA.

Heim, I. (1992). Presupposition projection and the semantics of attitude verbs. *Journal of Semantics, 9*, 183–221.

Heim, I. (1994). Interrogative semantics and Karttunen's semantics for *know*. In R. Buchalla & A. Mittwoch (Eds.). *Israel Association for Theoretical Linguistics 1*, 128–144.

Heim, I. (2006). Little. In M. Gibson & J. Howell (Eds.), *Proceedings of SALT 16* (pp. 35–58). Ithaca, NY: CLC Publications.

Henry, A. (1977). *Magnifique, la luxure*. Étude de syntaxe affective. In A. Heny, *Études de syntaxe expressive: Ancient français et français modern*. Brussels, Belgium: University of Brussels. (Original work published 1953)

Hernanz, M. L. (1999). Polaridad y modalidad en español: en torno a la gramática de *bien*. Retrieved from http://filcat.uab.cat/clt/publicacions/reports/pdf/GGT-99-6.pdf

Hernanz, M. L. (2001). ¡*En bonito lío me he metido!* Notas sobre la afectividad en español. *Moenia, 7*, 93–109.

Hernanz, M. L. (2006). Emphatic polarity and C in Spanish. In L. Brugè (Ed.), *Categorie funzionali del nome nelle lingue romanze* (pp. 105–150). Milan, Italy: Instituto Editoriale Universitario-Monduzzi Editore.

Hernanz, M. L. (2007). From polarity to modality. Some (a)symmetries between "*bien*" and "*sí*" in Spanish. In L. Eguren & O. Fernández Soriano (Eds.), *Coreference, modality, and focus* (pp. 133–169). Amsterdam, Netherlands: John Benjamins.

Hernanz, M. L. (2011). Assertive *bien* in Spanish and the left periohery. In P. Beninca & N. Munaro (Eds.), *Mapping the left periphery* (pp. 19–62). Oxford, United Kingdom: Oxford University Press.

Hernanz, M. L. (2012). Sobre la periferia izquierda y el movimiento: El complementante *si* en español. In J. M. Brucart & A. Gallego (Eds.), *El movimiento de constituyentes* (pp. 151–171). Madrid, Spain: Visor.

Hernanz, M. L., & Rigau, G. (2006). Variación dialectal y periferia izquierda. In B. Fernández & I. Laka (Eds.), *Andolin gogoan. Essays in honour of Professor Eguzkitza* (pp. 435–452). Bilbao, Spain: Euskal Herriko Unibertsitateko Argitalpen Zerbitzua.

Hernanz, M. L., & Suñer, A. (1999). La predicación: La predicación no copulativa. Las construcciones absolutas. In I. Bosque and V. Demonte (Eds.), *Gramática descriptiva de la lengua española* (vol. 2, pp. 2525–2560). Madrid, Spain: Espasa.

Herrero, G. (1991). El infinitivo exclamativo en español actual. *Thesaurus, 46*, 43–64.

Heycock, C. (2006). Embedded root phenomena. In M. Everaert & H. van Riemsdijk (Eds.), *The Blackwell companion to syntax* (vol. 2, pp. 174–209). Oxford, United Kingdom: Blackwell.

Hoeksema, J. (1983). Negative polarity and the comparative. *Natural Language and Linguistic Theory, 1*, 403–434.

Huang, C. T. J. (1982). *Logical relations in Chinese and the theory of grammar* (Unpublished doctoral dissertation). MIT, Cambridge, MA.

Iatridou, S. (2000). The grammatical ingredients of counterfactuality. *Linguistic Inquiry, 31*(2), 231–270.

Ishii, Y. (1991). *Operators and empty categories in Japanese* (Unpublished doctoral dissertation). University of Connecticut, Storrs, CT.

Israel, M. (1996). Polarity sensitivity as lexical semantics. *Linguistics and Philosophy, 19*, 619–666.

Jacobson, P. (1995). On the quantificiational force of English free relatives. In E. Bach, E. Jelinek, A. Kratzer, B. B. H. Partee (Eds.), *Quantification in natural languages* (pp. 451–486). Berlin, Germany: Springer.

Jónsson, J. G. (2010). Icelandic exclamatives and the structure of the CP layer. *Studia Linguistica, 64*(1), 37–54.

Joseph, B., & Philippaki Warburton, I. (1987). *Modern Greek*. London, United Kingdom: Croom Helm.

Kadmon, N., & Landman, F. (1993). Any. *Linguistics and Philosophy, 1*, 3–44.

Kaneko, M. (2008). Les phrases nominales événementielles exprimant une valeur affective. In J. Durand (Ed.), *Congrès Mondial de Linguistique Française* (pp. 2067–2084). Paris, France: Institut de Linguistique Française.

Kaplan, D. (1989). The meaning of "oops" and "ouch." Unpublished manuscript, UCLA, Los Angeles, CA.

Karttunen, L. (1973). Presuppositions of compound sentences. *Linguistic Inquiry, 4*, 167–193.

Karttunen, L. (1977). Syntax and semantics of questions. *Linguistics and Philosophy, 1*, 3–44.

Katz, G. (2005). Attitudes toward degrees. In E. Maier, C. Bary, & J. Huitink (Eds.), *Proceedings of Sinn und Bedeutung 9*. (pp. 183–196). Nijmegen, Netherlands: Radboud University.

Kayne, R. (1994). *The antisymmetry of syntax*. Cambridge, MA: MIT Press.

Kayne, R. (2005). *Movement and silence*. New York: Oxford University Press.

Kellert, O. (2010). L'interface syntaxique-sémantique de la phrase exclamative. In F. Neveu (Ed.), *Congrès Mondial de Linguistique Française* (pp. 2127–2139). Paris, France: Institut de Linguistique Française.

Kennedy, C. (1997). *Projecting the adjective: The syntax and semantics of gradability and comparison* (Unpublished doctoral dissertation). University of California, Santa Cruz, Santa Cruz, CA.

Kennedy, C. (2001). Polar opposition and the ontology of degrees. *Linguistics and Philosophy, 24*, 33–70.

Kennedy, C., & McNally, L. (2005a). Scale structure, degree modification, and the semantics of gradable predicates. *Language, 81*(2), 345–381.

Kennedy, C., & McNally, L. (2005b). The syntax and semantics of multiple degree modification in English. In S. Muller (Ed.), *Proceedings of HPSG-2005*, (pp. 178–191). Retrieved from https://web.stanford.edu/group/cslipublications/cslipublications/HPSG/2005/toc.shtml.

Kiefer, F. (1978). Adjectives and presupposition. *Theoretical Linguistics, 5*, 135–173.

Kim, K-S. (2008). English C moves downward as well as upward: An extension of Bošković and Lasnik's (2003) approach. *Linguistic Inquiry, 39*, 295–307.

Kiparsky, P., & Kiparsky, C. (1970). Fact. In M. Bierwisch & K. Heidolph (Eds.), *Progress in Linguistics: A collection of papers* (pp. 143–173). The Hague, Netherlands: Mouton.

Kratzer, A. (1990). How specific is a fact. In *Proceedings of the Conference on Theories of Partial Information*. Austin, TX: Center for Cognitive Science, University of Texas at Austin. Retrieved from http://www.semanticsarchive.net/Archive/mQwZjBjO/facts.pdf

Kratzer, A. (2002). Facts: Particulars or information units. *Linguistics and Philosophy, 25*, 655–670.

Krifka, M. (1995). The semantics and pragmatics of polarity items. *Linguistic Analysis, 25*, 209–257.

Krifka, M. (2007). Basic notions of information structure. *Interdisciplinary Studies on Information Structure, 6*, 13–55.

Krueger, F. (1960). *El argentinismo Es de lindo. Sus variantes y sus antecedentes peninsulares. Estudio de sintaxis comparativa*. Madrid, Spain: CSIC.

Laca, B. (2010). Mood in Spanish. In B. Rothstein & R. Thieroff (Eds.), *Mood in the languages of Europe* (pp. 198–221). Amsterdam, Netherlands: John Benjamins.

Ladusaw, W. A. (1980). *Polarity sensitivity as inherent scope relations*. NY: Garland.

Lahiri U. (1991). *Embedded interrogatives and predicates that embed them* (Unpublished doctoral dissertation). MIT, Cambridge, MA.

Lahiri, U. (1998). Focus and negative polarity in Hindi. *Natural Language Semantics, 6,* 57–125.

Lahiri, U. (2000). Lexical selection and quantificational variability in embedded interrogatives. *Linguistics and Philosophy, 23,* 325–389.

Lahiri, U. (2002). *Questions and answers in embedded contexts.* Oxford, United Kingdom: Oxford University Press.

Laka, Itziar. 1990. *Negation in syntax: On the nature of functional categories and projections,* Doctoral Dissertation, MIT, Cambridge, MA.

Lakoff, G. (1974). Syntactic amalgams. *CLS, 10,* 421–434.

Lazard, G. (1999). Mirativity, evidentiality, mediativity, or other? *Linguistic Tipology, 3,* 91–110.

Lazard, G. (2001). On the grammaticalization of evidentiality. *Journal of Pragmatics, 33,* 358–368.

Lewis, D. (1975). Adverbs of quantification. In E. Keenan (Ed.), *Formal semantics of natural language* (pp. 3–15). Cambridge, United Kingdom: Cambridge University Press.

Lewis, D. (1979). Scorekeeping in a language game. *Journal of Philosophical Logic, 8,* 339–359.

López Bobo, M. J. (2002). *La interjección. Aspectos gramaticales.* Madrid, Spain: Arco Libros.

Marandin, J-M. (2008). The exclamative clause type in French. In S. Müller (Ed.), *The proceedings of the 15th International Conference on HPSG* (pp. 436–456). Stanford, CA: CSLI.

Marandin, J-M. (2010). Les exclamatives de degré en français. *Langue française, 165,* 35–52.

Martí, L. (2003). *Contextual variables* (Unpublished doctoral dissertation). University of Connecticut, Storrs, CT.

Martínez Álvarez, J. (1997). Estructuras exclamativas con *si*. In M. Almeida & J. Dorta (Eds.), *Contribuciones al estudio de la lingüística hispánica. Homenaje a R. Trujillo* (vol. 1, pp. 223–230). Barcelona, Spain: Montesinos.

Masullo, P. J. (1992). Antipassive constructions in Spanish. In P. Hirschbüler & E. F. K. Koerner, *Romance languages and modern linguistic theory* (pp. 175–194). Amsterdam, Netherlands: John Benjamins.

Masullo, P. J. (1999). On hidden exclamatives in Spanish. Unpublished manuscript, Universidad Nacional del Comahue, Buenos Aires, Argentina.

Masullo, P. J. (2003). Hidden exclamatives in Spanish. Unpublished manuscript, University of Pittsburgh, Pittsburg, PA; Universidad Nacional del Comahue, Buenos Aires, Argentina.

Masullo, P. J. (2005). Covert exclamatives and LF. Paper presented at the 15th Colloquium on Generative Grammar, Barcelona, Spain.

Masullo, P. J. (2012). Covert exclamatives (in Spanish) and logical form. In M. González-Rivera & S. Sassarego (Eds.), *Current formal aspects of Spanish syntax and semantics* (pp. 147–178). Newcastle-upon-Tyne, United Kingdom: Cambridge Scholars Publishing.

Matushansky, O. (2013). More or better: On the derivation of synthetic comparatives and superlatives in English. Unpublished manuscxript, UiL OTS, Utrecht University, Utretch Netherlands; CNRS, Universitè Paris-8, Paris, France .

Mayol, L., & Castroviejo, E. (2013). How to cancel an implicature. *Journal of Pragmatics, 50,* 84–104.

Mayol, L. (2008). Catalan "Deu n'hi do" and levels of meaning in exclamatives. *Catalan Journal of Linguistics, 7,* 135–156.

McCawley, J. D. (1981). *Everything that linguists have always wanted to know about logic but were ashamed to ask.* Chicago, IL: University of Chicago Press.

Meibauer, J. J., & Steinbach, M. (2011). *Experimental pragmatics/semantics.* Amsterdam, Netherlands: John Benjamins Publishing Company.

Merin, A., & Nikolaeva, I. (2008). *Exclamatives as a universal speech act category. A case study in decision-theoretic semantics and typological implications.* Unpublished manuscript, University of Kostanz, Konstanz, Germany; University of London, London, United Kingdom.

Michaelis, L. (2001). Exclamative constructions. In M. Haspelmath, E. König, W. Oesterreicher, & W. Raible (Eds.), *Language universals and language typology: An international handbook* (vol. 2, pp. 1038–1050). Berlin, Germany: Walter de Gruyter.

Michaelis, L., & Lambrecht, K. (1996). The exclamative sentence type in English. In A. Goldberg (Ed.), *Conceptual structure, discourse and language* (pp. 375–389). Los Angeles, CA: CSLI Publications.

Milner, J-C. (1978). *De la syntaxe à l'interprétation. Quantités, insultes, exclamations.* Paris, France: Seuil.

Mindt, I. (2011). *Adjective complementation.* Amsterdam, Netherlands: John Benjamins.

Mondorf, B. (2009). *More support for more-support.* Amsterdam, Netherlands: John Benjamins.

Montes, R. G. (1999). The development of discourse markers in Spanish: Interjections. *Journal of Pragmatics, 31,* 1289–1319.

Montolío, E. (1999a). Las construcciones condicionales. In I. Bosque and V. Demonte (Eds.), *Gramática descriptiva de la lengua española* (vol. 3, pp. 3643–3737). Madrid, Spain: Espasa.

Montolíu, E. (1999b). *¡Si nunca he dicho que estuviera enamorada de él!* Sobre construcciones independientes introducidas por *si* con valor replicativo. *Oralia, 2,* 37–69.

Morón Pastor, A. (2004). *La frase de grado compleja con adjetivos en español* (Unpublished doctoral dissertation). Universidad Autónoma de Madrid, Madrid, Spain.

Morzycki, M. (2008). Adverbial modification of adjectives: Evaluatives and a little beyond. In J. Dölling, T. Heyde-Zybatow, & M. Schafer (Eds.), *Event structures in linguistic form and interpretation* (pp. 103–126). Berlin, Germany: Mouton de Gruyter.

Munaro, N. (2003). On some differences between exclamative and interrogative wh-phrases in Bellunese: Further evidence for a split-CP hypothesis. In C. Tortora (Ed.), *The syntax of Italian dialects* (pp. 137–151). Oxford, United Kingdom: Oxford University Press.

Munaro, N. (2005). On the role of FocusP in wh-exclamatives: Evidence from northern Italian dialects. Paper presented at the Workshop on the Structure of the Left-Periphery, University of Paris 1, Paris, France.

Munaro, N. (2006). Verbless exclamatives across Romance: Standard expectations and tentative evaluations. *University of Venice Working Papers in Linguistics, 16,* 185–209.

Nathan, L. (2006). *On the interpretation of concealed questions* (Unpublished doctoral dissertation). MIT, Cambridge, MA.

Navarro Tomás, T. (1918). *Manual de pronunciación española.* Madrid, Spain: Centro de Estudios Históricos.

Neeleman, A., van de Koot, H., & Doetjes, J. (2004). Degree expressions. *The Linguistic Review, 23,* 1–66.

Nouwen, R., & Chernilovskaya, A. (2013). Wh-exclamatives with and without scales. Retrieved from http://ricknouwen.org/rwfn/wp-content/uploads/2012/01/whexcl-submitted-version-for-web.pdf

Noveck, I. A., & Sperber, D. (Eds.). (2004). *Experimental pragmatics.* New York: Palgrave Macmillan.

Obenauer, H-G. (1994). *Aspects de la syntaxe A-barre: Effets d'intervention et mouvements des quantifieurs* (Unpublished doctoral dissertation). Université de Paris VIII, Paris, France.

Ocampo, F. (2009). *Mirá*: From verb to discourse particle in Rioplatense Spanish. In J. Collentine, M. García, B. Lafford, & F. Marcos Marín (Eds.), *Selected proceedings of the 11th Hispanic Linguistics Symposium* (pp. 254–267). Somerville, MA: Cascadilla Proceedings Project.

Octavio de Toledo, Á. (2001-2002). ¿Un camino de ida y vuelta? La gramaticalización de *vaya* como marcador y cuantificador. *Anuari de Filologia, 11–12*, 47–72.

Octavio de Toledo, Á., & Sánchez López, C. (2009). Cuantificadores II: Cuantificadores interrogativos y exclamativos. In C. Company (Ed.), *Sintaxis histórica de la lengua española* (vol. 2, part 2, pp. 961–1072). Mexico City, Mexico: El Colegio de México.

Octavio de Toledo, Á., & Sánchez López, C. (2010). Variación histórica y espacio dialectal: a propósito de los cuantificadores interrogativos y exclamativos. In *Actas del VI Congreso Internacional "El Español de América"* (pp. 839–855). Valladolid, Spain: Universidad de Valladolid.

Olbertz, H. (2009). Mirativity and exclamatives in functional discourse grammar: Evidence from Spanish. *Web Papers in Functional Discourse Grammar, 82*, 66–82.

Olbertz, H. (2012). The place of exclamatives and miratives in Grammar: A functional discourse grammar view. *Linguística (Universidade Federal do Rio de Janeiro), 8*, 76–98.

Ono, H. (2004). On multiple exclamatives. Paper presented at Georgetown University Roundtable, Georgetown University, Washington, DC.

Pastor, A. (2008). Split analysis of gradable adjectives in Spanish. *Probus, 20*, 257–300.

Pinker, S. (2007). *The stuff of thought: Language as a window into human mature*. New York: Viking.

Plungian, V. A. (2001). The place of evidentiality within the universal grammatical space. *Journal of Pragmatics, 33*(3), 349–357.

Pons, S. (2003). *Que* inicial átono como marca de modalidad. *ELUA, 17*, 531–545.

Porroche, M. (1998a). Algunos aspectos del uso de *que* en el español conversacional (*que* como introductor de oraciones "independientes"). In G. Rufino (Ed.), *Atti del XXI Congreso Internazionale di Linguistica e Filologia Romanza (Palermo, 1995)* (vol. 2, pp. 245–255). Berlin, Germany: Walter de Gruyter.

Porroche, M. (1998b). Sobre los usos de *si, que* y *es que* como marcadores discursivos. In M. A. Martín Zorraquino & E. Montolio (Eds.), *Los marcadores del discurso: Teoría y análisis* (pp. 229–242). Madrid, Spain: Arco Libros.

Portner, P., & Zanuttini, R. (2000). The force of negation in wh exclamatives and interrogatives. In L. Horn & Y. Kato (Eds.), *Studies in negation and polarity* (pp. 193–231). Oxford, United Kingdom: Oxford University Press.

Portner, P., & Zanuttini, R. (2005). The semantics of nominal exclamatives. In R. Stainton & R. Elugardo (Eds.), *Ellipsis and non-sentential speech* (pp. 57–67). Dordrecht, Germany: Kluwer.

Porto Dapena, J. Á. (1991). *Del indicativo al subjuntivo. Valores y usos de los modos del verbo*. Madrid, Spain: Arco Libros.

Postma, G. (1996). The nature of quantification of high degree: *Very, many* and the exclamative. In C. Cremers & M. Den Dikken (Eds.), *Linguistics in the Netherlands 1996* (pp. 207–220). Amsterdam, Netherlands: John Benjamins.

Potts, C. (2005). *The logic of conventional implicatures*. New York: Oxford University Press.

Potts, C. (2007). The expressive dimension. *Theoretical linguistics, 33*, 165–198.

Potts, C., & Roeper, T. (2006). The narrowing acquisition path: From expressive small clauses to declaratives. In L. Progovac, K. Paesani, E. Casielles, & E. Barton (Eds.), *The syntax of nonsententials: Multi-disciplinary perspectives* (pp. 183–201). Amsterdam, Netherlands: John Benjamins.

Potts, C., & Schwarz, F. (2008). Exclamatives and heightened emotion: Extracting pragmatic generalizations from large corpora. Unpublished manuscript, University of Massachusetts Amherst, Amherst, MA.

Prieto, P., & Roseano, P. (2010). *Transcription of entonation in the Spanish language*. Munich, Germany: Lincom.

Pustejovsky, J. (1995). *The generative lexicon*. Cambridge, MA: MIT Press.

Quer, J. (1998). *Mood at the interface*. The Hague, Netherlands: Holland Academic Graphics.

Real Academia Española y Asociación Academias de la Lengua Española (RAE-ASALE) (2009). *Nueva gramática de la lengua española* (2 vols.). Madrid, Spain: Planeta Publishing.

Rett, J. (2007). Antonymy and evaluativity. In M. Gibson & T. Friedman (Eds.), *Proceedings of SALT 17* (pp. 210–227). Ithaca, NY: CLC Publications.

Rett, J. (2008). *Degree modification in natural language* (Unpublished doctoral dissertation). Rutgers University, New Brunswick, NJ.

Rett, J. (2009). A degree account of exclamatives. In T. Friedman & S. Ito (Eds.), *Proceedings of SALT 18* (pp. 601–618). Ithaca, NY: CLC Publications.

Rett, J. (2011). Exclamatives, degrees and speech acts. *Linguistics and Philosophy, 34*, 411–442.

Rett, J., & Murray, S. (2013). A semantic account of mirative evidentials. In T. Snider (Ed.), *Proceedings of SALT 23* (pp. 453–472). Ithaca, NY: CLC Publications.

Ridruejo, E. (1983). Notas sobre las oraciones optativas. In *Serta Philologica F. Lázaro* (vol. 1, pp. 511–520). Madrid, Spain: Cátedra.

Ridruejo, E. (1999). Modo y modalidad. El modo en las subordinadas sustantivas. In I. Bosque and V. Demonte (Eds.), *Gramática descriptiva de la lengua española* (vol. 2, pp. 3209–3253). Madrid, Spain: Espasa.

Rifkin, J. I. (2000). If only *if only* were *if* plus *only*. *CLS, 36*, 369–384.

Rigau, G. (2003). Mirative and focusing uses of the particle *pla* in Catalan. Retrieved from http://filcat.uab.cat/clt/publicacions/reports/pdf/GGT-09-03.pdf

Rivero, M. L. (1977). *Estudios de gramática generativa del español*. Madrid, Spain: Cátedra.

Rivero, M. L. (1994). Negation, imperatives and Wackernagel effects. *Rivista di Linguistica, 6*, 39–66.

Rivero, M. L., & Terzi, A. (1995). Imperatives, V-movement and logical mood. *Journal of Linguistics, 31*, 301–332.

Rizzi, L. (1990). *Relativized minimality*. Cambridge, MA: MIT Press.

Rizzi, L. (1997). The fine structure of the left periphery. In L. Haegeman (Ed.), *Elements of grammar: A handbook of generative syntax* (pp. 281–337). Dordrecht, Germany: Kluwer.

Roberts, C. (1996). Information structure in discourse: Toward a unified theory of formal pragmatics. *The Ohio State University Working Papers in Linguistics, 49*, 91–136.

Roberts, C. (2011). Only: A case study in projective meaning. *The Baltic International Yearbook of Cognition, Logic and Communication, 6*, 1–59.

Rodríguez Espiñeira, M. J. (1996). Sobre *como* anunciativo. In *Scripta philologica in memoriam Manuel Taboada Cid* (vol. 2, pp. 649–666). Coruña, Spain: Universidade da Coruña.

Rodríguez Ramalle, T. M. (2007a). El complementante *que* como marca enfática en el texto periodístico. *Revista Electrónica de Lingüística Aplicada, 6*, 41–53.

Rodríguez Ramalle, T. M. (2007b). Las interjecciones llevan complemento, ¡vaya que sí! Análisis de las interjecciones con complemento en el discurso. *Español Actual, 87*, 112–125.

Rodríguez Ramalle, T. M. (2008a). El valor de las marcas enunciativas en la configuración del discurso en el ámbito de las lenguas romances. In A. Moreno Sandoval (Ed.), *El valor de la diversidad (meta)lingüística: Actas del VIII congreso de Lingüística General* (pp. 1714–1732). Madrid, Spain: Universidad Autónoma.

Rodríguez Ramalle, T. M. (2008b). Estudio sintáctico y discursivo de algunas estructuras enunciativas y citativas del español. *Revista Española de Lingüística Aplicada, 21*, 269–288.

Rodríguez Ramalle, T. M. (2008c). Valores de las interjecciones en el discurso oral y su relación con otras marcas de modalidad discursivas. *Oralia, 11*, 399–417.

Rodríguez Ramalle, T. M. (2011). La expresión del grado en las interjecciones y la función de la conjunción *que*. *Verba, 38*, 191–217.

Rojas, E. (1985). El valor afectivo del pronombre enfático *qué* en el habla de Tucumán. *Revista Argentina de Lingüística, 1*, 73–82.

Rojo, G. (1974). La temporalidad verbal en español. *Verba, 1*, 68–149.

Rojo, G, & Veiga, A. (1999). El tiempo verbal. Los tiempos simples. In I. Bosque & V. Demonte (Eds.), *Gramática descriptiva de la lengua española* (vol. 2, pp. 2867–2935). Madrid, Spain: Espasa.

Rys, K. K. (2006). L'exclamation: Assertion non-stabilisée? Le cas des exclamatives à mot *qu-*. *Revue Romane, 41*, 216–238.

Sadock, J., & Zwicky, A. (1985). Speech act distinctions in syntax. In T. Shopen (Ed.), *Language typology and syntactic description* (vol. 1, pp. 155–196). Cambridge, United Kingdom: Cambridge University Press.

Sæbø, K. J. (2010). On the semantics of embedded exclamatives. *Studia Linguistica, 64*, 116–140.

Sánchez López, C. (2014a). Person features and functional heads: Evidence from an exceptional optative sentence in Spanish. Paper presented at the Going Romance Meeting, Lisbon, Portugal.

Sánchez López, C. (2014b). Mirativity in Spanish. Paper presented at EMEL'14. Evidentiality and Modality in European Languages Workshop on Evidentiality, Mirativity and Modality, Universidad Complutense, Madrid, Spain.

Sánchez López, C. (2015a). Dos tipos de oraciones exclamativas totales en español. In *Studium grammaticae. Homenaje al profesor José A. Martínez* (pp. 771–730). Oviedo, Spain: Universidad de Oviedo.

Sánchez López, C. (2015b). The properties of force and the selection of mood in Spanish independent sentences. Paper presented at the 25 Colloquium on Generative Grammar, Paris, France.

Sánchez López, Cristina (2016). Person features and functional heads. Evidence from an exceptional optative sentence in Ibero-Romance. In E. Carrilho, A. Fiéis, M. Lobo and S. Pereira (Eds.), *Romance Languages and Linguistic Theory 10. Selected papers from 'Going Romance' 28, Lisbon* (pp. 259–278). Amsterdam: John Benjamins. DOI 10.1075/rllt.10.13san.

Sánchez Royo, M. I. (1976). *La interjección en la lengua castellana contemporánea* (Unpublished doctoral dissertation). Universidad Complutense de Madrid, Madrid, Spain.

Sancho Cremades, P. (2001–2002). La gradualidad de los procesos de gramaticalización: Sobre el uso idiomático del adjetivo *menudo* en español coloquial. *Cuadernos de Investigación Filológica, 27–28*, 285–306.

Sancho Cremades, P. (2008). La sintaxis de algunas construcciones intensificadoras en español y en catalán coloquiales. *Verba, 35*, 199–233.

Sansiñena, M. S, Cornillie, B., & De Smet, H. (2013). Free-standing *que*-clauses and other directive strategies in Spanish. *Leuven Working Papers in Linguistics, 2*, 50–83.

Sansiñena, M. S., De Smet, H., & Cornillie, B. (2015). Displaced directives: Subjunctive freestanding *que*-clauses vs. imperatives in Spanish. *Folia Linguistica, 49*(1), 257–285.

Sauerland, U., & Yatsushiro, K. (2009). *Semantics and pragmatics: From experiment to theory*. New York: Palgrave Macmillan.

Schlenker, P. (2007). Expressive presuppositions. *Theoretical Linguistics, 33,* 237–245.

Schneider, S., Glikman, J., & Avanzi, M. (Eds.). (2015). *Parenthetical verbs.* Berlin, Germany: Mouton/De Gruyter.

Schwager, M. (2009). What is amazement all about? In A. Riester and T. Solstad (Eds.), *Proceedings of Sinn und Bedetung 13* (pp. 499–512). Stuttgart, Germany: Opus.

Schwarzschild, R. (2006). The role of dimensions in the syntax of noun phrases. *Syntax, 9,* 67–110.

Schwarzschild, R., & Wilkinson, K. (2002). Quantifiers in comparatives: A semantics of degree based on intervals. *Natural Language Semantics, 10,* 1–41.

Schwenter, S. (1996). The pragmatics of independent *si*-clauses in Spanish. *Hispanic Linguistics, 8,* 316–351.

Schwenter, S. (1999). Sobre la sintaxis de una construcción coloquial: Oraciones independientes con *si*. *Annuari de Filología, 21,* 87–100.

Schwenter, S. (2012). Independent *si*-clauses in Spanish: Functions and consequences for insubordination. Paper presented at the Symposium Dynamics of Insubordination. Tokyo, Japan.

Searle, J. (1976). A classification of illocutionary acts. *Language in Society, 5,* 1–23.

Searle, J. (1979). *Expression and meaning.* Cambridge, United Kingdom: Cambridge University Press.

Seuren, P. (1984). The comparative revisited. *Journal of Semantics, 3,* 109–141.

Sibaldo, M. A. (2013). Free small clauses of Brazilian Portuguese as a TP-phase. In J. Cabrelli Amaro, G. Lord, A. de Prada Pérez, & J. E. Aaron (Eds.), *Selected proceedings of the 16th Hispanic Linguistics Symposium* (pp. 324–337). Somerville, MA: Cascadilla Proceedings Project.

Simons, M. (2003). Presupposition and accommodation: Understanding the Stalnakerian picture. *Philosophical Studies, 112,* 251–278.

Solt, S. (2010). *Much* support and *more*. In M. Aloni & K. Schulz (Eds.), *Amsterdam Colloquium 2009 (LNAI 6042)* (pp. 446–455). Berlin, Germany: Heidelberg Springer.

Spaulding, R. K. (1934). Two elliptical subjunctives in Spanish. *Hispania, 17,* 355–360.

Stalnaker, R. C. (1974). Pragmatic presuppositions. In M. Munitz & P. Unger (Eds.), *Semantics and philosophy* (pp. 197–213). New York: New York University Press.

Stalnaker, R. C. (1978). Assertion. In P. Cole (Ed.), *Syntax and semantics, vol. 9: Pragmatics* (pp. 315–332). New York: Academic Press.

Stalnaker, R. C. (2008). A response to Abbott on presupposition and common ground. *Linguistics and Philosophy, 31,* 539–544.

Szabolcsi, A. (2004). Positive polarity-negative polarity. *Natural Language and Linguistic Theory, 22,* 409–452.

Szczegielniak, A. (2012). Degree phrase raising in relative clauses. In V. Camacho-Taboada, Á. L. Jiménez-Fernández, J. Martín-González, & M. Reyes-Tejedor (Eds.), *Information structure, agreement and CP* (pp. 255–274). Amsterdam, Netherlands: John Benjamins.

Tirado, I. (2013). *Vaya* como cuantificador en expresiones nominales. Paper presented at the XXVIIe Congrès international de linguistique et de philologie romanes, Nancy, France.

Tirado, I. (2015a). Interacción entre pragmática y estructura sintáctica: construcciones encabezadas por *vaya*. In C. Álvarez, B. Garrido Martín, & M. González Sanz (Eds.), *Jóvenes aportaciones a la investigación lingüística* (pp. 153–168). Seville, Spain: Ediciones Alfar.

Tirado, I. (2015b). La gramaticalización de *vaya* como cuantificador. In J. M. García Martín (Ed.), *Actas del IX Congreso Internacional de Historia de la Lengua Española* (pp. 1123–1138). Madrid, Spain: Iberoamericana.

Tonhauser, J., Beaver, D., Roberts, C., & Simons, M. (2013). Towards a taxonomy of projective content. *Language, 89*, 66–109.

Torrego, E. (1988). Operadores en las exclamativas con artículo determinado de valor cuantitativo. *Nueva Revista de Filología Hispánica, 36*(1), 109–122.

Torres Bustamante, T. (2013). *On the syntax and semantics of mirativity. Evidence from Spanish and Albanian* (Unpublished doctoral dissertation). University of Rochester, Rochester, NY.

Torres Sánchez, M. A. (2000). *La interjección*. Cádiz, Spain: Universidad de Cádiz.

Tovena, L. (1998). *The fine structure of polarity items*. New York: Garland.

Van der Wouden, T. (1997). *Negative contexts: Collocation, polarity and multiple negation*. London, United Kingdom: Routledge.

Van Olmen, D. (2014). Past imperatives. Paper presented at the SWL6 Conference, Pavia, Italy.

Vicente, L. (2010). Past counterfactuality in Spanish imperatives and its implications for the analysis of imperatives. Paper presented at the 20th Colloquium on Generative Grammar, Barcelona, Spain.

Vigara Tauste, A. M. (2005). *Morfosintaxis del español coloquial*. Madrid, Spain: Gredos.

Villalba, X. (2001). The right periphery of exclamative sentences in Catalan. *Catalan Working Papers in Linguistics, 9*, 119–135.

Villalba, X. (2003). An exceptional exclamative sentence type in Romance. *Lingua, 113*, 713–745.

Villalba, X. (2004). Exclamatives and negation. Retrieved from http://semanticsarchive.net/Archive/2FkOWM1M/exclamatives&negation.pdf

Villalba, X. (Ed.). (2008a). Exclamatives at the interfarces [Special issue]. *Catalan Journal of Linguistics, 7*.

Villalba, X. (2008b). Exclamatives: A thematic guide with many questions and few answers. *Catalan Journal of Linguistics, 7*, 9–40.

Villalba, X. (2016). Oraciones exclamativas. In J. Gutiérrez-Rexach (Ed.), *Enciclopedia lingüística hispánica* (pp. 737–749). Abingdon: Routledge.

Villalta, E. (2007). *Context dependence in the interpretation of questions and subjunctives* (Unpublished doctoral dissertation). University of Tübingen, Tübingen, Germany.

Villalta, E. (2008). Mood and gradability: An investigation of the subjunctive mood in Spanish. *Linguistics and Philosophy, 31*, 467–522.

Vinet, M-T. (1991). French non-verbal exclamative constructions. *Probus, 3*(1), 77–100.

von Fintel, K. (1994). *Restrictions on quantifier domains* (Unpublished doctoral dissertation). University of Massachusetts Amherst, Amherst, MA.

von Stechow, A. (2006). Times as degrees: *früh(er)* "early(er)," *spät(er)* "late(r)," and phase adverbs. Unpublished manuscript, Universität Tübingen, Tübingen, Germany.

Watanabe, A. (2001). Wh-in-situ languages. In M. Baltin & C. Collins (Eds.), *The handbook of contemporary syntactic theory* (pp. 203–225). Oxford, United Kingdom: Blackwell.

Westerstal, D. (1995). Logical constants in quantifier languages. *Linguistics and Philosophy, 8*, 387–413.

Wiese, H. (2003). Wh-words are not "interrogative" pronouns: The derivation of interrogative interpretations for constituent questions. In M. Hoey & N. Scott (Eds.), *Questions: Multiple perspectives on a common phenomenon*. Liverpool, United Kingdom: University of Liverpool Press.

Zaefferer, D. (2001). Deconstructing a classical classification: A typological look at Searle's concept of illocution type. *Revue Internationale de Philosophie, 2001/2*, 209–225.

Zanuttini, R, & Portner, P. H. (2000). The characterization of exclamative clauses in Paduan. *Language, 76*, 123–132.

Zanuttini, R., & Portner, P. H. (2003). Exclamative clauses at the syntax-semantics interface. *Language, 79*, 39–81.

Zanuttini, R., Pak, M., & Portner, P. (2012). A syntactic analysis of interpretive restrictions on imperative, promissive, and exhortative subjects. *Natural Language and Linguistic Theory, 30*(4), 1231–1274.

Zwarts, F. (1998). Three types of polarity. In F. Hamm & E. Hinrichs (Eds.), *Plurality and quantification* (pp. 177–238). Dordrecht, Germany: Kluwer.

Contributors

IGNACIO BOSQUE is Honorary Professor of Spanish Linguistics at Complutense University (Madrid). His main research interests include Spanish grammar (syntax, morphology, and the lexicon-syntax interface), as well as theoretical linguistics, lexicology, and grammar instruction. His publications deal with topics such as negation, mood, exclamatives, indefinites, plurals, coordination, anaphora, passives, subextraction, lexical restrictions, light verbs, auxiliaries, informational structure, lexical aspect, and lexical integrity, among others. He is the author of *Las categorías gramaticales* (1989; 2nd edition in 2015) and *Sobre la negación* (1990); co-author, with J. Gutiérrez-Rexach, of *Fundamentos de sintaxis formal* (2009); editor of *Indicativo y subjuntivo* (1990) and *El sustantivo sin determinación* (1996); co-editor, with V. Demonte, of *Gramática descriptiva de la lengua española* (1999); coordinator of the Morphology and Syntax volumes of *Nueva gramática de la lengua española* (2009); and director of two combinatory dictionaries of Spanish (2004, 2006).

PATRICIA ANDUEZA is Assistant Professor of Spanish Linguistics at the University of Evansville, Indiana. Her areas of research are pragmatics, semantics, exclamative constructions, and irony in language use. Her PhD dissertation (The Ohio State University, 2011) is entitled *Rhetorical Exclamatives in Spanish*.

RAQUEL GONZÁLEZ RODRÍGUEZ is Associate Professor of Spanish Language at University of Castilla-La Mancha (Spain). She received her PhD from Complutense University (Madrid, 2008). Her major research interests focus on the syntax and semantics of Spanish grammar. She has written on positive polarity items, degree quantifiers, and event structure. Her publications on these topics include "Reconstruction and Scope in Exclamative Sentences" (in Eguren and Fernández Soriano eds., *Current Studies on Syntax and Interpretation*, 2007), "Exclamative Wh-Phrases as Positive Polarity Items" (*Catalan Journal of Linguistics*, 2008), "Negation of Resultative and Progressive Periphrases" (*Borealis. An International Journal of Hispanic Linguistics*, 2015), and "Polaridad: Afirmación y negación" (in Gutiérrez-Rexach, ed., *Enciclopedia de Lingüística Hispánica*, 2016).

JAVIER GUTIÉRREZ-REXACH was Professor of Spanish and Linguistics at The Ohio State University. His research areas included the syntax and semantics of Spanish as well as formal semantics and pragmatics. His books include *Los indefinidos* (2004) and *Interfaces and Domains of Quantification* (2014). He was also co-author of *Fundamentos de sintaxis formal* (2009) and editor of the *Enciclopedia de Lingüística Hispánica* (2016).

PASCUAL JOSÉ MASULLO is currently Professor of Linguistics at Universidad Nacional de Río Negro (Bariloche, Argentina). Previously he has held positions at Universidad Nacional del Comahue (Argentina); University of Pittsburgh; University of Illinois, Urbana-Champaign; Middlebury College (USA); and Durham University (UK). He received his PhD in Linguistics from University of Washington, Seattle, in 1992. His dissertation, *Incorporation and Case Theory in Spanish: A Crosslinguistic Perspective*, proposes the first unified account of dative constructions and non-nominative subjects in Spanish. His research has focused primarily on syntactic structures at the interface with lexical semantics, as well as on recent lexical, morphological, and syntactic changes in Argentinian Spanish. He has published on topics such as bare noun phrases, light verbs, and prepositions; complex predicates; lexical relational structures; unaccusativity; argument alternations; null objects; conflation patterns; and implicit exclamatives, among others. He is the main editor of *Romance Linguistics 2007* (John Benjamins).

LUIS SÁEZ is Professor at the University Complutense of Madrid. His publications include papers on ellipsis (such as "Sluicing with Copula," *LSRL* 34), Spanish Possessives (such as "Peninsular Spanish Pre-nominal Possessives in Ellipsis Contexts: A Phase-Based Account," *LSRL* 40 and "On Certain

Distributional Gaps of Spanish Possessives: A Phrasal Spell-Out Account," in *Of Grammar, Words, and Verses*, ed. Torrego, 2012). He has also published on Spanish clitics ("Applicative Phrases Hosting Accusative Clitics," in *Little Words*, ed. Leow, Campos, and Lardiere, 2009; and "Restrictions on Enclitics and the Imperative in Iberian Spanish," in *Movement and Clitics*, ed. Torrens et al., 2010). More recently he edited the book *Las construcciones comparativas* (in collaboration with Cristina Sánchez López). He is currently working on amalgam-related constructions, among other grammatical topics.

CRISTINA SÁNCHEZ LÓPEZ is Professor of Hispanic Linguistics in the Department of Lengua Española at the Universidad Complutense of Madrid (Spain), where she has taught since 2000. She has been Assistant Professor at the Universidad Autónoma of Madrid (1993–2000) and Visiting Researcher at the Harvard University (2010–11). Sánchez's research in linguistics mainly focuses on the syntax and semantics of Spanish. Her publications include *Las construcciones con 'se'* (2002), *El grado de adjetivos y adverbios* (2006), and *Las construcciones comparativas* (ed. with Sáez, 2015). She is the author of two chapters, one on negation and another one on quantifiers, in the *Gramática descriptiva de la lengua española* (ed. Bosque and Demonte, 1999) and many other articles and book chapters. She is also interested in comparative Romance syntax and historical linguistics, and has contributed two chapters to the *Sintaxis histórica de la lengua española* (ed. Company, 2009–15).

XAVIER VILLALBA is Assistant Professor of Catalan Linguistics at the Universitat Autònoma de Barcelona (Spain). He has published extensively on exclamative sentences ("Las exclamativas" *Enciclopedia de Lingüística Hispánica*, 2016; "Predicate Focus Fronting in the Spanish Determiner Phrase" with Anna Bartra-Kaufmann, *Lingua*, 2010; "Exclamatives: A Thematic Guide with Many Questions and Few Answers," *Catalan Journal of Linguistics*, 2008; and "An Exceptional Exclamative Sentence Type in Romance," *Lingua*, 2003). He has also published on information structure ("Ambiguity resolution and information structure," with M. Teresa Espinal, *The Linguistic Review*, 2015; "Right-dislocation in Catalan: Tails, Polarity and Activation," with Laia Mayol, *International Review of Pragmatics*, 2013; "The Right Periphery of Interrogatives in Catalan and Spanish: Syntax/Prosody Interactions," with Sílvia Planas-Morales, *Catalan Journal of Linguistics*, 2013; "A quantitative comparative study of right-dislocation in Catalan and Spanish," *Journal of Pragmatics*, 2011). Finally, he is author of the books *The Syntax and Semantics of Dislocations in Catalan* (2009) and *El orden de las palabras en español* (2010).

Index

al menos, 85
alto (in Argentinian Spanish), 120
amount exclamatives. See *cuánto-cuán*; quantitative exclamatives
anda, 207
anti-additive contexts, 166–68
anti-factivity, 84, 97–100, 101. See also factivity
anti-morphic contexts, 167. See also negation
articles in exclamatives. See definite article degree exclamatives
así, 36
at-issue meaning, 145–54

banda (in Argentinian Spanish), 120, 121
bien, 26, 27, 208
binomial exclamatives, 10, 32–34
bocha, una ~ (in Argentinian Spanish), 120
bueno, 26

cada, 35, 94, 95, 109, 114, 127, 134
classifications of exclamatives, 7–50, 189–96. See also exclamative words
clefts, 41, 42

cómo, 4, 21, 40, 41, 193, 194
comparatives and exclamatives, 53, 54
complementation. See wh- exclamatives; doubly filled COMP; embedded exclamatives; concealed exclamations
complementizers in exclamatives. See matrix complementizer exclamatives; *que, si*
concealed exclamations, 47, 198–200. See also embedded exclamatives
conditional exclamatives, 31, 32. See also *si*
conque, 10
consecutives. See suspended exclamatives
conventional implicatures, 7, 52, 141, 143–46, 154
counterfactive optatives. See optatives
covert exclamatives, 110–19, 144. See also concealed exclamatives
cuándo, 38, 195
cuantísimo, 40
cuánto-cuán, 12–15, 21–23, 38–41, 60–65, 75, 102, 103, 111, 165, 193, 194
cuidado, 208
cyclicity in exclamatives, 25, 43–44. See also wh-exclamatives

232

de + adj., 35, 109, 111–13, 127, 134, 152, 116–18, 144–145
declarative exclamatives, 9, 31, 137–38, 192
definite article degree exclamatives, 22–25, 187, 189, 197–200
DegP. *See* degree expressions
degree expressions, 4n2, 12–19, 53, 59–68, 81, 159–73; extreme degree, 115–33, 139–54, 159–73, 184, 185. *See also* elatives; *extremadamente*; definite article degree exclamatives
degree relatives. *See* definite article degree exclamatives
denial in replies to exclamatives, 145–58; denial of presupposed information, 147–54. *See also* negation
dependencies, long distance ~, 133–36. *See also* wh- exclamatives
de re reference/belief, 182, 184, 192–96
desiderative exclamatives. *See* optative exclamatives
desire, predicates of ~, 102; feasible or unfeasible desires, 32, 90, 99–101, 105, 107. *See also* optatives
dónde, 102, 195
doubly filled COMP, 19–22, 26–28, 40, 91–96, 112, 113. *See also* wh- exclamatives
downward entailment, 167–68, 172–76. *See also* negation

echoic exclamatives. *See* matrix complementizer exclamatives
elatives, 11, 108–38, 160, 162; plain elatives, 133–38. See also *extremadamente*; degree expressions
embedded exclamatives, 18, 23, 39, 44–47, 95, 96, 102, 112, 148, 181–210. *See also* concealed exclamations
embedded root phenomena. *See* matrix complementizer exclamatives
emotive content, 3, 82, 183–85. *See also* surprise
emotive factives, 186–89, 196, 206
emphatic articles in exclamatives. *See* definite article degree exclamatives
emphatic polarity exclamatives. *See* polarity exclamatives

evidential exclamatives, 27, 28. *See also* matrix complementizer exclamatives
evidentiality, 5–6
exaggeration, 11
exclamatives with emphatic articles. *See* definite article degree exclamatives
experimental evidence, 145–58
expressive constructions, 2–7, 150
extremadamente, 159–73. *See also* degree expressions; elatives
extreme degree. *See* degree expressions

factivity, 6–7, 84, 98, 140–45, 186–88. *See also* emotive factives; anti-factivity; miratives
fíjate (and its variants), 45, 203–4
focalized exclamatives, 10, 22, 25–28, 31, 33n9, 94, 116–19, 122, 131. *See also* sentential exclamatives; wh- exclamatives
focus fronting in exclamatives. *See* focalized exclamatives; FocusP
ForceP, 20, 25–28, 90, 91, 94, 106

gradability. *See* degree expressions
gradation. *See* degree expressions; elatives
grounded belief/knowledge, 181–89

hidden exclamatives. *See* covert exclamatives; concealed questions
humor, 12. *See also* irony

idioms, 8
illocutionary force. *See* ForceP; speech acts
imperatives and exclamatives, 30, 203, 204. See also *mira*; *fíjate*; *anda*
increíblemente, 176
indirect exclamatives. *See* embedded exclamatives
infinitives in exclamatives, 11, 33, 37, 45, 86
initial particle exclamatives. *See* matrix complementizer exclamatives
in situ wh- exclamatives, 42, 43. *See also* wh- exclamatives
insubordination. *See* matrix complementizer exclamatives

interjections, 8, 207
intonation, 7–9, 34, 35, 54, 192
irony, 11, 18, 19, 26
irrealis (as a feature), 31
islands. *See* dependencies, long distance ~; cyclicity; wh- exclamatives

jussive, 37, 83n1, 112. *See also* optative subjunctive

la de + N, 24, 197
last resort, 73–81
lo in exclamatives. *See* definite article degree exclamatives
lo más (in Argentinian Spanish), 120

mal (in Argentinian Spanish), 110, 120, 123–33
más, 53–81, 110
masa, una ~ (in Argentinian Spanish), 120
matrix complementizer exclamatives, 10, 27–32, 83. *See also* root exclamatives; *que, si*
measure phrases. *See* degree expressions; elatives
measure verbs, 41
menudo, 18–19, 26
mira, 5, 28n8, 45, 202–6. *See also* miratives
miratives, 5, 6, 45, 202–6; directive mirative factives, 204–6. See also *mira*
mood in exclamatives, 29–32, 33n9, 46, 96–101, 112
MoodP, 84, 90, 91, 94, 96
muchísimo, 110
mucho-muy, 57–61. *See also* degree expressions; elatives
multiple exclamatives, 42–43

negation, 47–50, 113–14, 117n7, 118, 162–68. *See also* anti-morphic contexts; denial
non-sentential exclamatives. *See* phrasal exclamatives
noteworthiness, 4
null operators in exclamatives. *See* operators in exclamatives

ojalá, 36–37, 83, 84, 90–96, 122, 208
only, 32, 87, 145
operators in exclamatives, 16, 35, 53–81, 84–91, 103, 105–7, 115–19, 134, 141, 146, 183, 188, 200–202, 209
optatives, 10, 30, 32, 34–38, 82–107, 206. See also *quién; ojalá*
optative subjunctive. *See* jussive

parasitic gaps, 24
particles in exclamatives. *See* matrix complementizer exclamatives
person features in exclamatives, 104–7
phrasal exclamatives, 12–19, 53–81, 197–200
poco, 26, 59–60
polarity exclamatives, 10, 25–28, 85, 89
polarity items. *See* negation; positive polarity
por qué, 38
por supuesto, 208
positive polarity, 159–73
pragmatic inferences, 16, 17n5. *See also* conventional implicatures
predicational exclamatives. *See* binomial exclamatives
prepositional exclamatives, 33, 34
presupposition, 185. *See also* grounded belief/knowledge; factivity; conventional implicatures
primary exclamatives, 8–10
projective meaning, 146
prosody. *See* intonation
psycholinguistic evidence, 153–62

qualifiers. *See* qualitative exclamatives
qualifying nouns, 11
qualitative exclamatives, 12–19, 24, 25, 46
quantification-at-a-distance effects, 28, 31, 35
quantitative exclamatives, 12–17, 24, 25, 162–66. See also *cuánto-cuán*
qué, 12–22, 41, 65–68, 111, 115–19, 146, 154, 159, 183, 185, 193–95
que as an initial particle in matrix exclamatives, 29–30, 36, 83–86, 97–98. *See also*

matrix complementizer exclamatives; doubly filled COMP
qué de + N, 13, 15, 25, 50, 66, 67, 69, 116
que «galicado», 42
questions. *See* rhetorical questions and exclamations
quién, 38–40, 83, 104–7. *See also* optatives
quiénes, 193
quizá(s), 91–92
quotative exclamatives. *See* reportative exclamatives; matrix complementizer exclamatives

raramente, 167
re- (in Argentinian Spanish), 121–22, 131n17. *See also* elatives
relativized minimality, 118
reportative exclamatives, 29. *See also* matrix complementizer exclamatives
rhetorical questions and exclamatives, 12, 26, 39, 42, 50n13, 184n1
romperla (in Argentinian Spanish), 120
root exclamatives, 18, 188, 196. *See also* wh-exclamatives; matrix complementizer exclamatives

scales, 31, 40, 96; open and closed, 4n2, 4, 5, 168–76. *See also* degree expressions
se (aspectual uses), 121–29. *See also se . . . todo*
se . . . todo (in Argentinian Spanish), 109, 121–29
secondary exclamatives, 7, 9, 10
sentential exclamatives, 19–38. *See also* wh-exclamatives; doubly filled COMP exclamatives; focalized exclamatives
si as an initial particle in matrix exclamatives, 29–32, 36, 85–88. *See also* conditional exclamatives; matrix complementizer exclamatives
siempre, 200
sin, 167
sorprendentemente, 160, 176–79
speech acts, 2–7. *See also* ForceP

subjunctive, 86, 87, 102. *See also* mood in exclamatives
subordinated exclamatives. *See* embedded exclamatives
surprise (and other emotive reactions), 3, 54, 89, 96, 183, 189, 194, 206, 207
suspended exclamatives, 10, 34–35, 68, 81, 109–15, 144, 145

tal(es), 16, 114
tan(to), 17, 34, 35, 62–65, 113
tense in exclamatives, 93, 96–101
tetic exclamatives, 34
todo (in Argentinian Spanish). *See se . . . todo* (in Argentinian Spanish)
type exclamatives. *See* qualitative exclamatives
types of exclamatives. *See* classifications of exclamatives; words, exclamative ~

valiente, 8, 18–19
variable binding in exclamatives, 42
vaya, 5, 18, 26, 28n8, 52n13, 67n5, 207
venga, 207
verbless exclamatives. *See* binomial exclamatives
verum focus, 26
very, 57–51

warning, 207
wh- exclamatives, 10, 12–22, 101–6, 137; wh-words in optative sentences, 101–7. *See also* cyclicity; *in situ* wh- exclamatives; phrasal exclamatives; embedded exclamatives; sentential exclamatives; doubly filled COMP exclamatives; variable binding in exclamatives; qualitative exclamatives; quantitative exclamatives; quantification-at-a-distance effects; polarity exclamatives; dependencies, long distance ~
wh- exclamative words, 12–19, 38–41. *See also* words, exclamative ~
widening of quantificational domains, 3–5, 138, 141, 143, 144, 172, 173, 188, 172–76. *See*

also optatives, wh- exclamative words; wh- exclamatives

words, exclamative ~. *See* wh- exclamative words; classes of exclamatives; *anda*; *cuánto-cuán*; *dónde*; *fíjate*; *mira*; *ojalá*; *qué*; *quién*; *vaya*; *venga*

ya, 28n8

THEORETICAL DEVELOPMENTS IN HISPANIC LINGUISTICS
Javier Gutiérrez-Rexach, Series Editor

This book series aims to be an outlet for monographs or edited volumes addressing current problems and debates within Hispanic linguistics. The series will be open to a wide variety of areas and approaches, as long as they are grounded in theoretical goals and methodologies. Contributions from the disciplines of syntax, semantics, pragmatics, morphology, phonology, phonetics, etc. are welcome, as well as those analyzing interface issues or the historical development, acquisition, processing, and computation of grammatical properties. Research topics of interest are those dealing with Spanish or other Hispanic languages, in any of their dialects and varieties.

Advances in the Analysis of Spanish Exclamatives
    EDITED BY IGNACIO BOSQUE

The Afro-Bolivian Spanish Determiner Phrase: A Microparametric Account
    SANDRO SESSAREGO

Interfaces and Domains of Quantification
    JAVIER GUTIÉRREZ-REXACH

www.ingramcontent.com/pod-product-compliance
Lightning Source LLC
Chambersburg PA
CBHW030110010526
44116CB00005B/182